Seven Stories, How to Study and Teach the Nonviolent Bible

Copyright © 2017 Anthony W. Bartlett

The Scripture quotations contained herein are from the New Revised Standard Version Bible, copyright, 1989, by the Division of Christian Education of the National Council of the Churches of Christ in the U.S.A. used by permission. All rights reserved.

Screenshots of Hebrew Interlinear from Biblehub.com, used by permission.

Design and layout by Marina Goba. Contact at marinagoba.com

Fair public use of this text can include the copying of a few pages, but not whole lessons or chapters.

Hopetime Press

ISBN-13: 978-0692931943 (Custom Universal)

ISBN-10: 0692931945

Seven Stories

**How to Study and Teach
the Nonviolent Bible**

Anthony W. Bartlett

To the Wood Hath Hope Christian Community

TABLE OF CONTENTS

FOREWORD

In 1999 Linda and Tony Bartlett began a Bible study and prayer community, with the name of "Wood Hath Hope" (www.woodhathhope.org). Its meetings were leavened by the insights of anthropologist/Bible-interpreter, René Girard, while positively accenting God's plan for human transformation, the deep and thrilling content of today's "Good News." Over the years people gathering around this teaching have grown into a community, with progressively stronger roots and personal relationships. In 2015 Wood Hath Hope found a stable home, "Bethany House" in Syracuse, New York, a space which offers a center for its activities and a visible reference point for its message and witness. *Seven Stories* is the product of hundreds of meetings over eighteen years, producing little by little a dynamic new reading of the Bible. We believe that Wood Hath Hope has evolved a new style of Biblical interpretation, grafting a number of vital strains into a wonderful new vinestock. We hope the present coursebook will bring this fresh new wine of God's Kingdom to multiple individuals and communities.

About the Author

Anthony Bartlett read philosophy and theology at Heythrop Athaneum in Oxfordshire, England, and at London University. Following his ordination to the Roman Catholic priesthood he spent a year studying in Rome. After ten years of ministry, he resigned the official priesthood. In this period of transition he lived in a community of prayer near Assisi in Italy, under the guidance of writer and teacher, Carlo Carretto. The experience around Carretto welcomed many different individuals at the crossroads of traditional Catholicism and the search for fresh perspective and spiritual practice. It was natural that news of a major recent book by René Girard and his extraordinary cross-disciplinary understanding of Christianity should arrive among members of this group. The seed of information planted then eventually matured into contact between Tony and James Williams, professor of the Hebrew Bible in the Syracuse University Department of Religion and prominent Girardian scholar. With Williams' support and encouragement Tony was accepted for doctoral studies in the Department, emigrating to the U.S. with his family, and gaining his degree in 1999. As well as being a founding member of Wood Hath Hope he is the author of numerous articles and books, including *Virtually Christian, How Christ Changes Human Meaning and Makes Creation New* (2011).

Editor

Linda Bartlett completed a Bachelor of Divinity at Heythrop College, London University, and a Masters of Science in Nursing from the State University of New York. She is a Nurse Practitioner and currently works in HIV treatment and prevention in the Syracuse area. She is a charter member of the Wood Hath Hope community and an integral part of the vision and evolution of the *Seven Stories*, also serving as the coursebook editor.

ACKNOWLEDGMENTS

Special thanks for essential contributions go to Jessamyn and Alphonso Magri, Heather Scanlon, Jennifer Wissman, Cathy Gibbons, Jerry and Carola Shave, Earl Arnold, Maggie Carter and Yvonne Swanson. Their help and support ranged from organization and administration, through teaching, to copy reading and editing. But beyond these individuals, enormous thanks are due to the whole Wood Hath Hope Christian Community, a group which provided both a vital sounding board and unfailing spiritual support for the life and growth of *Seven Stories.*

Finally, Linda and Tony would like to thank their children, Christopher, Susannah and Liam, who grew up with Wood Hath Hope and responded always with patience, good humor and love.

INTRODUCTION

There is a quote attributed to Richard Rohr, and even if he didn't say it, it is certainly worth repeating. "Many Christians have to go through a time and experience of atheism, because the God we have been taught to believe in does not exist."

This book is nothing less than a schooling in necessary Christian atheism about a God of violence. But underlying and vitally more important than that, it is the revelation of the God of love who has been there all along, and whose very character of love prods this kind of atheism into being!

The course of study provided here shows how Jesus' teaching and practice of nonviolence are rooted in the deepest and most dynamic levels of the Old Testament, and ultimately are nothing less than the full revelation of the Biblical God and God's plan for us. Divine nonviolence is the core of the Bible's journey of revelation, from Eden to the New Jerusalem.

If you are picking up this book for the first time do not doubt that it contains the germ of something capable of transforming everything. Not only does it show that the God of the Old Testament is consistent with the God of the Sermon on the Mount, but it carries a sea-change in the meaning of church. Rather than an institutional guarantee for an afterlife, Christian identity is a profound journey of human change in this life, one always intended by a God of unimaginable love and vitality. The resurrection of Jesus is a pledge of a transformed Earth where all of history is invited into a fullness of life, a time and place where violence has no part.

If God is nonviolent then God's identity in the world has to struggle against the default violence of human identity. How can God's face be seen clearly when the eyes we see with are framed and focused by cultural roots and memes of violence? Here is the contribution of the theoretical anthropology of René Girard, itself deeply influenced by the Biblical record. The Girardian perspective enables us to see how humanity has been formed from originating events of violence and how the Bible both reveals this and calls us into an entirely new way of being human. Girardian insight provides a major driving force for this textbook and its method of interpretation.

If the Bible is anthropological revelation — showing us the violence of human cultural origins — then the Bible must carry within itself a critique of its own theological forms. If on the one hand the Bible tells about human violence and on the other about God, texts about the latter will always be written and read in tension with texts about the former. It is only over the course of development of the whole Bible that resolution will be possible, but the tension must be always kept in mind. We get the kind of God our minds are equipped to understand. Violent minds understand God violently; and perhaps nothing more violently than "God," the generative concept at the source of human cultural evolution. But the Bible is never univocal about God: there are always stresses and strains, like a landscape bending and warping around a geological fault. Genesis is particularly suggestive of the way our thought of God has to be decoded according to awareness of generative human violence. If God, after the devastating universal flood, decides "I will never again destroy every living thing, as I have done," what clues for deciphering are being given us? But then the whole labor of the text, from Genesis to Revelation, is a journey of decoding the Bible by the Bible.

Today we are on the cusp of an enormous shift, from colluding with inherited tropes of violent divinity, to surrendering completely to the dramatic truth revealed through the whole Bible: nothing less than a nonviolent God bringing to birth a nonviolent humanity. We offer this coursebook as a heartfelt contribution to this worldwide movement.

⸻

Seven Stories satisfies the requirements of a good hermeneutics: persuasive principles of interpretation making sense of the whole text. The principles we use are essentially three: an historical-critical sensibility, one that would be encountered in most seminaries; the novel ingredient of Girardian anthropology; and running through everything a faith relationship with a God of nonviolence, a God who reveals his/her character over time, coming to transcendent focus in the crucified and risen Jesus.

The first cycle of three classes, titled "Method," introduces this hermeneutic. It presents the evolutionary composition of the Biblical canon together with the disciplines of historical and literary criticism—the thinking which tells us historical situation and literary device always condition meaning. Another class provides a thorough grounding in Girardian anthropology. In the middle there is a session on "The Problem of Atonement." Atonement doctrine, especially in Western Christianity, stands like a fierce cyclops guarding the path back to a more authentic understanding of the scripture. If the one thing we know about Jesus is that he paid to God the price of our sins then there is no way we will be able to work our way through the violence in some of the Biblical stories. In an understanding like this, God is the most violent and vindictive of all beings, demanding the brutal death of his Son in order to be able to look at the rest of humanity with equanimity. Our class on "atonement" demonstrates the historically and culturally conditioned character of this viewpoint, and allows us to begin our journey into the truly transformative vision of the Bible. It represents the breakthrough to a Biblical spirituality of nonviolence.

In some ways this first cycle is the most difficult, because it lacks the excitement of immediate study of the text and perhaps comes across as academic or abstract. It is very important, however, not to be put off. Only by preparing the ground in this way will the student be able to appreciate the full thrill of the amazing new perspective once we embark on the following *Seven Stories*.

So what is a "story," in the sense we are using it here?

Five of the story cycles have titles which express movement "from" something "to" something else: "from" something established and ingrained "to" something unexpected and new. It is a real movement, one happening at the level of human perspective and meaning. If we think for a moment about normal changes in human life, say from childhood to adolescence, or from being single to being married, we can easily understand how the change will bring a real shift in how we see and relate to the world. Different things become important to us, our values change, the very things and the words we use about them change. But what is being talked about in *Seven Stories* is not a normal mutation built into the pathway of human life. We are talking about a shift in the fundamental way in which the world is constructed for everyone, in every situation and at every level.

Imagine that the actual eyes we see with are filters which only let in a certain amount and certain type of information. Then, somehow, we are given new eyes which reveal to us completely new perspectives and possibilities! But even this metaphor doesn't quite do it. Because what the Biblical transformation is offering are new eyes and the reality to go with them. Without the new eyes the new reality is simply not there. With new eyes a new reality dawns. As Jesus says, "The eye is the lamp of the body. So, if your eye is focused ['single' in the Greek], your whole body will be full of light!"

Let's take, for example, the second story cycle, "From Violence to Forgiveness." What is happening is not simply some way of dealing with violence through a subsequent forgiveness; say, for a particular episode of offense. No, it is a matter of going from a world constructed in and through violence to one constructed in and through forgiveness. With this shift in perspective creation is authentically new.

The phrase used here for this huge change is "semiotic shift." It means a shift in the way the world is figured and shaped at the most basic level, the level at which the signs that give and convey meaning are generated. There is a new generation of meaning altogether. So forgiveness is no longer in a kind of equal partnership or back-and-forth with violence. Instead, it replaces it entirely.

Another thought about the way story works can help. In many thrillers or detective stories there is the big moment of revelation, what is sometimes called "the reveal!" This is the point when all the bits fit together and the reader finally understands what has been going on in the many details of the story. The jigsaw suddenly makes sense. There also may be a "twist" at the end that turns the whole thing on its head once more. The semiotic shift is both the reveal and the twist, a credible explanation and a sudden astonishing re-dimensioning that changes everything. At the end of John's Gospel the Risen Jesus meets Mary Magdalene in the garden near to the tomb. In the text she is seen to "turn" twice, before she recognizes Jesus. Mary experiences a "twist" and yet another "twist," before finally she gets the radical "reveal" of the whole story, the one that changes the meaning of everything.

However, in order to get to that final twist we first must have a continuity of narrative which can bring us to that point. In order for the new to arrive there must first be the familiar and known. Thus *Seven Stories* includes cycles on the Land of Israel and the Jerusalem Temple. These institutions and their symbolic value provided the necessary historical and narrative arc within which the plot of the new could emerge. In the *Seven Stories* understanding, the Land of Israel and the Jerusalem Temple are the stable rock of ordinary human culture in and through which the stresses of the new show themselves, and finally break through into new creation.

The upshot of all this is a very clear understanding of the authority of the text. To claim authority for scripture does not depend on an abstract notion of inerrancy, so that somehow every single statement in its literal and grammatical form has the weight of a courtroom statement by or about God. To assert this is to create nothing more than a weapon of authority where the authority is more important than the story, than the transformation wrought by the stories. No, the authority of scripture is much more consistent with a God of creative love, and of loving creation. Its authority lies within the transformative process itself, within its slow, gentle but unfailing agency to bring creation to perfection in peace and love. Is this not a much more credible notion of authority, represented in the slow patient progression of Biblical texts and their final realization in the person of Jesus? Rather than a rock falling from the sky the Bible is a seed sprouting from the earth. Whatever is consistent with this generative process has authority. Everything else is the rock of human culture against which the seed is slowly but irresistibly straining.

Therefore, to be a skilled student of the Bible someone has to read texts on at least two conscious levels. First a text must be read at the critical level, thinking in terms of the author and the actual and symbolic world in which s/he worked. And then the same text must be read within the frame or pathway of transformation. The student will look out for the slight or sometimes major shifts the writer brings about despite, and yet still within, their world. It is this evolving pattern of shifts that counts as revelation, and to see it you have to pay attention at every level.

The Bible is always in discussion with itself and the informed student will see and feel this at every point. Genesis is in discussion with Exodus-through-Kings, Job with Deuteronomy, Ecclesiastes with Proverbs, Jonah with Nahum, Ruth with Nehemiah, Song of Songs with Genesis, and Daniel with almost all of the above. For a Christian the point where the discussion is resolved is with Jesus. And so the persona and teaching of Jesus always constitute the third lesson in each cycle, folding into his story the transformative changes detected in his scriptural tradition. He is also mentioned freely in the course of the Old Testament lessons, because he is indeed the final interpretive lens, the final twist that makes sense of everything.

This pivotal character of Jesus brings us to the issue of New Testament criticism. Did Jesus say and do many of the things that are attributed to him; or was it the early church that made them up as needed? Naturally a course method that employs historical criticism is not indifferent to these questions. Not at all. However, in the compass of the course it would be terribly pedantic to have to vindicate critically every reference to Jesus' words and actions. (Not to say, in the setting of the argument, something that would soon be felt as tendentious!) At a few points arguments will in fact be presented to establish the historical credibility of a certain Gospel saying or incident. However, what we always have in view is the overall quantum leap of meaning accomplished in Jesus' story: from a world based on oblivion of the victim, to one where the victim is displayed for all to see, in and through forgiveness and love. The overall leap provides its own critical frame, one vindicating the ultimate truth of the text.

The Girardian argument of the disclosure of the victim can only work if there is no feedback loop of violence, no reciprocal hostility which would maintain the generative order of violence and, with that, the guilt of the victim. Thus the gospel of absolute nonviolence and love has to be integral to the gospel of disclosure. The assumption then is that the New Testament tradition has to be basically true to accomplish this whole leap, to provide us with the full arc of semiotic shifts. So great is the change, and so difficult and controverted at every step, there had to be a uniquely creative figure (and a history to match) to make it possible. Therefore, as will be evident in the Gospel studies, the critical sense is that the Gospels are substantively true records. They conform historically to their historical results.

HOW TO READ THIS BOOK

There are two ways to use this book. An individual can read it for her own sake, in her own time. She can follow the journey of the stories as if indeed it were a story, but also at the same time an informative discipline of study. To approach the book this way will certainly prove a rewarding and fruitful experience.

Alternatively, *Seven Stories* can be teacher-led, where at least one individual with background in the study of scripture and theology will undertake to lead a group of students through the material. Human change can ultimately only take place in face-to-face settings where people have the chance to absorb at first hand the whole-self response of love and peace characteristic of disciples of Jesus. In this case, where the group embarks on a journey of transformation together, it is recommended that sessions for feedback be incorporated into the schedule. With an appropriate number of such sessions (depending on how many weeks overall the group can commit to) the joint classes will become something more—a community growing together toward the new humanity God desires for them. Each cycle is made up of three lessons. Excluding the initial cycle on methodology, the first two lessons focus on the Old Testament scriptures, the final lesson on Jesus and the Gospels. The cycle always looks to how Jesus interpreted and drew from his scriptures and traditions to create and complete his transformative agenda. At the beginning of each cycle there is a summary giving a broad overview of the complete cycle, including lesson plan, learning objectives, and synopsis of the story as a whole.

Then each lesson has its own overview, with learning objectives, core texts, and key points and concepts. Following the lesson, there are content questions to promote discussion after group study, as well as more reflective questions aimed at personal and communal spiritual growth. Finally, further resources for in-depth study are included, as well as cultural references, such as movies and novels, which help situate and illustrate major themes. At the back of the book there is a glossary of key terms with definitions; and these are indexed to the chapter and lessons where they appear.

The book has most of the technical material needed to back up its arguments, including the necessary scriptural citations, references to words in original languages, and references to academic sources with general publication details. All citations and quotes are taken from the New Revised Standard Version Bible with Apocrypha/ Deuterocanonical Books (1989), unless otherwise stated.

Finally, this book uses the name "Father" for the God of Jesus, as given in the New Testament. However, the meaning understood is always inclusive, that is, "Father/Mother God."

Method

Lesson Plan

Lesson 1: Critical Tools
Lesson 2: The Problem of Atonement
Lesson 3: Original Violence

Learning Objectives

· To gain a preliminary understanding
of the critical tools used by this course.

· To understand that the question
of the "atonement" is critical to the
meaning of Biblical Christianity.

· To encounter the thinking of the French
theoretical anthropologist, René Girard.

Synopsis

We always use a lens in reading the Bible.
The vital thing is to know what this lens is
and whether it fits convincingly with the
revelation we find in the person of Jesus.
The meaning of Jesus' death stands
at the center of Christian faith. It
is essential to know what meaning
has been given to it in the past and
what is available to us to discover.

Key Words/Concepts

· Historical and Literary
  Criticism

· Atonement

· Violence

METHOD
Lesson 1: Critical Tools

Method: Lesson 1

Learning Objectives

· To understand the composition of the canon and its variation between diverse church traditions.

· To gain an appreciation of the historical nature of the Bible, how it was written over a long period of time, reflecting a developing experience of divine revelation.

· To comprehend the character of fundamentalism, and, in contrast, the nature of literary and historical criticism.

· To gain an initial understanding of an anthropological-revelatory lens for reading the Bible.

Core Biblical Texts

· Lk 4.16-30
· Mt 5.21-48

Key Points

· The Bible is composed over a long period, and a human community decided (and still decides) what is in it and what is not.

· The underlying dynamic of revelation is what counts. What is important is where God is trying to lead us, in and through the text and its story. Not the literal reference of each individual word or phrase.

· Our understanding of how a text gets constructed, and what the goal of the writing is, enables us to get a handle on the dynamic of revelation.

· The Bible is a revelation of human violence and God's desire to change the human condition. This is the crucial underlying engine of Biblical writing.

Key Words/ Concepts

· Canon
· Historical-critical method
· Literary criticism
· Literalism; fundamentalism
· Hermeneutics

The Seven Stories are seven key themes in the Bible which together provide both a framework and overview of the whole Hebrew and Christian Scriptures. Each story will be studied over three lessons — the first two lessons primarily looking at the Hebrew Scriptures, the third lesson looking at how Jesus utilized this material and interpreted it.

We study the Scriptures using the following methodologies: (i) the historical-critical method, (ii) literary-criticism, and (iii) an anthropological lens coming from the work of René Girard.

The first and third lessons are an introduction to this methodology. The second lesson provides an overview of the main atonement theories in church history.

Atonement (the purpose and effect of Christ's death) lies at the heart of Christian Bible meaning and interpretation. How we understand the atonement colors how we read the Bible and vice versa. To propose a method of understanding the Bible does not impose a false layer between us and the text. Every possible reading has its method. Denying this simply means that you refuse to recognize you are wearing a pair of glasses while you're reading! It is to claim that your prescription lenses belong to the text and are a natural part of it. The usual evangelical reading is legalistic: this means that evangelicals often wear legal lenses while they're reading. It is equally possible to use critical and anthropological lenses. The point is to acknowledge our reading glasses and move on from that point, seeking always the reading most consistent with love and its necessary condition, freedom.

At the same time, we see the Bible as revelation. It is not purely a human document. It is God's light shone on humanity. To seek the correct method of reading is to seek the method that arises from the depth of the text itself. Reading the Bible reveals both who we are and who God is. We believe it reveals a nonviolent God who calls us to a new humanity and a transformed Earth.

The Old Testament Canon

First: what books are actually in the Old Testament, how did they get there, and are there others which we should be interested in?

The Hebrew Old Testament is the Jewish Tanakh which contains 24 books of Torah, Prophets and Writings. These come from the Masoretic text which is the authoritative Hebrew and Aramaic manuscripts of Rabbinic Judaism, compiled between the 7th and 10th centuries of the Common Era

(CE) but based upon earlier texts dating from the first centuries. There are other manuscripts out there — for example those written in Syrian, and the one written in Greek known as the Septuagint (abbreviated as LXX). The Septuagint is a translation by Jewish scribes of the Hebrew Old Testament compiled from the 3rd century before the Common Era (BCE) and used a lot by the New Testament authors. However, it is the Masoretic text that defines the books of the Jewish canon. This canon was developed between 200 BCE – 200 CE, in part as a response to emerging Christianity. Two of the criteria used to fix the Jewish canon were that its books be written in Hebrew or Aramaic and that they be written no later than the book of Ezra. (The Book of Daniel is the exception — written closer to the time of Jesus, but its story claims to be from the time of the exile.)

As we just said the Tanakh is divided into three parts:

• The Torah, which means "the teaching" or "the law," is the first five books of the Bible, also known as "the Pentateuch."

• The *Nevi'im*, meaning "prophets," include what Christian Bibles call the historical books. These historical books are known by Jews as the "former prophets."

• The *Ketuvim*, meaning "writings," include Wisdom books like Job, Proverbs and Ecclesiastes, plus other late-comers like Chronicles and Daniel.

The Christian Old Testament contains, at minimum, the above twenty-four books but divided in the Christian version or recension into thirty-nine books and ordered differently. Traditions and denominations have changed the order, or divided or combined the books in different ways. Many include additional books in their Old Testament canons, most of which derive from the Septuagint (LXX). The Roman Catholic and Eastern churches hold that certain books found in the LXX are "deuterocanonical," i.e. they are not in the Hebrew canon but nevertheless have canonical value (a "second canon"). These are Tobit, Judith, Wisdom of Solomon, Sirach, Baruch, and 1 & 2 Maccabees, plus various additions to Daniel and Esther. These books and passages are always included in the Bible by those ancient church traditions. Luther rejected these books and additions because he believed the Masoretic Jewish canon to be more authentic. In the Protestant churches they are called "Apocrypha," i.e. of challenged authenticity. However, in the Anglican tradition these books are "not considered equal to the Holy Scriptures, but are useful and good to read." Many of these deuterocanonical/apocryphal books were written in the period when the Jewish canon was still in the process of being fixed, and are informative of Jewish thought in that period. Some of these books were written originally in the more contemporary Greek or Aramaic.

The number of books in the Christian Bible therefore ranges from 39 Books of the Protestant Bible to 46 in the Roman Catholic Bible, and as many as 54 books in the canon of the Ethiopian Orthodox Tewahedo Church.

New Testament Canon

The New Testament is written entirely in Greek. It is accepted by the great majority of churches that the New Testament canon has 27 books. These are the four canonical Gospels (the stories of Jesus' life and death), the Acts of the Apostles (the follow-up to Luke's Gospel, relating the story of the early church), 20 Epistles (or letters), and the Book of Revelation.

Table 1

Hebrew Old Testament Jewish Bible	Protestant Old Testament	Roman Catholic Old Testament	Greek Orthodox Old Testament
Torah	Pentateuch	Pentateuch	Pentateuch
Genesis	Genesis	Genesis	Genesis
Exodus	Exodus	Exodus	Exodus
Leviticus	Leviticus	Leviticus	Leviticus
Numbers	Numbers	Numbers	Numbers
Deuteronomy	Deuteronomy	Deuteronomy	Deuteronomy
Nevi'im (former prophets)	Historical Books	Historical Books	Historical Books
Joshua	Joshua	Joshua	Joshua
Judges	Judges	Judges	Judges
	Ruth	Ruth	Ruth
	1 Samuel	1 Samuel	1 Samuel (1 Kingdoms)
	2 Samuel	2 Samuel	2 Samuel (2 Kingdoms)
	1 Kings	1 Kings	1 Kings (3 Kingdoms)
	2 Kings	2 Kings	2 Kings (4 Kingdoms)
	1 Chronicles	1 Chronicles	1 Chronicles
	2 Chronicles	2 Chronicles	2 Chronicles
			1 Esdras
	Ezra	Ezra	Ezra (2 Esdras)
		Tobit	Tobit
		Judith	Judith
	Esther	Esther	Esther (with additions)
	Nehemiah	Nehemiah	
		1 Maccabees	1 Maccabees
		2 Maccabees	2 Maccabees
			3 Maccabees
			4 Maccabees

Hebrew Old Testament Jewish Bible	Protestant Old Testament	Roman Catholic Old Testament	Greek Orthodox Old Testament
	Wisdom/Poetry	**Wisdom/Poetry**	**Wisdom/Poetry**
	Job	Job	Job
	Psalms	Psalms	Psalms
	Proverbs	Proverbs	Proverbs
	Ecclesiastes	Ecclesiastes	Ecclesiastes
	Song of Solomon	Song of Solomon	Song of Solomon
		Wisdom	Wisdom of Solomon
		Sirach	Wisdom of Sirach
Nevi'im (latter prophets)	**Major Prophets**	**Major Prophets**	**Major Prophets**
Isaiah	Isaiah	Isaiah	Isaiah
Jeremiah	Jeremiah	Jeremiah	Jeremiah
	Lamentations	Lamentations	Lamentations
		Baruch	Baruch
			Letter of Jeremiah
Ezekiel	Ezekiel	Ezekiel	Ezekiel
	Daniel	Daniel	Daniel (with additions)
	Minor Prophets	**Minor Prophets**	**Minor Prophets**
Hosea	Hosea	Hosea	Hosea
Joel	Joel	Joel	Joel
Amos	Amos	Amos	Amos
Obadiah	Obadiah	Obadiah	Obadiah
Jonah	Jonah	Jonah	Jonah
Micah	Micah	Micah	Micah
Nahum	Nahum	Nahum	Nahum
Habakkuk	Habakkuk	Habakkuk	Habakkuk
Zephaniah	Zephaniah	Zephaniah	Zephaniah
Haggai	Haggai	Haggai	Haggai

Hebrew Old Testament Jewish Bible	Protestant Old Testament	Roman Catholic Old Testament	Greek Orthodox Old Testament
Zechariah	Zechariah	Zechariah	Zechariah
Malachai	Malachai	Malachai	Malachai
Ketuvim (writings)			
Psalms			
Job			
Proverbs			
Ruth			
Songs of Songs			
Ecclesiastes			
Lamentations			
Esther			
Daniel			
Ezra/Nehemiah			
Chronicles			

Basic Timeline of the Bible

It is useful to see how the stories and events of the Bible connect in a historical timeline. Table 2 provides the basic sweep of the Biblical era and the beginning of Christianity. (Some of these dates are best estimates or approximate.)

The two key events in the development of the Old Testament are the Exodus and the exile, especially the latter. It is through these events that the Jews found their identity and meaning. The Torah is both a narrative of and commentary on the Exodus and it reaches its final edited form at the time of the exile. The four major prophets (Isaiah, Jeremiah, Ezekiel and Daniel) are all written (or set) during the exile period. Just as in our own lives, a pivotal event of loss and trauma will interpret everything before or after, so the exile served to grow a crucial layer of reflective meaning for almost all Israelite history.

Literal & Fundamental vs. Historical-Literary Critical reading of the Bible

A document composed over the better part of one thousand years needs careful assessment as to when an account was composed, alongside the judgment of when and in what manner the events described actually occurred. There is also the question of what literary form a writer is using

to make a point. Clearly poetry differs from prose, and if Jesus could create powerful parables is it not possible that some key Old Testament passages — for example, the Garden of Eden — were written as parables rather than factual narratives? Finally, over that length of time it is all but certain that attitudes and perspectives changed, and this movement of thought is reflected as the different writings progress.

In the late 19th and early 20th centuries American Protestant fundamentalism arose in response to the scientific method and secular viewpoint of the modern era. A fundamentalist reading of the Bible takes a strict literal approach to the text. The statements written are interpreted to be exactly true as written. For example if a book claims to have a certain author then this is the person who wrote the text (rather than being attributed — a favorite literary device in antiquity). What fundamentalism achieved was a mental bulwark against the creeping relativism of science and modernist criticism. If every word is true because God said so, then nothing, absolutely nothing, can argue against it. A fundamentalist reading, therefore, makes every element of the text equal to every other. And so, naturally, expressions of God's command to "utterly destroy" an enemy are equal and somehow equivalent to "God is love."

In the 19th century, scholars began to study the Bible writings as literature: the birth of Biblical literary criticism. It involves, for example, appreciating the function of symbolism, metaphor, paradox, irony, style, story and plot in the text. The book of Job is a poster example of a text crying out for literary evaluation. (See Story 5, Lesson 1.) The historical critical method overlaps with this approach, seeing Biblical literature as historical products and investigating sources, problems of authorship, and questions of context. Historical criticism looks at the internal evidence of the book (references to contemporary or later historical events, and arguments in their likely historical context), as well as external evidence (archeological artifacts and contemporary documents). It does this in order to accurately determine the text in the place and time in which it was written, along with the plausible historical roots of the events described. In this way historical criticism seeks to get a better sense of the writer's meaning in narrating the events, and, with that, the underlying dynamic of revelation.

Examples of historical-literary criticism

Read Genesis 1.1–13 (excerpt from the six days of creation).

Read Genesis 2.4–14 (excerpt from the Garden story).

Compare the two creation stories. They have two different voices. The author of Chapter 1 uses the word "God." The style is poetic, sonorous — almost liturgical. In Chapter 2 the word for God is "YHWH" ("The Lord" — Hebrew, Adonai — is added as a scribal annotation in place of the unsayable name). The Garden of Eden story uses older material, parallels of which can be found in other ancient literature (for example, the snake and tree in the Babylonian Gilgamesh epic). And the Lord appears in a much more familiar, almost human role, than the more remote, majestic God of the first chapter. Genesis 1, while placed at the beginning of the book, is more modern and developed in sensibility. God creates by his word alone, and there is the notable absence of primordial battles so dear to world mythology, and represented in fact elsewhere in the Bible (for example Isa 27.1, Pss 74.14, 89.10). This would suggest Genesis 1 is a later composition than the early books of Isaiah. The author of chapter 1 is sometimes known as the "Priestly author;" the author of chapter 2 is known as the "Yahwist author," because of the way they name God.

Editing in the form of translating still goes on today. We have already looked at the different canons of the Christian Bible. There are also many different Bible translations. Often the translation is influenced by the theological concerns of the editor. Sometimes it is necessary to get back to the original Greek or Hebrew to investigate the original meaning. (For example, Job's "repentance" at Job 42.6 can be translated in a different, quite contradictory way — as a deliberate double meaning which maintains all his previous complaints. See Story 5, Lesson 1.)

Interpretation is a word for the meaning derived from the text, and the process of deriving that meaning. Interpretations can be grounded or fanciful. One example of fanciful interpretation is the concept of "the rapture" which was invented by a minister in the Church of Ireland, John Nelson Darby, in the 19th century and then set out as an addendum in the Scofield Bible which was very popular in the U.S. throughout the early 20th century. Over the years it came to be regarded as a part of scripture, but the interpretation is achieved by stringing together a number of texts without regard for the context of each. (This in turn is a result of a fundamentalist reading, where words and sentences more or less stand on their own, apart from context, thus lending themselves to random connection.)

A New Hermeneutics

The scholarly name for the work of interpretation is "hermeneutics." Biblical hermeneutics is the formal study of interpretation of the Bible. As argued above, the literary and historical critical method is one set of tools we will be using to understand and interpret the Bible. Another crucial interpretative tool in this course is an anthropological lens derived from the work of René Girard. Girard argues that the Bible reveals the violence at the heart of human culture and points to the way to overcome this violence. In other words, the Bible progressively demonstrates the "generative" nature of human violence — the way in which it gives birth to human culture. Hand in hand with this it opens up the possibility of a new and different humanity not based in violence. More will be said about this in Lesson 3 of this cycle, but we can say at once that if the mainspring of the Bible is not the legal weight of each word, but a progressive engine of disclosure, overturning a root human condition, then we are discovering a radically new hermeneutics. One which provokes human transformation.

In a nutshell, the Bible is a living dynamic document that reflects and projects a changing understanding of God and humanity.

Read Jehu's slaughter of the house of Ahab in 2 Kings 10.1–11, and then the critique of this action by the prophet Hosea (Hos 1.4).

Jesus also re-interpreted his own scriptures (of course!).

Read Lk 4.16–30 (Jesus reads from the scroll of Isaiah in Nazareth).

Compare Isa 61.1–2. Jesus leaves out the final part of the Isaiah prophecy which proclaims a day of vengeance.

Read Mt 5.21–48 (here Jesus is explicitly rejecting previous interpretations, including negating traditional texts; e.g. Mt 5. 31–32, 38).

In conclusion this course will aim to place the Bible texts in their historical context, try to capture the original meaning of the text, and see how Jesus interpreted the Hebrew scriptures and followed them through to their transformative end goal.

Lesson Questions

· Do you think that understanding the Bible as an evolving historical human document rather than a sacrosanct text with a legal, once-and-for-all meaning, increases or decreases its validity/authority?

· Does a text have to be literal to be true? If not, how does this affect your understanding of divine revelation?

· Why do you think the Bible contains texts that appear to contradict each other? (For example, Gen 1.12 — vegetation created before human beings, and 2.5-8 — human beings before vegetation. How can both be revelation?)

Personal Reflection

· What is/has been the dominant hermeneutic of my church/ Christian experience?

· How important is/has been the Bible, and Bible study, in my Christian life?

· Which parts of the Bible have I found difficult to read or understand? Which books do I turn to most? Why?

· What am I hoping to get from this course of study? What are my personal goals?

Glossary

· Canon — the rule or list which establishes which books are to be included in the Bible.

· Septuagint (LXX) — Greek translation of the Old Testament produced by Jewish scholars around 200 BCE, used frequently in first century CE New Testament.

· Torah — first five books of the Bible, comprising the "Teaching" or "Law" of the Jewish faith.

· Nevi'im — "Prophets" in the Hebrew Bible, including narrative from Joshua through Kings, and "Latter Prophets," Isaiah, Jeremiah, Ezekiel and the twelve minor prophets.

· Ketuvim — the writings of the Jewish canon coming after the Torah and Prophets

· Deuterocanonical — the "second canon," consisting of books approved as part of the Old Testament in a number of Christian traditions, including the Roman Catholic, but not included in the Hebrew Bible, and named Apocrypha in most Protestant churches.

· Apocrypha — a number of books included in the LXX (Septuagint) considered to be not authoritative for faith; Luther included the deuterocanonical books under this heading.

· Historical-Critical Method — investigation of the historical reliability of events described in the Bible, and of the circumstances of their being written down.

· Critical — refers to the exercise of judgment about the thought-world and social pressures affecting the composition of a text.

· Literary Criticism — the investigation of the literary and rhetorical character of Bible writings affecting their interpretation.

· Fundamentalism — a faith attitude to the Bible which considers the text to be inerrant (without error) and literally true, in order to preserve the "fundamentals of the faith." It arose in response to the scientific method of higher criticism.

· Hermeneutics — a scholarly discipline offering coherent principles of interpretation.

· Tanakh — Hebrew acronym for the Torah–Prophets–Writings.

· Gilgamesh Epic — an ancient Babylonian writing, dating from the 2nd millennium BCE, describing the adventures of a king, Gilgamesh; a number of its concerns and stories are paralleled in the first chapters of Genesis.

Resources/Background Reading

· Brian McClaren, A New Kind of Christianity (2011)

· For Fundamentalism see the original set of volumes "Fundamentals" (https://archive.org/details/fundamentalstest17chic). Also a useful article describing the Fundamentals project at http://www.theopedia.com/the-fundamentals.

Cultural References

· Movie, Noah, dir. Aronofsky (2014) as a fairly fundamentalist reading of the story, with apocryphal references from the book of Enoch, emphasizing the destruction of life.

Movie, Higher Ground, dir. Vera Farmiga (2011) depicting the tensions within a fundamentalist Christian community.

Table 2 — Basic Timeline of the Bible

From Beginning of Second Millennium
Canaanite Myths and Prehistory

1750–1300 BCE
Patriarchal Traditions, Israel's Family Ancestry

1400–1200 BCE
From Hebrew Experience in Egypt to God of Exodus & Covenant Tribes

1200–1050 BCE
Judges

1050–930 BCE
United Monarchy (Saul, David, Solomon)

930–587 BCE
Rise and Fall of the Two Kingdoms, Israel and Judah

587–539 BCE
Exile to return

537–332 BCE
Early Post-Exilic or Second Temple period

334–167 BCE
From Alexander the Great to Antiochus Epiphanes persecution

164–63 BCE
From Hasmoneans to conquest by Rome

63 BCE–6 CE
Period of puppet rulers (e.g. Herod the Great)

6–30 CE
Direct Rule of Judea by Rome (Prefects) to death of Jesus

32 CE
Jesus Mission to Gentiles begins

Start of the Second Millennium BCE
Canaanite and Babylonian myths, employed as matrix for Genesis 1–11

18th - 13th Century
Oral Patriarchal traditions, matrix for Genesis 12–50

From 13th Century BCE
Memories, stories and early records basis for narratives in
Exodus, Leviticus, Numbers, Joshua, Judges

From 11th - Early 6th BCE
Court records as basis for 1&2 Samuel, 1&2 Kings

8th Century
Prophets, First Isaiah (Chapters 1–39), Amos, Hosea, Micah

7th Century
Prophet Nahum

6th Century Before and During exile
Prophets Habakkuk, Obadiah, Jeremiah, Ezekiel. Deuteronomic authors and editors
begin to produce book of Deuteronomy and give final form to 1&2 Kings

End of 6th century, Return from exile
Prophets, Second & Third Isaiah, Haggai, Zechariah. Genesis finalized and made preface
to whole Bible, critiquing original violence of early myths and rivalry in patriarchal stories

5th century
Ezra and Nehemiah, 1&2 Chronicles, Malachi (Job, Jonah and Ruth arguably
composed in this period as critique of dominant narratives)

3rd - 2nd centuries BCE
Sirach, Daniel, 1&2 Maccabees

Psalms is a compilation of material stretching from the beginning
of the Israelite tradition through the post-exilic period

METHOD
Lesson 2: The Problem of Atonement

Learning Objectives

· To see how Christian atonement doctrine is the product of an historical development over almost fifteen hundred years.
· To understand the generative role of violence in the topics of exchange, honor, satisfaction, penal substitution.
· To see that the New Testament should not be used to underpin satisfaction doctrine or penal substitution.
· To begin to understand that Jesus reveals a nonviolent God at the same time as he reveals human violence, and it is this twin revelation that transforms us.

Core Biblical Texts

· Jn 12.20–33
· Rom 3.21–26

Key Points

· Atonement doctrine is a cultural product of Western Christianity.
· Violence not forgiveness is the generative force of this doctrine.
· The transcendent nonviolence of Jesus both reveals the truth of God and changes the nature of humans.

Key Words/Concepts

· Tricking the Devil
· Satisfaction
· Penal Substitution
· God's Nonviolence

This class is about "atonement." It gives a brief overview of the history of the church that led to the point we are now at in our Christian theology.

Why are we concerned with this topic? The question of atonement is crucial to an account of how the gospel works. The prevailing understanding of atonement is loaded with violence. It interprets the gospel in terms of violence. The *Seven Stories* program can be understood as a profound alternative. It overturns the traditional violent construct by which the message of Christianity has been conceived and proclaimed.

It is important to grasp this alternative right from the start.

The common parlance understanding of "atonement" is to right a wrong via some kind of penance or punishment. We say a man who has completed a prison sentence has "atoned" for his crime. In the specific Christian context "the atonement" refers to the death of Jesus and the way it has been read as compensating the offense of sin against God's honor and justice. The purpose of the compensation was to effect the reconciliation of the sinner to God.

Over the course of history there have been varying interpretations of Christ's death. None of them was ever adopted as doctrine by an early Council of the church. The understanding given above is a relatively late version, from the eleventh century.

The First Millennium — Ransom from the Devil by a Trick!

In the first millennium the understanding in the West was generally related to the figure of Satan or the Devil. The idea was that the Devil had humanity in his power and the inevitable expression of this was death for all humankind. This interpretation was a result of a combination of texts in the Bible, beginning with the story of the Serpent in the Garden of Eden and running, for example, through Heb 2.14–15 and First Corinthians 2.6–8.

The death of Jesus then set people free from this bondage to Satan. How? In one early 20th century book on atonement *Christus Victor* (Gustaf Aulen, 1931), it is presented as a simple victory or triumph. Christ's death and resurrection are a victory over the power of the Devil, and no more needs to be said. But from very early on there was a distinctive concept of how this actually took place. It was a trick or a ruse played on the Devil. Because through Adam's sin we were all doomed to death, the Devil had rights over all humanity and he exercised those rights in the death of Jesus. But exactly in this instance he had no rights, because Jesus was innocent and was God. The Devil fatally overreached himself and forfeited his claim on humanity. There are various slight permutations in the formula, but what became fixed in popular imagination were images like those of a fish and a fishhook, or a mouse, cheese and a mousetrap. The Devil is the greedy fish or mouse and Jesus is the bait or cheese. The Devil takes the hook which is the Deity he cannot devour, or is caught in the mousetrap which is Jesus' death far in excess of what he can claim. (Believe it or not, Augustine is the author of the mousetrap image.)

It's easy to see in this thinking and its imagery the role played by the motif of exchange. One thing of value is handed over for another. The guarantee of the exchange is violence, and we see that because the moment a creditor oversteps his due he instantly becomes a debtor himself. Only the latent mutual violence in exchange can guarantee this instant switch.

We can also see in the "trick on the Devil" scheme the enormous role given to the Devil, almost on the level of God himself. So much so that a ruse had to be devised to overcome the master agent of evil.

It was partly in response to this excessive role given to the Devil that a major reaction took place during the 11th century. It was seen as demeaning to God to have to stoop to tricking the Devil or according him any rights. Rather it was understood that it was always a matter of God's justice that humankind was handed over to death as consequence of Adam's sin. If the Devil had any power it was because God had given it to him. Thus it was an easy transition to think it was not the Devil we were in debt to, but God himself!

Enter Anselm of Canterbury!

Through Anselm especially we begin to see the historically conditioned character of atonement doctrine.

The Second Millennium — Anselm and Satisfaction Made to God

Anselm shifts the theology. Instead of a figure of evil, it is now God who is our enemy!

Anselm was the son of a Lombard nobleman, born in North Italy. He became a priest and rose through the ranks until, in the last decade of the 11th century, he became Archbishop of Canterbury. He wrote a major document *Cur Deus Homo* ("Why God Man?") published in 1096. He wrote it in response to an inquiry from Crispin, the archdeacon of Westminster Abbey, who had been in dialogue with a group of educated Jews. They claimed the teaching of Jesus as God–made– flesh was demeaning to God, because of the normal indignities of human life, but most of all because of Jesus' brutal death.

Anselm replied by turning the critique on its head: it was precisely because of the dishonor to God made by human sin that the Son of God had to become human and eventually die. Jesus' death compensated the Creator's offended honor because he himself was also divine and so gave an infinite and free service to the Father which no other human could give. Just to live as a man would have been enough, but dying in the way he did was the biggest and best service of all.

We can detect in this answer the cultural context of aristocratic honor and the absolute need to maintain it should it be in any way offended. It was the calculus of honor-debt that made sense of Jesus' death for Anselm.

Honor is a social commodity the force of which is a controlled and sanctioned violence. Dueling with pistols or swords is its classic expression, preceded by the standard line "I demand satisfaction." Anselm used exactly that term and it became pivotal to his, and then our, understanding. He said that Jesus "made satisfaction" to God for sin.

There is also the context of the Crusades, motivated by much of the same sentiment. In the same year as the book's publication (1096) Pope Urban II called the first crusade, to take back the holy sepulcher in Jerusalem from its dishonoring Muslim invaders. It was a Christian holy war backed by God's holy will.

Once these metaphors and themes were released in relation to Jesus' death, then the heart of Christianity was twisted to a violent, vengeful set of relationships.

Protestant Reformation: From Honor to Wrath

The Protestant Reformation brought this violence to the fore with the concept of "penal substitution." The notion of "satisfaction" masked violence under the thin veil of honor; the demand for punishment made it explicit.

Luther does not use the word substitution, but the logic of Jesus as a stand-in for human sinners is plain (plus, in this instance, the continued use of the concept of satisfaction). "Christ was made to become the greatest thief, adulterer, robber, desecrater, blasphemer…. In short, He has and bears all the sins of all men in His body — not in the sense that He has committed them but in the sense that he took these sins, committed by us, upon his own body in order to make satisfaction for them with his blood" (Luther, *On Galatians*). Christ "really and truly offered Himself to the Father for eternal punishment on our behalf. His human nature behaved as if He were a man to be eternally condemned to Hell" (Luther, *Commentary on Romans*).

Calvin goes from the stand-in figure of Christ, vividly presented by Luther, to its subjective effect in the mind of the believer, i.e. to the concept of substitution. The term becomes a shorthand, a concise legal formula, for the saving function of the death of Jesus. It is continually reinforced by the terror of what substitution is saving from.

"This is our acquittal: the guilt that held us liable for punishment has been transferred to the head of the Son of God (Is 53.12). We must, above all, remember this substitution, lest we tremble and remain anxious throughout life — as if God's righteous vengeance, which the Son of God has taken upon himself, still hung over us." (Calvin, *Institutes*, II.xvi.5)

"Suppose a man learns that he was estranged from God through sin, is an heir of wrath, subject to the curse of eternal death, excluded from all hope of salvation, beyond every blessing of God, the slave of Satan, captive under the yoke of sin, destined finally for a dreadful destruction and already involved in it; and that at this point Christ interceded as his advocate, took upon himself and suffered the punishment that, from God's righteous judgment, threatened all sinners; that he purged with his blood those evils which had rendered sinners hateful to God; that by this expiation he made satisfaction and sacrifice duly to God the Father; that as intercessor he has appeased God's wrath; that on this foundation rests the peace of God with men; that by this bond his benevolence is maintained toward them. Will the man not then be even more moved by all these things which so vividly portray the greatness of the calamity from which he has been rescued?" (*Institutes*, II.xvi.2. Note again the continued use of Anselm's "satisfaction.")

Through this process, from Anselm to Calvin, there was laid down the classic Western Christian mindset of divine violence directed against humanity, only held back by the substitutionary death of Jesus. It is here, this course argues, that there is a profound mis-diagnosis of the human problem. It says our most fundamental problem is God's anger, not human anger.

The Eastern Orthodox church has always had a different, more restorative approach. It is deeply influenced by Athanasius' *De Incarnatione*. (But it is worth noting that here Christ still takes on the role of substitute or stand-in for God's judgment of death due to all.) "He [the Word] took to himself a body which could die, in order that, since this participated in the Word who is above all, it might suffice for death on behalf of all, and because of the Word who was dwelling in it, it might remain incorruptible, and so corruption might cease from all men by the grace of the resurrection."

"Seven Stories" Atonement

The *Seven Stories* concept of atonement comes from a place of redemption from violence. We believe the correct diagnosis of our condition is the way that violence controls our existence, to the extent that it gives birth to human thinking itself. Not surprisingly human thinking works to frame God in terms of violence.

To grasp this is necessarily to embrace an evolutionary attitude — humankind cannot change a root behavior all at once. It is a process. And it leaves in a kind of mystery the question of how God could set up a violent creation in the first place. This is a major driver for fundamentalist thought — that creation did not have death in it to begin with: it was sin which produced death. However, this is to think in a very linear fashion and denies the possibility that creation is a work–in–progress; that if God built freedom into creation then violence was always going to be a risk. If God is to create a genuinely non-determined creation, independent of his control, then perhaps forces of opposition and destruction cannot be avoided. In any event, we can see in the Bible a movement to overcome all violence in the created order.

Redemption comes from the revelation that we are caught up in human systems of violence and that God's desire, and very nature, is to free us from these and lead us into life. Redemption is not about debts or a law that must be fulfilled. It is a positive program of giving life. The only cry for blood comes from us. Jesus becomes the victim in order to reveal the whole system of victims and scapegoats, and at the same moment the bottomless forgiveness and nonviolence that releases us to a new way of being.

We have shown that the construction of "penal substitution" is an historically conditioned process. We then "find" it in scripture. In reality, the New Testament is very imprecise about how Christ's death works. There is an overwhelming experience that it works, and the writing reflects that experience without trying to analyze.

Paul has been read in a number of ways, but there are none of the mechanics of satisfaction/substitution in his letters, only vague allusions to sacrifice as a metaphor, full of confidence that Christ's death "for us" changes everything. At Romans 3.25a we have a key text which uses sacrificial metaphor. But God, not man, puts forward the effective element, and if we read it in its original Greek, it is nothing like a "sacrifice" or "an atonement." Rather it is *hilasterion*, translated in the Old Testament as "mercy seat," and meaning a place in the Holy of Holies where the desired effect of sacrifice happens — where mercy takes place. The implications are massive. Only in the most convoluted and

barbaric thinking can this event be interpreted as "God offering sacrifice (of Jesus) to himself." Rather, in Christ, God is introducing into the human scene a completely new "holy space," one where what was sought before in the violent mechanics of sacrifice now happens by the free revelation of God's nonviolence (grace) in Christ.

John's Gospel centers on "the lamb of God who takes away the sin of the world" (1.29). The lamb is of or from God (not a sacrifice offered to God). It is the same as the Son of God. It comes from God and shows us who God is. Later Jesus asks himself whether he should pray to the Father "to save [him] from this hour?" (of his suffering and death, 12.27). But then he says "No, it is for this reason that I have come to this hour," followed directly by a prayer to the Father to "glorify" his name (v. 28). In other words, the purpose of Jesus' death is to shine forth God's identity and character in the world. "Glory" is the transforming public manifestation of God's nonviolence.

Resurrection is the fulfillment of this glory. Jesus' nonviolent life is restored and made transcendent. It is declared and recognized as the same life as God's. Because Jesus rose again we all are caught up in this new nonviolent reality. The world has changed.

The resurrection is not about the hereafter, rather about transformed life now and into the ages to come.

Taking Transaction and Transference out of Atonement

In this understanding there is no exchange or transaction, one thing given for another. If this still exists in salvation it means that God has to obey a higher law of exchange economy. He can't just forgive. Exchange is the law of money, one thing for another. Literally, it "makes the world go 'round."

In our understanding atonement is non-transactional. It is a free gift. It is grace, as always understood. If there is transaction then grace is not really grace. The receipt is also free: we must be open to receive it. The gospel reveals and unfolds a totally free relationship not based in any violence.

Sanctification in the penal substitution world in fact represents the re-entry of legalism: you have to be this way (holy) to show you are saved. Instead, there is the revelation of a new way of human life, one which we will want to be part of, and more and more so.

Transference is a term that refers to a subjective process, while transaction is more objective.

Transference has a classic meaning in psychoanalysis where the therapist can become a stand-in for a missing father/mother/lover. In transference we transfer onto the other an emotional energy or polarity in order to receive in turn what we feel we are missing.

In Anselmian atonement, we transfer onto Jesus our guilt and we get back our innocence.

In this new model there is no transference from the human side. There is a revelation of the energy of violence which makes such transference possible, the making of victims and scapegoats to prove our innocence. At the same moment there is the communication of God's bottomless love in Christ, God's non-retaliation before our violence.

We are given new and crucial life information, and invited into the new way of being it offers.

Lesson Questions

· The popular first millennium atonement theory was of the Devil being tricked. Why did it fall out of favor?

· How did the crusades and the medieval concept of "honor" and "satisfaction" influence Anselm's understanding of the atonement?

· In what ways are both of these theories transactional? Why is this inherently violent?

· To what extent does a transaction or price still remain at the heart of dominant atonement theory today?

Personal Reflection

· What has been your received understanding of the atonement?

· How is God the Father presented in this understanding? How is Jesus? Has this influenced your relationship with God/Jesus?

· Why do you think the meaning of the atonement is so important for how we understand God and God's work in the world?

Glossary

· Satisfaction — the surrender of some element of life on the part of an offender to make good the loss of status on the part of the one offended.

· hilasterion — literally "a covering place," a place where the effect of sin is covered over and annulled by blood; used to refer to the cover above the Ark in the Holy of Holies.

· Penal Substitution — the need for divine justice to make Christ a substitute to endure punishment in the place of human sinners if they are to be forgiven.

· Generative Violence — René Girard's theory that violence gives rise to human culture and yet always continues to produce more violence.

Resources/Background Reading

· *Cross Purposes, The Violent Grammar of Christian Atonement*, chapters two and three, Anthony Bartlett (2001)

· Anthony Bartlett's blogs on Bible interpretation at http://hopeintime. com/category/bible-interpretation/

· *Divine Dance: The Trinity and Your Transformation*, Richard Rohr and Mike Morrell (2016)

· *Christus Victor*, Gustaf Aulen (1931)

· *Cur Deus Homo*, Anselm of Canterbury (1096)

Cultural References

· *The Lion, the Witch and the Wardrobe*, C.S.Lewis (1950) — the sacrifice of Aslan as an example of tricking the Devil/White Witch.

· *The Portrait of Dorian Gray*, Oscar Wilde (1890) — transactional thinking: Dorian transfers his corruption to his portrait in order to stay beautiful, but in the end receives it all back in his own body.

· Movie, *Memento*, dir. Christopher Nolan (2000), "Somebody has to pay, Lenny, somebody always pays."

METHOD
Lesson 3: Original Violence

Learning Objectives

· To grasp the seismic shift in thought emerging with René Girard's anthropology.

· To understand something of the intellectual pathway producing this shift.

· To become familiar with the three stages of Girard's thought.

· To see how Biblical revelation breaks open the violent construct of human origins in order to transform it.

Core Biblical Texts

· Mt 26.69-75
· Lk 23.34

Key Points

· Mimetic desire is the specific human quality that both threatens overwhelming violence and produces its sacrificial solution.

· Girard follows a course of reflection from mimesis, through sacrifice, to Biblical revelation.

· Original violence is subverted and transformed by original love.

Key Words/Concepts

· Mimesis

· Scapegoat/ surrogate victim

· Sacrificial crisis

· Revelation

Girardian Anthropology

In the latter part of the Twentieth Century, after two World Wars, the Holocaust of the Jews, the Atomic Bomb ... there comes a profound reflection on human violence. More than simply biological animal responses (Konrad Lorenz), or drives and learned behaviors (Maslow), René Girard introduced a relational structural understanding. His work opened up the question of human violence as a fundamental human issue, and thus offered a whole new take on the death of Christ and the meaning of atonement.

But Girard did not produce his understanding out of whole cloth. He builds on thinkers like Durkheim, Freud and Lévi-Strauss who were working in the fields of sociology, psychology and anthropology — the human sciences. He is part of the intellectual progress of his era.

Structuralism

One example of the intellectual background is the work of Claude Lévi-Strauss. Without going into complex detail Lévi-Strauss invented structuralism, beginning with a study of elementary forms of kinship. We need to understand a little of the shift in thinking he produced in order to get a handle on Girard.

Lévi-Strauss developed a picture of kinship as a changeable structure of relationships. The resulting theory of structuralism claimed to see an underlying pattern of thought in all human activity. Normally we think of kinship in terms of degrees of closeness or separation from the nuclear family — husband, wife and children. Thus we have the wife and husband's birth families as in–laws, and blood relations as sons, daughters, cousins, second-cousins etc. Everything is a strictly conceived tree of descent and kinship. It is a hierarchical picture necessary for controlling rights of inheritance and property.

Table 4: Traditional Family Tree

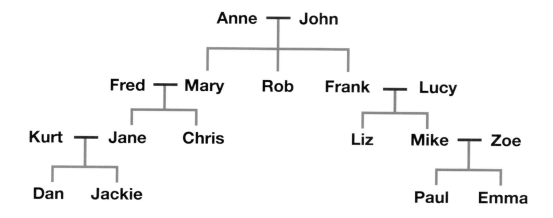

Lévi-Strauss argued that elementary or primitive forms of kinship were different. They did not consist of a tree of descent, but of lateral arrangements between families. They had one overriding purpose which was getting women from outside a family unit to marry men within it, and making available those within the unit to other, external family units with the same need. They are essentially systems of exchange between families.

There were different organizational solutions bringing this about, not based upon family trees. By far the most important factor was a set of relationships which were connected and interchangeable: for example, the one between the son and the father was linked to the one between son and his maternal uncle. When Lévi-Strauss tracked these relationships he noticed that if there was a harsh or rigid relationship in the first case (between father and son), there was a warm and familiar one in the second (between son and uncle), and then vice versa. There was also always a corresponding shift in relationship with the familial sister.

Alternative Relationships Between Pairs

Family Structure One:

Son	✗	Father
Son	♥	Maternal Uncle
Son	♥	Sister

Family Structure Two:

Son	✗	Maternal Uncle
Son	♥	Father
Son	✗	Sister

He concluded these related pairs were the elementary structure of kinship, but they could always be changed around. What was essential was the structure, not a particular set. Girard derived from Lévi-Strauss the insight that the relationships between pairs were indeed arbitrary, but it was always violence that governed the structure.

Now before you lose it trying to figure this out, remember kinship (and archaic sexism) are not our concern! Girard did not examine these relationships psychologically. What is important is Lévi-Strauss' general observation: relationships between pairs can be turned around (inverted) and it doesn't matter, so long as some overall structure is maintained. Here is Lévi-Strauss' famous conclusion:

"A kinship system does not consist in the objective ties of descent or consanguinity between individuals. It exists only in human consciousness; it is an arbitrary system of representations, not the spontaneous development of a real situation." (*Structural Anthropology,* 50)

"It is not the families (isolated terms) which are truly 'elementary' but rather the relations between these terms." (*Structural Anthropology*, 51)

With this reflection "structuralism" is born, the way of thinking which suggests that truth is relationships between pairs and the way we choose to set this up, rather, than any objective or real situation.

Girard both agreed and disagreed. He noticed that the taboo of incest lay at the heart of the system. For Lévi-Strauss the taboo was fundamental but it simply served the exchange of women.

"The primitive and irreducible character of the basic unit of kinship is actually a direct result of the universal presence of the incest taboo. This is really saying that in human society a man must obtain a woman from another man who gives him a daughter or a sister." (*Structural Anthropology*, 46)

Girard says, "Not so fast!" In the absence of a rational pre-conceived plan (remember representations are arbitrary!) a universal taboo cannot get put in place out of nowhere. Girard intuits that it is the experience and threat of violence which is the key. The possibility (and preceding events) of deadly competition between males (father, son, uncle) for an available female (daughter, sister) — this is what creates the incest taboo. The violence loaded in the taboo is stronger than any possible desire for the female. The unconscious taboo then acts as a way to protect the clan from self-destruction. For Girard, it is only violence and its generative power of creating order that provided the stability necessary for humanity to survive. (This will become fully clear when we get to the section below on Scapegoat and Sacrifice.)

We can conclude, therefore, that in elementary kinship it does not matter where the figure of prohibition and control is — father or uncle — so long as there is one. It is the terror of intra-familial rivalry for women that finally determines any kinship relationship. Reasonably, there has to be a very strict figure somewhere in the system to signal the taboo. It does not matter who it is; there just has to be one.

In other words, a violent structure of relationships is necessary to control violence. It is a cultural reality rather than biological drives which protects the human family. (Note: in animal societies it seems incest is generally avoided by the instinctual migration/driving out of young males/females from the family group. There is a lot of discussion about how biologically important incest avoidance may or may not be. Certainly incest allows a narrow pool of genes to gain a hold. Girardian violence-avoidance would then have a biological side-effect of greater diversity.)

In sum, the relational structure between human family units is arbitrary, the reason for it is essential. Girard discovered that arbitrary structural relationships had violence as their origin and sanction. It was not family tree (hierarchy) which controlled elementary kinship, but the internal taboo (violence) which was critical.

This is just one example of Girard's intellectual parentage. There are several other intellectual influences on Girard. They all come to him, in a kind of cascade of evidence, resulting in his pivotal book *Violence and the Sacred*. But we must now back up to trace the first stage of his reflection that will lead him consecutively to the point of *Violence and the Sacred*.

1st Stage of Girard's Thought — Mimesis or Imitative Desire

The very first stage of Girard's work came from literature. He discovered the imitative nature of desire, something he calls "mimesis." We desire because someone else shows us what to desire. Reading Cervantes, Shakespeare, Dostoevsky, Proust, he discovered a pattern in these great writers: they always come to a point of abandoning the belief that desire is something coming entirely from within us — ideal "spontaneous desire." Instead they discover that desire is really always imitating someone else. He wrote a whole book on Shakespeare in this line — *A Theatre of Envy*. He finds *Midsummer Night's Dream* to be a lucid example of the principle: Shakespeare understood mimesis. Thus Hermia loves Lysander, Helena loves Demetrius, but Demetrius is crazy about Hermia. Oberon and Puck plan to put love potion on the eyes of Demetrius to turn him around. But first by mistake they put it on Lysander, and then finally on Demetrius. So now they are both crazy about

Helena when before they were crazy for Hermia .... Girard says the love potion is a device and the real play going on under the surface of the fantasy is the imitative nature of desire. As Helena says "Oh Hell! To choose love by another's eyes!"

Mirror Neurons

Girard produced the thought of mediated or learned desire in 1961. In the nineties a converging source of evidence came from the hard sciences: the discovery of mirror neurons. The brain possesses motor neurons which enable the body to perform actions, for example, running, jumping, crying, speaking. A discovery, from Parma in Italy, showed that some of these motor neurons fire when we simply watch someone else perform the same action, without doing the action ourselves. In other words these neurons mirror actions of others. Perhaps most essentially, they mirror acquisitive actions, thus forming a basis for desire. If I mirror you eating a pie, I want that pie! Check out the Nova short film, at http://www.pbs.org/wgbh/nova/body/mirror-neurons.htmlat.

Violent Consequences

It is not hard to deduce the consequences of imitated desire. If we learn from each other to desire the same thing, and the desire in one reinforces the desire in the other — in any order — then rivalry, conflict and violence seem inevitable.

See also this interview for Girard's own account of mimesis. http://www.cbc.ca/radio/ideas/the-scapegoat-the-ideas-of-ren%C3%A9-girard-part-1-1.3474195

2nd Stage of Girard's Thought - Scapegoat and Sacrifice

After the idea of mimesis coming from literature, Girard then made the leap into anthropology— a fundamental human structure. The work of Lévi-Strauss was a key stepping stone, as we have described above. But the crucial concepts are "mythology" and "sacrifice." These developments came in *Violence and the Sacred* (1972). If human beings are intensely mimetic and this very quickly becomes conflict, their species would seem doomed to immediate self-destruction. At the level of early hominids, where the brain function of mimesis had overtaken inherited and instinctual dominance-and-submission patterns, a self-destructive war of all-against-all could be the only outcome. However, a solution presented itself, enabled by the same imitative capacity. In a crisis of desire everyone imitates everyone else's violence, all against all, but then very quickly, as one appears weaker and/or more hateful, it becomes all against one. If one hominid falls and is being horribly beaten everyone will join in, attracted by the triumphant violence. The single victim becomes the evil source, guilty of the whole crisis; but his/her killing brings transcendent peace, so he/she also becomes the god who brings sacred order.

Girard drew key evidence from the world of Mythology, showing multiple examples where someone is accused of something and then they disappear, fly off, go to live at the bottom of a lake etc. He argues that mythology is the distorted recollection of a crisis in which someone is killed in order that communal peace will prevail. Once human beings learned the reconciling effect of the group victim, they also learned to repeat the event, and the name for the repetition is "sacrifice." So the founding victim is the origin of mythology and ritual, and with that also the taboos and prohibitions that seek to prevent future crises (Girard's "three pillars of culture"). Here is an example of a story/ myth which both tells the truth and masks it. The crisis is hunger and access to a food source.

Origins of Corn

A large number of Native American myths deal with the origin of corn and how it came to be grown by humans. Many of the tales center on a "Corn Mother" or other female figure who introduces corn to the people.

In one myth, told by the Creeks and other tribes of the southeastern United States, the Corn Woman is an old woman living with a family that does not know who she is. Every day she feeds the family corn dishes, but the members of the family cannot figure out where she gets the food. One day, wanting to discover where

the old woman gets the corn, the sons spy on her. Depending on the version of the story, the corn is either scabs or sores that she rubs off her body, washings from her feet, nail clippings, or even her feces. In all versions, the origin of the corn is disgusting, and once the family members know its origin, they refuse to eat it.

The Corn Woman solves the problem in one of several ways. In one version, she tells the sons to clear a large piece of ground, kill her, and drag her body around the clearing seven times. However, the sons clear only seven small spaces, cut off her head, and drag it around the seven spots. Wherever her blood fell, corn grew. According to the story, this is why corn only grows in some places and not all over the world.

Read more: http://www.mythencyclopedia. com/Ca-Cr/Corn.html#ixzz3pmbXNXqm

In another account, the Corn Woman tells the sons to build a corn crib and lock her inside it for four days. At the end of that time, they open the crib and find it filled with corn. The Corn Woman then shows them how to use the corn.

Marks of the Victim:

Girard takes preferential marks of the victim from these stories:

crisis (hunger, drought, flood etc.)

an outsider, on the edges of the community (old, weak, dirty, diseased)

extreme accusation (eating

feces; in the story of Oedipus it is parricide and incest)
the sacred (presence of gods)

For archeological evidence of ritual human sacrifice see

http://westerndigs.org/victims-of-human-sacrifice-at- cahokia-were- locals-not-captives-study- finds/

Note also The Hymn to Purusha in the *Rig Veda* (see Girard's *Sacrifice, p.p.* 36-40) which explicitly describes the foundation of the human world through human sacrifice. The whole social order is born from sacrifice. So we can see how Girard's thought explained human origins and can claim to have identified our cultural DNA.

3rd Stage of Girard's Thought — Biblical Revelation of the Victim

This for us is the vital stage where Girard's thought reaches the point of Biblical interpretation. In 1978 Girard published *Things Hidden since the Foundation of the World*, in which he claimed the Bible reveals the scapegoat/victim.

Instead of deifying the victim, the victim is disclosed: for example, the stories of Abel, Hagar, Joseph, Tamar, Job, Jonah, Suffering Servant, and finally Jesus (whose story also includes "The Woman Taken in Adultery"). Girard argues that the Bible reveals the innocence of the victim and thus the human construct which scapegoats the victim and perpetuates sacrifice.

Peter's Actions

Another example of revelation are the actions of Peter on the occasion of Jesus' arrest (Mt 26.69-75). He cannot withstand the power of the mob — of mass mimesis. Peter is not peculiarly weak. He is in fact a strong and passionate man. But he crumbles before the crowd gathered round the fire and the victim, and the Gospels are intent on showing this.

Forgiveness

The story of the passion, death and resurrection of Jesus shows him an innocent victim. An essential part of his innocence is his forgiveness — not perpetuating the cycle of violence (see Lk 23.34). It is this nonviolence that is raised up on the third day to become a new transcendent theme in place of violence. The Bible, and in particular the gospel, continues to disclose the falsehood of the scapegoat process, at the same time as proposing forgiveness and love as the new way forward for human beings. This then becomes our new understanding of atonement.

Notes:

Lesson Questions

· Girard argues that humanity's ability and desire to imitate is so strong that it has overcome animal instinct. How does the modern marketplace and media utilize mimesis?

· Mimetic desire leads to rivalry and violence which would spiral out of control without the cultural restraints that emerged through sacrifice, scapegoats and taboos. Can you think of examples in our world today of these? How do they control/discharge social violence?

· Girard says that the discharge of violence and resulting order that emerges through these human constructs are perceived/experienced as "the divine." This was the first human experience of "god." Is this the Biblical God?

· Girard states that the Bible reveals the scapegoating process through key figures, and especially with Jesus. How does revealing the process help overcome it?

· If we are mimetic by nature, how can we translate that into something non–violent, and non–rivalrous?

Personal Reflection

· How has what I most desire been mediated through mimesis? Is mimesis always bad? When does it become dangerous?

· Can I think of times where I have experienced or witnessed scapegoating?

· Have I understood sacrifice as something that God demands or as a human construct displaced onto the divine? How does changing the way I look at sacrifice change how I see God?

Glossary

· Mimesis — the highly developed human quality of imitation, especially imitation of another's perceived desires.

· Scapegoat — a Biblical term used in common parlance for a designated group victim unjustly blamed for a general social crisis.

· Revelation — in this *Seven Stories* study the word refers to revelation of generative human violence alongside its progressive transformation through divine love.

· Mirror Neurons — function of brain neurons discovered in 1980s and 1990s through experiments with monkeys, demonstrating ability internally to imitate the action of others through motor neurons firing when those actions are observed.

· Sacrificial Crisis — the moment when the order of a group breaks down and violence builds to the point where the remembered solution of killing a victim is activated, and sacred order is re-established.

Resources/ Background Reading

· Books by René Girard (English versions), *Deceit, Desire and the Novel* (1966); *Violence and the Sacred* (1972); *Things Hidden Since the Foundation of the World* (1978); *The Scapegoat* (1986); *A Theatre of Envy* (2000); *I See Satan Fall Like Lightning* (2001); *Sacrifice* (2011)

Cultural References

· Movie, *The Hunt*, dir. Vinterberg (2012), example of a community quickly convinced of the guilt of an innocent man.

Movie, *Twelve Angry Men*, dir. Sidney Lumet (1957), the novel, *To Kill A Mockingbird Harper Lee* (1960), and its movie, dir. Robert Mulligan (1962), for examples of scapegoating.

Movies, *Face/Off*, dir. John Woo (1997), *Dangerous Liaisons*, dir. Stephen Frears (1988), and *The Count of Monte Cristo*, dir. Kevin Reynolds (2002), for mimetic desire and rivalry.

Oppression to Justice

Lesson Plan

· Lesson 1: The Hapiru

· Lesson 2: Exodus

· Lesson 3: Sermon on the Mount

Learning Objectives

· To discover that the God of the Bible begins the work of revelation among the poor and dispossessed.

· To grasp that this starting point is consistent if structural human change is the goal of Biblical revelation.

· To understand that Jesus brings this revelation to its term as the perfect human being.

· The Bible begins with the poor, showing that God is concerned to change the oppressive way in which human beings make their world. But because humans are violent from their origins, and their generative relationships are violent, they also read God's action as violent. Little by little the Bible comes to see that the God of true justice cannot be violent. The figure of Jesus completes and fully models this revelation.

Key Words/Concepts

· *Hapiru*

· **Mixed Multitude** (*rab ereb*)

· **Semiotic Shift**

Synopsis of the Story as a Whole

OPPRESSION TO JUSTICE
Lesson 1: The Hapiru

Learning Objectives
· To recognize the connection between the class of people in the Ancient Near East called Hapiru and the Biblical Hebrews.

Core Biblical Texts
· Genesis 14.13–16
· Exodus 12.38

Key Points
· The "Hebrews" originated as a socio-economic class not a racial group.
· Hapiru was the name given to this class in the contemporary near eastern world.
· The "mixed multitude" is a Biblical term that bridges between the Hapiru and the classical Israelite Hebrews.
· Descendants of Abraham and Jacob were part of this mixed multitude and were themselves *Hapiru*.
· Because of the conflation of "Hebrews" and "Israelites" the sense of socio-economic group is lost.
· God's act of liberation was to draw out one group from this class of dispossessed people and to reveal to them his/her identity and purpose.

Key Words/Concepts
· *Hapiru*
· **Mixed Multitude** (*rab ereb*)

The purpose of this lesson is to change our concept of the Hebrews, from a race of people descended genetically from Abraham, Isaac and Jacob, to a dispossessed social class among whom the revelation of a God of justice first appeared. This does not mean that the patriarchs were not real individuals, nor that some of the group leaving Egypt under Moses were not actually related to them, nor does it mean that the term did not come to denote a distinct covenant group. What it does mean is that there is a broad social class among whom and to whom the God of the Bible is revealed, and this is consistent with God's Biblical character. The God of the Bible wishes to bring freedom, justice, truth, peace and life to humanity, beginning with those most evidently deprived of these things.

Hebrew/*Hapiru* — Racial Descent vs Socio-Economic Class.

The Biblical story given in Genesis focuses on named individuals whom God called and made a covenant with. This enables us to see how the God of the Bible works with individuals one by one, and through these individuals is committed over time to the cause of human transformation. But when the events of the Exodus take place we are dealing with a category of people defined first of all by oppression, not racial descent. The metaphor of a family (descendants of Abraham) comes to express and underline the new style of community and identity God is seeking to create, but this biological meaning is not the source of the Biblical term "Hebrew."

There existed throughout the Ancient Near East a group known as *Hapiru* (var. *Habiru*). The name is recorded in clay tablets or stone inscriptions over the course of a thousand years spanning the second millennium BCE.

Hapiru are "... a loosely defined, inferior social class composed of shifting and shifty population elements without secure ties to settled communities." They are referred to as "outlaws, mercenaries, and slaves" in ancient texts. (Carol Redmount, Bitter Lives: Israel in and out of Egypt.)

Here is a description of the context in which *Hapiru* arose. We begin with a war-torn countryside. An imperial nation is land grabbing and throwing around its weight, absorbing small city-states and exacting tribute from their citizens.

The city-states are organized for defense against this nation, or are in alliance with it, and in the process establish control of a surrounding area, dispossessing the peasantry. But then often in turn they are conquered by invasion or rebellion. Constant warfare produces displaced persons, refugees, outlaws. In this war-torn countryside these people frequently become slaves, or debt-servants, and are treated as less than human. Or they become mercenaries, hiring themselves out as bands of soldiers to the highest bidder. Back then the common understanding for their plight was that they deserved it because of some infraction they had committed. Or that their gods were not strong enough to protect them against a stronger nation. Thus the stronger the gods you have the stronger the nation. So, you have a group of ethnically diverse people from many city-states and areas pushed into extreme circumstances and sometimes forced-labor at the whim of a large imperial nation. These people are seen in socio-economic terms as the lowest of the low. A possible example would be the "untouchable" class in India. Periodically as the imperial nation expands its operations the demand for work from this eclectic group increases to the point of servitude and oppression.

We may add then that among some of the group a religion forms, and with that an identity. These people have a God they believe is on their side, not on the side of the empire. A prophet is raised up to communicate to them the truth of this God and to lead the people from slavery.

What we want to focus on is the diversity of this group, and at the same time, the fact that they are brought together by oppression. They are made up of people from all over the neighboring areas bound together by violence, dispossession, and poverty.

Reference Websites

See https://en.wikipedia.org/wiki/Habiru.

Also case study of Labaya (https://en.wikipedia.org/wiki/Amarna_letters) mentioned in the 14th century BCE Amarna letters, giving a good picture of the situation we are describing.

Mixed Multitude

The Bible begins in Genesis with individual violence and the answering revelation of nonviolence. We will look at this meaning of the first book of the Bible in the next story cycle. Here, in Exodus, the Bible turns to the harsh reality of human history from which the experience of the Israelites emerged. It is important now to get rid of the idea that the Israelites were a pure racial group. Much more likely Abraham and Jacob were semi-legendary ancestral figures of a number of families, which were then adopted as the ancestral stories of a wider, ethnically diverse group. It is the actual story of Exodus that makes them a people, not strict genetic descent. Egypt was an imperial force, as were Mesopotamian states and the city-states of Canaan. They all fought many wars and conquered foreign territory. All this disturbance created *Hapiru* and the name of the Biblical Hebrews has a very similar word form. And if we look at the Biblical descriptions they were exactly a group in a *Hapiru* situation

Also we can consider this: why, in fact, after so many years, would the descendants of Jacob still be in Egypt at the start of Exodus, and not back in their ancestral lands, unless social and economic circumstances forced them to be there? Surely they should have left before things got so bad? It seems evident, therefore, that the Biblical Hebrews are a group drawn from a class of dispossessed and stateless people.

Read Ex 12.38:

"A mixed crowd also went up with them, and livestock in great numbers, both flocks and herds." The Hebrew is *rab ereb* (*ereb* translates mixed; *rab* is multitude). This is the journey out of Egypt. It is not "only" the descendants of Jacob; mixed crowd means foreigners not all one race.

For added evidence read Neh 13.3 where the law requires the Israelites to separate themselves from the people of "foreign descent" (*ereb*).

Read Num 11.4.

Another Hebrew expression here is given as "rabble" in most modern translations. Who are these people? The King James Bible translates the term as "mixed multitude," identifying it with the group at Exodus 12:38.

See also Gen 14.13-16; 1 Sam 22.1–2 & 29.1–5.

The same word "Hebrew" is used to describe Abram in Genesis and David and his men in Samuel. The context in both instances presents Abram and David as warlords, able to field a battalion of warriors. In I Sam 22:1-2 David's men are comprised of all those who were in debt or distress, the downtrodden, outsiders, i.e. *Hapiru*.

In 1 Sam 29.3 Hebrews are mentioned in functional distinction from the nation of Israelites. They are identified first as Hebrews, and then, subsequently, as "servants of the King of Israel."

Yahweh is called the God of the Hebrews, at Ex 3.18, 5.3, 7.16, 9.1, 9.13 & 10.3. The insistent designation makes much more sense in its context if it refers to a God who has taken the side of an oppressed group, rather than the God of an arbitrary ethnic tribe.

Elsewhere it has been argued (in order to prove the racial identity of the Hebrews) that this ethnic group gets its name from Eber in Gen 10.25. This does not seem to make sense. Did the Exodus Hebrews then consist of descendants of Peleg and Joktan etc., as well as Abraham and Jacob? Why are there no patriarchal stories related to Eber, or these other figures? The descent from this figure is completely insignificant, unless indeed it is another rendering of Hebrew/*Hapiru*.

Read also the shocking stories of Abraham and Isaac effectively pimping their wives at Gen 12. 10–16, 20.1–18, 26.1–11. These stories are maintained because they preserve the memory of the total insecurity of these people. They have the sociological identity and desperation of the *Hapiru*.

What if all this means that the God of Moses chose a group of *Hapiru* to be his people and to give them a land? Then, when they established themselves in the land as the nation of Israel they continued to remember their *Hapiru*/Hebrew roots, but over time this name became routinized, losing more and more of its social connotation? (Just as "Smith" does not anymore mean someone who smites metal things.) But underneath the clear meaning remains of a social class and of a God who chooses them.

"I have observed the misery of my people who are in Egypt; I have heard their cry on account of their taskmasters. Indeed, I know their sufferings, and I have come down to deliver them from the Egyptians, and to bring them up out of that land to a good and broad land, a land flowing with milk and honey .... The cry of the Israelites has now come to me; I have also seen how the Egyptians oppress them ...." (Ex 3.7-9).

Lesson Questions

· Does it matter that Biblical revelation begins with God's choice of a group from a dispossessed class rather than a chosen race?

· If God's people are not exclusively identified with a particular nation or race does this make a difference to how we understand God's purpose?

· How does this fit with Jesus' message of good news to the poor?

· How does this relate to human desire for national identity and opposite attitudes toward those who do or do not "belong?"

Personal Reflection

· If God's call is to the powerless and dispossessed, what does that mean to me?

· Does God's call to follow him come through my weakness? If so, how have I experienced this?

· How much does national identity, race, or other ways humans define who is "in" or "out," matter to me? What does the Exodus story tell me about what is important to God?

Glossary

· *Hapiru* — a form of a common name given in the Ancient Near East to a dispossessed class of people characterized as vagrants, mercenaries, migrant laborers, living on the margins of society (sometimes also spelled *Habiru*).

· *rab ereb* — Hebrew for "mixed multitude." A Biblical term that describes the group that left Egypt under Moses.

Resouces / Background Reading

· Useful Jewish perspective on *Hapiru*: http://www.newenglishreview.org/Robert_Wolfe/From_Habiru_to_Hebrews%3A_The_Roots_of_the_Jewish_Tradition/

· See https://en.wikipedia.org/wiki/Habiru

· Carol A. Redmount, "Bitter Lives: Israel in and out of Egypt," article in *The Oxford History of the Biblical World*, ed: Michael D. Coogan, (Oxford University Press, 1999)

· *The Tribes of Yahweh, A Sociology of the Religion of Liberated Israel*, 1250--1050 BCE, Norman Gottwald (1999)

· Labaya reference: https://en.wikipedia.org/wiki/Amarna_letters

· *Ancient Israel's Faith and History: An Introduction to the Bible in Context*, Norman Gottwald (2001)

· *The New Jim Crow: Mass Incarceration in the Age of Color Blindness*, Michelle Alexander and Cornel West (2012)

Cultural References

· "Race is a social construct" http://www.livescience.com/53613-race-is-social-construct-not-scientific.html

· *Spartacus* and *Robin Hood* (multiple movies) are examples of groups banded together from diverse origins and desperate circumstances.

· Movie, *The Birth of a Nation*, dir. Nate Parker (2016), rebellion of African-American slaves uniting under the leadership of Nat Turner.

· A Conversation With Toni Morrison, https://www.youtube.com/watch?v=Q5D5PLI7kvc

OPPRESSION TO JUSTICE
Lesson 2: Exodus

Learning Objectives

· To recognize that the Biblical God's first act within the context of recognizable public history is to set free an oppressed group of people.

· To identify that the first semiotic shift is when God formed a people from the poor and dispossessed, rather than the rich and powerful previously favored by the gods.

· To explain the ten plagues as an account of natural events seen from the perspective of the oppressed, rather than acts originating in divine violence.

Key Points

· The Exodus is the first act of God in the Bible within the context of clearly identifiable ancient history.

· The Exodus is also the first semiotic shift in the Bible because God sides for the first time with the powerless, rather than with those in power.

· The language used to describe God's solidarity with the poor and powerless is also new because it is personal.

· The Exodus is an incomplete revelation of God's action because God's actions to liberate are described in terms of divine violence.

· The Bible reveals as much about human violence as it does about the nature of God.

Core Biblical Texts

· Ex 1.8–14

· Ex 15.1–6

Key Words/Concepts

· Semiotic Shift

Review of Last Lesson

The land of Israel was located in a transitional zone or "corridor" between empires of Egypt and Mesopotamia. This means that it was an area hard to hold on to, but continually destabilized. All this friction and upheaval created groups of displaced people, people deprived of land or rights. They were forced to hire themselves out as mercenaries or for hard labor. These people were known as Hapiru (in the contemporary inscriptions, clay tablets etc.) and the name of the Biblical Hebrews has a very similar word form. The Hebrews were exactly a group in this kind of situation — a shifting population of displaced people (mercenaries, slaves, migrant workers, outlaws). The Hebrews are not primarily a racial/ethnic group, rather a socio-economic class. It is a set of shared stories and the experience of Exodus that makes them a people, not genetic descent.

The Exodus experience is the starting point of Bible study. It is the place where God first publicly intervenes in human history. (The creation narratives and stories of the patriarchs are written as reflections on the origins of the world and humanity, drawing on traditional ancestral and wisdom stories. They reflect important meanings but are not public historical events like the birth of a nation and its law.) The first five books of the Bible (the Torah) were knit together/edited into a final whole much later than the events described. The beginning of Exodus is a clear editorial suture and segue from the preceding Joseph story.

Read Ex 1.1–8.

The Exodus as a Semiotic Shift

In each of the *Seven Stories* we are focusing on a semiotic shift — a step forward in the way humans understand themselves and God. Semiotics is the study of signs and their meaning. A shift is brought about by means of a set of words and a story which change the way humans think. The first semiotic shift occurs when God hears the cry of the oppressed. To focus on the change of signs and meaning recognizes that human transformation is not primarily conceptual or moral, but depends on the stories we tell and the relative value of the signs that get fixed in our minds.

There is a misconception today that we live in a rational universe in which human rights, democratic ideals, etc. are naturally inherent and have been discovered by rational human beings over the course of time (the Enlightenment). That belief finds its basis in Greek thought — the existence of the logical ideal in each mind. However, Greek thought is not the basis of human rights as we understand them today. Greek thought does not reject the idea of slavery, for example. Aristotle, a pupil of Plato, taught that some were destined to be slaves. Also Greek democracy was only for the citizens of the city state, not the peasantry, or other nations. The original "divine" principles of Greek thought are indifferent to humanity, e.g. the "First Mover." Greek thought is more concerned with bringing order rather than justice. There have been kind, compassionate people throughout history but structurally things did not change. The understanding of the role of the gods before the Exodus — and the power of which they were signs —remained impersonal and violent. Exodus is the first major semiotic shift. Pharaoh did not hear the poor; rather the Hebrews were disgusting to the Egyptians (Gen 43.32). In Exodus the poor and oppressed (instead of the rich and powerful) are identified as the chosen people of the God proclaimed by Moses. For this God to be seen as on the side of the downtrodden there has to be new human meaning, because it is so foreign to the way humans think. It is a radical change in perception which can only be brought about by some kind of dramatic intervention and by the story and language which carries it in people's minds.

God moves in history and his interest is personal on behalf of the oppressed. The text makes this very clear:

Read Ex 1.8–14.

The Israelites are oppressed.

Read Ex 2.23–25.

"God **heard** their groaning … **remembered** his covenant … **looked upon** the Israelites … **took notice** …."

Read Ex 3.7–9.

"… **observed** the misery … **heard** their cry … **know** their sufferings … cry has **come to me** … **seen** how the Egyptians oppress …."

This is a new/transformational language that is personal, relational. No God before has expressed solidarity with human suffering in this way.

Giving of the Law

Exodus is also the first time a change in the way God is understood is written down and codified as law.

Read Ex 23.1–9. "… You shall not oppress a resident alien; you know the heart of an alien, for you were aliens in the land of Egypt."

The character of the Law is based on the lived experience of the Hebrews — because they were oppressed and set free by God, they should not oppress others.

The Law was given to an oppressed people without roots or powerful group coherence — to give them an identity, a belief system, a way of understanding themselves in relation to their God. They are given a personal relationship with a God of justice. The Law gives identity and worth to all those who have not had these things. The poor and the oppressed are never again to be forgotten.

Nevertheless the Revelation is Incomplete

The Exodus transformation in our understanding of God's work in the world remains incomplete. The Hebrews were still living in a world constructed on generative violence. This means that mimetic violence and events of foundational violence still controlled human culture. If one is totally immersed in that world it is very difficult to see things differently, to break free of the paradigm. Achieving a sense of justice was the first step, something completely new — but only half the change. Foundational violence is still evident in the text.

Read Ex 12.1–13 then 12.29–32 (the killing of the firstborn followed by sending away of the Israelites).

Read Ex 14.26–29 (the drowning of the Egyptians in the Red Sea).

Read Ex 15.1–10 (the Song of Moses. "… Yahweh is a warrior … Pharaoh's chariots and his army he has cast into the sea ….").

Looking at these texts, how did the Hebrews perceive their God? How is the God who liberates them described? How does he bring about liberation?

These texts assert that Israel's God is supreme, but acts through violence.

This picture is also contained in the Psalms where God is on the side of the victim, and avenger of the righteous

Read Pss 11, 52, 64, 94.

The cry for vindication can easily become the cry for revenge

Read Nah 3.1–9 (against Nineveh) & Ob 10–16 (against Edom).

The Law's justice also includes reciprocal violence. For example, Ex. 21.29–30 (if an ox kills someone then the ox and owner must be killed). This acts as a deterrent to breaking the law — a fear of retributive violence. It also attempts to be commensurate, not excessive. Nevertheless, it remains the effect of generative violence.

A Nonviolent Read of the Ten Plagues

This reciprocity is at work in the death of the first born, the ultimate violent act of God to free the Hebrews. How can we reconcile the story with a nonviolent God? The answer lies in how the Exodus Hebrews produced an interpretation of real events. The Bible reveals as much about us as it does about God. If we explain the narrative of the ten plagues as a cultural lens by which those who told the story saw God then it becomes simply a layer of text which points beyond itself. The ten plagues can be explained from a factual point of view: natural events which are then constructed as divine violence.

For example, the Ten Plagues theory of Dr John Marr (epidemiologist) and Curtis Malloy (medical researcher) understands the plagues as a series of closely linked natural events.

At http://www.nytimes.com/1996/04/04/ garden/biblical-plagues-a-novel-theory.html

The Ten Plagues

1. Rivers of blood: dinoflagellate microorganisms are capable of turning rivers blood-red — then releasing toxins which attack fish leaving them bleeding and helpless.

2. Plague of frogs: lack of oxygen forces frogs to escape from the water, but then out of the water they die.

3. Plague of lice: midge-like creatures breed in the dust, cause louse-like irritation and transmit viruses that can kill livestock in hours.

4. Swarm of flies: resulting from dead fish/frogs/animals.

5. Sickness of livestock: possibly the result of stable fly which carries bacterial infection which also causes ...

6. Boils on man and beast.

7. Hail: not uncommon in Middle East.

8. Plague of locusts: still occurs in Middle East.

9. Three days of darkness on the land: possibly a sandstorm or outbreak of Rift Valley Fever known to cause temporary blindness.

10. Death of the First Born: resulting from attempt of the Egyptians to deal with previous plagues. A meager harvest of grain after locusts and hail is stored damp in silos, becoming a source for molds/ mycotoxins. The eldest child would receive double rations leading to increased death rates among the first born. With no visible external cause these deaths would be perceived as an act of God.

The basic point is there is a plausible natural explanation for disasters which then, in the tradition, are read as a direct effect of divine action. But it is the root change in human perspective that counts and which is the work of revelation — God is on the side of the oppressed and is creating a new people based in this relationship.

The Egyptian Perspective

From a Girardian–anthropological point of view, the Egyptians could also see the plagues as caused by a cursed people who actually had to be expelled (cf. Ex.11.1). Egyptian historians from the 3rd century BCE in fact report this viewpoint — the Exodus Hebrews were diseased and expelled. (See *The Bible, Violence and the Sacred*, by James G. Williams.)

The Hebrews fleeing Egypt perceive that God is on their side in terms of generative violence, while the Egyptians see the same events based on the same generative violence, but in terms of a cursed group. Both parties interpret the events according to the default human frame of meaning. Nevertheless, in the overall Biblical narrative something amazing is happening: a God of human transformation is being revealed. From the anthropological perspective the Exodus picture of divine violence is an interpretation of natural events, but the underlying truth is God's intervention on behalf of a group of oppressed people, laying the foundation of a transformative divine and human journey. This is the true work of the Biblical God, changing our human perspective progressively and continually, including our perception of God as violent. In the following cycle we will see how the book of Genesis prefaces the book of Exodus with a profound critique of human violence. So, a deeper change of meaning (semiotic shift) is already set up in the Bible text before we even get to read Exodus! In our next lesson we will see how Jesus reinterprets the Law, reading its radical intent, and teaches us the full revelation of a God of nonviolence.

Lesson Questions

· How have Christians traditionally reacted to the violent God of the Old Testament? Affirmed or embraced it? Skipped over it?

· Does understanding the Bible as an evolving document, that is both a revelation of human violence and a progressive revelation about God, help to reclaim parts of the Bible that might have been problematic for you before?

· Do you think that seeing the violence attributed to God in the Bible as a human construct takes away power from God?

Personal Reflection

· If the violence of the Bible is a revelation of human violence rather than divine - how does this change how I think about reciprocal violence, revenge?

· If change comes through revolutionary violence, does anything actually change? What stays the same?

· If I take the violence out of God, how do I then understand his/her power?

· Does this increase or decrease God's power to bring about human transformation?

Glossary

· Semiotic Shift — the concept of how human meaning changes through pivotal stories, signs and symbols, above all through the Biblical narrative.

· Liberation Theology — a theology that grew out of the big changes in thought in Latin America and elsewhere from 1968 onwards. It tells us that God's revelation is properly to be interpreted and understood from the perspective of the poor and oppressed.

Resources/Background Reading

· Ernesto Cardenal's *Psalms of Struggle and Liberation* (1971), and *The Gospel in Solentiname* (1984), for perspective of Liberation Theology

Cultural References

· Exodus movies: *The Ten Commandments*, dir. Cecile B. DeMille (1956), *The Prince of Egypt*, dir. Brenda Chapman (1998), and *Exodus: Gods and Kings*, dir. Ridley Scott (2014)

· Bob Marley: "Exodus," "Redemption Song"

· U.S. African-American experience of oppression, see for example: https//www.youtube.com/watch?v=Rekp7rRcSFs https://www.youtube.com/watch?v=kFBHOtN5ssc

OPPRESSION TO JUSTICE
Lesson 3: Sermon on the Mount

Learning Objectives
· To understand how Jesus claims authority over his own Biblical tradition, announcing blessing rather than law, a blessing that was always at the heart of the law.
· To understand how this blessing becomes possible, through both the teaching and action of Jesus.

Core Biblical Texts
· Ex 20.1–21
· Mt 5.1–48

Key Points
· The Sermon on the Mount presented by the Gospel of Matthew is Jesus' reformulation of the Decalogue
· There is a shift from prohibitive and retributive law to a transformation of the human heart.
· The fulfillment of the law is understood in terms of nonviolence and relationship.

Key Words/Concepts
· Decalogue
· Antitheses
· Beatitudes
· Retributive
· Proscriptive
· Consequential
· Relational

In this lesson we are looking at some very iconic Biblical texts. We are going to examine parallels between the Ten Commandments and the Sermon on the Mount. As with all of these studies you are encouraged to try to imagine the radical newness of the message for the contemporary audience at the time of Jesus.

The Ten Commandments

The Israelites have been wandering in the desert for three months and arrive at Mount Sinai.

Read Ex 19.3–6. God speaks to Moses on the mountain: if the people keep God's covenant they shall be his holy nation.

Read Ex 19.10–13. God to come down on the holy mountain; anyone who touches the mountain will be put to death.

Read Ex 19:16–25. God appears in smoke and thunder on Mount Sinai.

Read Ex 20:1-21. Ten Commandments, or "Decalogue," given to Moses.

- What is the setting? What is the tone?

- What is the dynamic between God and the people?

- What is the overall purpose of the commandments?

- What is the verbal mechanism by which they are announced? (Hint: prohibitions!)

- What is the sanction if they are broken?.

Keep all this in the back of your mind as we head to Mt 5 and the Sermon on the Mount.

The Sermon on the Mount

In modern Bibles the Gospels are divided into chapters but in the original Greek manuscripts these did not exist and the Sermon on the Mount was one seamless teaching.

Overview of the Sermon on the Mount

Mt 5.1–12. The Beatitudes.

Mt 5.13–16. Salt of the earth; light of the world.

Mt 5.17–48. Fulfilment of the Law — the Antitheses.

Mt 6.1–18. On alms, prayer and fasting (the three major works of piety).

Mt 6.19–34. Teaching on wealth, purity of heart, non-anxiety and seeking the Kingdom.

Mt 7.1–7. Teaching on not judging.

Mt 7. 8–23. Teaching on trusting prayer, the narrow gate, and false prophets.

Mt 7. 24–27. Parables on true discipleship.

The Beatitudes

*Read Mt 5.1–16 (compare Lk 6: 20-23).
- What is the setting? Who is Jesus speaking to? What is the tone?*

The Beatitudes are a series of nine "Blesseds," the last one doubled with a "rejoice," adding up to ten statements that parallel the ten commandments. "Blessing" is a Wisdom concept, meaning fullness of life: "blessed are you" means "you are filled with life!" The first four are directed towards different public classes or states of people — the poor, the grieving, the meek (those who do not offer violence), the hungry. The next four relate to active relationships and the spirit that goes with them — those who are merciful, pure in heart, peacemakers and the persecuted. All relate to a condition or an activity that is non-violent, non-competitive.

Luke's Gospel has "you poor" rather than "poor in spirit." Matthew's phrasing refers to a condition of poverty that is also an inner state of non-possession, rather than poverty plus envy or resentment. Luke also has "you who are hungry" rather than "those who hunger and thirst for righteousness." Luke's more concrete expressions are likely more original; but Matthew's expansions are fully consistent.

Finally, the expansion of the "blessing" of persecution to three expressions demonstrates the crucial character of this experience for early Christianity, and the need to underline that the state of persecution without retaliation is part of the joy of the Kingdom.

All in all Jesus announces not law but a life-blessing, one that is deeply paradoxical because it goes along with poverty and powerlessness. Jesus is saying that the purpose of the law is fulfilled in the voluntary nonviolent embrace of these conditions. An entirely new relationship with the violence of existence is proclaimed — one of love, trust, letting-go, forgiveness.

The Antitheses

The statements known as the antitheses begin with "You have heard that it was said" and follow with "but I say to you …."

These relate directly to the Ten Commandments. The commandments are as follows:

1. You shall have no other gods

2. You shall not make idols

3. You shall not take the Lord's name in vain

4. You shall observe the Sabbath

5. You shall honor your father and mother

6. You shall not murder

7. You shall not commit adultery

8. You shall not steal

9. You shall not bear false witness

10. You shall not covet (rivalry that leads to violence)

The first four of the commandments pertain to our relationship with God; the last six to our relationship with our neighbor. A parallel can be drawn between the antitheses and the last six commandments, with a slight adjustment. There is one commandment which is left out (the fifth), and the seventh is given a double expression.

• You shall not murder … do not even be angry (Mt 5.21–26).

• You shall not commit adultery … doubled into two teachings, do not lust/divorce (Mt 5. 27–32).

• The saying on divorce comes after and expands the statement of lust.

• You shall not steal … do not even resist the evil-doer … if someone wants to take your coat give your cloak as well …. no mimetic revenge/retaliation (Mt 5.38–42).

• You shall not give false witness … do not swear at all (Mt 5.33–37).

• You shall not covet: love your enemy, pray for those who harm you — love breaks the cycle of desire and violence (Mt 5.43–48).

All the antitheses relate to violence and the violent consequences of our desires and actions. The social reason behind no-divorce is that in the conditions of the time it leaves the woman vulnerable and without protection; but Jesus goes further, insisting on relationship over sexual desire. His teaching on swearing recognizes that any kind of swearing invokes violence, on one's self or another.

Jesus does not seem to address the fifth commandment, "You shall honor your father and mother." Why?

Jesus is speaking to a Jewish audience with a powerful tradition of family ritual and expectations. Human beings naturally extend to family, clan, tribe what we want for ourselves (possessions, security, identity, belonging). Jesus throughout the Gospels teaches against the dangers of putting family before the kingdom:

Read Mt 8. 21–22 (let the dead bury the dead).

Read Mt 12.46–50 (Who are my mother and brothers?)

The original purpose of the commandment — to protect the older members of dispossessed groups from abandonment — is clearly fulfilled in the wider love and service of the Kingdom.

A shift from prohibitive and retributive to consequential and relational

In the Sermon on the Mount Jesus frees us from the mechanism of Law, one which is prohibitive and retributive. He sets instead a new standard, one which is consequential and relational and brings blessing. At the same time he fulfills the purpose of the Law (Mt 5.17–20).

The Decalogue was proscriptive. It expresses itself as an absolute "You shall not …." If you disobey then you can expect retribution/punishment. Laws are fear based, reinforced by sanctions. The result is to create some human protection from our basic human tendency towards destructive desire and violence. Jesus shifts the focus from rules and prohibitions to a different way of being human. By adopting nonviolence as the standard of behavior it radically changes who we are in relationship with others. The focus is on the consequent blessings of God's Kingdom, but also the negative consequences to ourselves if we fail to change. Mt. 5.25–6 is a good example: if we battle to the end with someone who makes a claim against us then they will do the same and we will not be forgiven any one of our debts. Blessings or sufferings result not from whether a person does or does not keep rules, and whether or not they avoid God's punishment, but rather from the mimetic consequences of our actions — forgiveness or violence.

Jesus is making a point about the true nature of God

God is love, compassion, relationship. The semiotic shift of Exodus was the realization that God is on the side of the poor and oppressed and not the powerful. God's act of liberation, however, was still interpreted in the old ways of power and violence, and the result was possibly an increased fear and dread of the divine. The old human ways of thinking about God as violent are still evident in the Exodus passages. Jesus reinterprets the Decalogue in the Beatitudes and Antitheses, through the lens of a nonviolent God who seeks profoundly to enter into relationship with us and to transform our hearts and lives.

Jesus claims a divine authority.

"You have heard that it was said, but I say to you …" By using this language that invokes words of God given to Moses on Mount Sinai ("you shall not murder … commit adultery ..."), and then expanding or changing them, Jesus is claiming a privileged understanding of God, one that goes far beyond Moses'. Doing so in the first person — rather than citing arguments or texts — implies a standing next to God himself. This claim is coherent with collapsing the distance between the human practice of love and the character of God (Mt 5.48).

The disciples are given the task of transformation

Read Mt 5.13–16 (salt of the earth, light of the world).

Read Mt 7.15–28 (a tree and its fruit, the house built on rock).

Through nonviolence, blessing and meaning come to the earth. It is through their fruits that people will know the disciples are doing the will of the Father.

Lesson Questions

· It has been argued that the Sermon on the Mount is idealistic and unachievable. What do you think?

· If it is achievable, on the basis of what kind of mindset?

· If the Israelite identity as God's people was formed through the Law, is there a new identity of God's people formed by the beatitudes?

· Do you think Christians today are living according to the Decalogue or the Sermon on the Mount?

· How does the Sermon on the Mount change our understanding of God?

Personal Reflection

· Have I ever felt under judgment that was then overcome by blessing?

· What are my grace-filled moments?

· Do I feel inspired to live a life guided by the beatitudes?

Glossary

· Decalogue — the ten commandments.

· Antitheses — the passage in the Sermon on the Mount where Jesus contrasts previous Biblical teachings with his new teaching.

· Beatitudes — the passage in the Sermon on the Mount consisting of wisdom sayings beginning with "blessed are you …."

· Retributive — the ethic that justice is achieved by reciprocal compensating violence against the perpetrator.

· Proscriptive — a command imposing a restraint or prohibition.

· Consequential — the ethic of positive or negative consequences flowing naturally (mimetically) from nonviolent or violent actions, thus bringing their own judgment.

· Relational — referring to the structure of human relationships rather than a system of rules.

Resources/Background reading

· *The Upside-Down Kingdom*, Donald B. Kraybill (2011)

· *I Francis*, Carlo Carretto (1982)

Cultural References

· Short stories by Flannery O'Connor, for example *A Good Man is Hard to Find*, or *The Lame Shall Enter First*

· Movie, *Babette's Feast*, dir. Gabriel Axel (1987)

Violence to Forgiveness

Lesson Plan

· Lesson 1: Prehistories
· Lesson 2: Patriarchs
· Lesson 3: Prodigal Son

Learning Objectives

· To see the pre-histories of Genesis as an integrated account of the human problem, not a single isolated story of "original sin."

· To understand that desire, rivalry and violence are at the heart of human existence and culture.

· To see the Patriarchs as working to a solution to the problem of violence rather than simply ancestor folklore and/or the descent line of covenant tradition.

· To understand that Joseph is a type of the forgiving victim, the Messiah to come.

· To recognize that Jesus draws from his tradition by using Genesis themes in parables teaching about violence and forgiveness.

Synopsis of the Story as a Whole

· All the stories found in Genesis 2–11 are equally valid as a template of human existence. The focus should not just be on the Garden of Eden. Looked at as a recurring pattern they point out how desire, rivalry and violence continually escalate in our world.

· Genesis should be considered in relation to what comes after– the bloody history of Exodus and the stories of the Israelite kingdoms all the way through to Maccabees. It acts as a critical reflection and preface to these accounts.

· Genesis is not the story of "The Fall" of humanity with its metaphysical connotations, and the ramifications of these for Christian theology. (The need for a Savior who could bring us to Heaven.)

· Genesis should be read as a unity. It is an anthropological commentary all the way through — from the intense reflection on desire in the Eden story, and in its doublet, the murder story of Cain; through the flood; to the tower of Babel; and finally the Abraham and Jacob sagas filled with violence.

· Neither is it just about the development of a covenant people as a type or fore-runner of the Christian covenant — these are purely formal and legal interpretations.

· This anthropological (rather than legal/moral) interpretation is the Biblical breakthrough of our time.

Key Words/Concepts

· Original Sin
· Covenant
· Wisdom

VIOLENCE TO FORGIVENESS
Lesson 1: Prehistories

Learning Objectives

- To see the pre-histories of Genesis as an integrated account of the human problem, not a single story of "original sin."
- To understand that desire, rivalry and violence are at the heart of human existence and culture.
- To see that the Bible is dealing with this problem progressively, step by step and that the image of God at this early stage is itself still permeated by the problem.

Core Biblical Texts

- Gen 3.1–24
- Gen 4.1–24

Key Points

- The stories in Gen 2–11 are equally valid, looking at the human condition from different angles. They are a breakthrough anthropology.
- The root of the human problem is desire, rivalry and violence not a single "original sin" or personal morality.

Key Words/Concepts

- Original Sin
- *Nephilim*

The second story is Violence to Forgiveness. This lesson focuses on how the first chapters of Genesis describe what they see to be the main problem associated with the human condition.

Although it contains many ancient stories and traditions, Genesis is in fact one of the later books of the Bible (later than many of the prophets, for example). It achieved its final form about 500 BCE, along with the other four books of the Torah. Genesis is designed to be read as a whole. The first part (chapters 2–11) comprises the "prehistories" and sets out the human problem; the second part tells the stories of the patriarchs and points to God's solution to the problem.

In this lesson we will look at the prehistories and next lesson we will look at stories of the patriarchs. The very first chapter of Genesis (the seven day creation account) is not treated here in detail. It acts as a preface to the whole of Genesis and in fact the whole of the Bible, underlining the nonviolence of the God of creation. Its picture of God is later, more conceptually refined than what follows in chapter 2. And it is clearly an alternative creation account. Chapter 2.4–9 has the Lord creating "man" before there is vegetation on earth, thus before the third day, and not on the sixth, as in the Chapter 1 account!

The main event in Genesis has been understood to be the disobedience of our first parents, Adam and Eve, in the Garden. In the broad Christian tradition the phrase that sums up the problem is "The Fall."

For various reasons the Christian tradition has given disproportionate weight to the first of the prehistory stories, while naming it in a way that implies a vertical Platonic scheme — "the Fall" (from a heavenly to an earthly condition). In doing so it has shifted the message of Genesis to one of individual morality and legal/metaphysical consequence. In this lesson we will study each story as having equal weight. Each approaches the human crisis from a different angle but with always the same anthropological components.

Overview of the Prehistories

1. The Garden story is about the emergence of human desire and freedom of choice; and then the crisis of human survival (work and suffering). God sets the scene of original desire by the drawing of a boundary around the tree. He resolves the problem by making another one — exclusion from the Garden. Note this is a horizontal exclusion, not a vertical fall.

2. The story of Cain and Abel is another scene of desire set by God. This time the object is God's favor, producing rivalry, violence, death, alienation, and — eventually — civilization. Cain becomes a wanderer, yet protected by God, and founder of the first city. His descendant, Lamech, threatens mass murder, but his children are the founders of culture.

3. The "sons of God and the daughters of men" is another crisis of transgressive desire, this time explaining the origins of mighty men/ professional warriors (the *Nephilim*).

4. The Flood story is about the crisis of all human culture and its exploding violence.

5. Babel is the crisis of human transcendence separate from God.

The Garden Story

Read Gen 3.1–7.

The fruit of the tree of knowledge of good and evil is desirable in many ways: "the woman saw that the tree was good for food, and that it was a delight to the eyes, and that the tree was to be desired to make one wise."

The Garden story is a way of explaining how human beings are different from the other animals. The fruit represents the imitative desire that René Girard speaks about — so powerful that it overcomes animal instinct as the dominant source of action. It is this that makes us different, free, and "like God" (Gen 3.22, "the man has become like one of us ...."). The Garden sets the scene of the birth of our humanity and freedom of choice. But freedom only comes about through desire, and Eve takes the first step. God is responsible for setting the scene of desire; he created the serpent and produces the first boundary — around the tree placed in the middle of the garden. Talk about advertizing! This is not a test: a test is never mentioned, and you cannot be tested without freedom. The narrative in fact reflects on the uselessness of prohibitions and boundaries, despite the fact they have divine sanction. The story is instead all about the production of desire, and freedom through desire, a uniquely human experience. Humans remain responsible for their actions, because in the moment of desire they also experience freedom.

Free choice arises paradoxically in a fundamental crisis of rivalry. This parallels Girard's primary anthropological scene of rivalry and violence. (Note that in Genesis it is the woman who is the agent of humanization.)

The sanction for eating from the tree of the knowledge of good and evil is that, should they eat it, they will die. This actually did not happen. The text does not even mean, at this point, that by eating the fruit they would eventually die — because at the end of the chapter God is worried they will also eat from the tree of life and so be able to live forever. This is why he expels them from the Garden. God in the prehistory narratives is depicted in rivalry with humans, and his solutions are locked in the frame of rivalry and violence. It seems the author is suggesting that because this is the way human beings are, this is also the way they see God.

Read Gen 3.16–18, describing the human condition of suffering.

Woman will endure pain of childbirth and desire for her husband who rules over her. Man must toil to eat from the ground which has become cursed.

This condition is archaic and patriarchal, reflecting a system of (male) control which is a response to the crisis of desire. At this point, freedom remains so closely intertwined with rivalry, that sanctions and hierarchy are the only way to contain the problem.

Cain and Abel

Read Gen 4.1–24.

René Girard talks about the Cain and Abel story as the foundational murder. It is here that violence and actual sin enter the world. It is the first Biblical mention of sin (4.7) and it relates to violence. It is with Abel that temple religion is born (blood sacrifice) and after Cain kills Abel (human sacrifice) civilization and culture are born. It is a story of the foundational victim.

Read Gen 4.3–7.

God sets up the scene of desire, as in the Garden story. He prefers Abel's blood sacrifice to Cain's vegetable offerings. There is no sense in this as, previously, God explicitly made Adam and his successors tillers of the soil. From where has the practice of animal husbandry and sacrifice come from? The writer knows in fact that blood sacrifice is foundational for humanity, and so implicates God in the practice. Essentially the story again implies that God is responsible for the origin of human desire (he prefers one gift over the other), while human freedom also remains responsible. As mentioned, this is the first reference to sin in the Bible. It is "crouching at the door" and its desire is for Cain. This is an accurate description of overwhelming desire: it is a dislocation of the self resulting in chaotic, destructive behavior. Desire is so powerful it assumes its own violent identity. It is a much more profound and appropriate description of "sin" than mere "disobedience": it is this that destroys the self and kills the other.

After he is murdered, Abel's blood cries out from the ground. Cain's punishment is to be a fugitive and a wanderer upon the earth — an alienation from the earth parallel to alienation from self. But then God puts a protecting mark on Cain: "Whoever kills Cain will suffer a sevenfold vengeance" (v.15). In effect God accepts the "sacred order" resulting from the foundational murder. However, the results then play out in Gen 4.17–24. Cain founds the first city, naming it after his son, Enoch. The descendants of this line introduce culture — animal husbandry, music, artisanship. But alongside culture, there is continually escalating violence. This is voiced by Lamech who says "I have killed a man for wounding me, a young man for striking me. If Cain is avenged sevenfold, truly Lamech seventy-sevenfold." Violence is the DNA of human culture. Scrape the surface and it is there. God seems to collude with this. His solutions to the problems of desire seem at this point to be conditioned entirely by violence. However, God does call Cain to account for the murder, echoing the outcry of the blood. ("Where is your brother … your brother's blood is crying out to me from the ground.")

The writer gives an authentic expression of human existence and of God's essential concern for life, prior to the emergence of the real solution which is the call of Abraham and the transforming pathway this initiates. "God" remains a highly ambiguous term at this stage, immersed in sacrifice and violence, with clear hints of how destructive this all is, but without a clear way out.

In contrast read Mt 18.21–22.

"How often should I forgive? As many as seven times? … Not seven times, but, I tell you, seventy-seven times." Jesus reverses and undoes the violence of Genesis, and says his Father is "perfect" in exactly this character of forgiveness (Mt 5.44–48).

The Garden and Cain & Abel Stories Are To Be Read Together

The way that the first two stories are written clearly makes them doublets interpreting each other. They mirror each other and are meant to be read together. Doing so allows us to see that the core issues are desire, rivalry and violence, not disobedience.

Comparison of the Two Stories

• The humans have familiar personal conversation with God. This only happens in these two stories.
• There is a supreme object of desire — for the fruit in the Garden; for God's favor in Cain and Abel.
• The serpent and croucher are different personifications of the power of desire. They are projected as beings outside of ourselves — greater than us.
• There are prohibitions and sanctions.
• There is hiding, shame and

evasion — Adam and Eve hide their nakedness; Cain asks: "Am I my brother's keeper?"
• God asks key questions: "Who told you that you were naked?" "Where is your brother?"
• Crime and punishment — toil for Adam/pangs of childbirth for Eve; for Cain the earth will not yield its fruit.
• Exile — Adam and Eve are cast out of Eden; Cain becomes a wanderer on the earth.

The stories read together show how rivalry and desire result in violence and alienation and this problem lies at the heart of the human condition. Separating out the Garden story makes it a human doom with only a legal waiver as a solution, rather than an anthropological condition needing to be healed.

The Fall

The "Fall" is not a term found anywhere in the Bible. Adam and Eve were "expelled" from the Garden to a land outside of it. A fall conjures up the Greek concept of a separate divine realm in the heavens and a descent to the material earth. A focus on the fault of Eve in the Garden story has also led to the scapegoating of women in the Christian tradition. In the Gospel of John's resurrection narrative, Jesus is mistaken for a gardener, evoking the Garden story of Genesis. In this account, it is the woman (Mary Magdalene) who is the first to recognise Jesus and receive the good news of life. An inversion and transformation of

the Eden story. The Garden story and the story of Cain and Abel give a comprehensive picture of the human situation, rather than the legal formula of a "single clause" fault. The legal formula puts the lawyers in charge, resulting in a penal system. Salvation becomes a matter of "doing time" (Jesus paying a penalty for us) rather than abolishing the jail itself.

Overall Genesis is a reflection on the human condition and its progressive crisis rather than the record of a single "original sin." Instead of sin and law the focus here is violence and desire.

Sons of God, Daughters of Men

Read Gen 6.1–4.

The sons of God take for themselves the daughters of men. Again there is boundary-breaking desire producing violence — this time involving "divine beings" mating with humans. The children born of these relationships are violent figures (the *Nephilim*.) At Numbers 13.32–33 these are described as giants. They are "the heroes of old and warriors of renown" (like Hercules in Greek mythology, born of Zeus and a human woman). Evidently we are dealing with mythological figures, but the point is that very violent beings (professional warriors) come from transgressive desire. God's response is the withdrawal of his spirit and the curtailment of the human lifespan: the first time God actively sets a limit to human life, and it is again a mirroring of human violence. Still today we look to violent "superheroes" and idolize them because of their violence and power, but that is part of the problem. It is as a result of idolizing violence that human lifespan is cut short! Humanity does not reach the fullness intended for it.

The Flood

Read Gen 6.5–13.

Why is God destroying mankind?

"Now the earth was corrupt in God's sight, and the earth was filled with violence" (no mention of sin). As civilization grows, violence grows exponentially, and so also the corruption of the earth — the breakdown of its life. Violence results from unbridled rivalry and desire. "Every inclination of the thoughts of their hearts was only evil continually." All this leads to a progressive loss of relationships, a world of despair, devoid of love. The flood story projects the core problems found in the other stories onto the scale of peoples and nations.

Flood stories are present in many different cultures. They are a symbol of complete devastation. In ancient near eastern mythology, the earth is surrounded by water, the symbol of primeval chaos. In the Biblical account of creation God divided the waters — those above are kept from the earth by the dome of the heavens, and those below are shut out by the Earth. God can choose to release openings in the dome and open the fountains of the deep. In this story he opens the floodgates until all the Earth is covered with water. God returns the world to its original chaos — which is a cosmic expression of human violence.

Yet God provides for a solution to the problem through Noah re-beginning the human project. And afterward God promises never again to curse and destroy the Earth (8.21–22). We can see the character of God moving little by little from violence. The author is subtly moving the thought of God forward. However, it is also telling that the author suggests it is because of animal sacrifice that God relents in this way. God appears capricious, unintelligent and affected by animal sacrifice. It seems clear that the author is deftly ironizing and critiquing received understandings of God.

Tower of Babel

Read Gen 11.1–9.

A story that explains the multitude of languages and diversity of human tribes and groups. Here again God is in rivalry with human beings as in Eden: he behaves like human beings. He prevents "megalopolis" pretensions by scattering people, creating barriers of language and understanding between groups. The tower of Babel is a story that recognizes that people are divided and work against each other. It seeks to explain how this came to be. The explanation is that God sees human beings establishing their own transcendence, and works forcefully against them. This seems unworthy on God's part. Ultimately it demonstrates that the Biblical God is working against the pretensions of human tribes, nations and cities of being absolute to themselves. The Tower with "its top in the heavens" implies victory over the "other" whoever that might be. God sets out to undo this, but still, at this point, by means of violence.

Compare Acts 2.1–11 where the Spirit of Jesus poured out, enables each person to understand the apostles' preaching "in their own language."

Like "forgiving seventy times seven" this inverts the solutions of God in Genesis, while actually fulfilling their intention.

Summary

Genesis chapters 2-11 describe human desire and its consequences. Each story is as important as the others. They are five stories of human desire resulting in violence and despair. God is often the one who sets things up and then reacts within the same parameters as the problem. He creates the human condition — the desire that produces rivalry and violence— then tries violently to contain the problem. Human beings chose this condition and remain responsible for it (it is *their* humanity) but it does not stop the picture of God in these stories being very unsatisfactory. In fact, Genesis may well demonstrate that the general human concept of "God" is itself produced out

of generative violence. At the least, we can say that reading Genesis both demonstrates the core problems of human existence and strongly suggests our default ideas about who God is and how s/he works are badly skewed by a violent human mindset. Genesis 2–11 is a deeply ironic text and must be seen that way. The only solution to its questions is by moving forward through the whole story of Genesis, and progressively through all the stories of the Bible.

Lesson Questions

· What do you think about this approach to understanding the message of Genesis 2–11?

· Traditionally the church has stressed personal morality and "original sin" as the root cause of our fall from grace. Why do you think this is so?

· Do you think that desire, rivalry, and violence are the root problem of the human condition?

· What parallels can we draw between these stories and our contemporary world (advertising, consumerism, addiction, violence, city life)?

Personal Reflection

· How would it feel to think that Christianity is not about redeeming me from original sin but transforming me from a condition of desire and violence?

· Can I identify with the prehistory figures like Cain and Eve in terms of my desire and its consequences?

Glossary

· Original Sin — the idea of a primary sin, committed by Adam, that is passed on to his descendants, with deadly legal and metaphysical consequences.

· The Fall — traditional theological concept figuring a vertical fall from communion with God, with a background Platonism of the soul becoming immersed in the material world.

· Nephilim — giant mythic heroes and figures of violence in the early Biblical worldview.

Resources/Background Reading

· An Introduction to the Old Testament, Walter Brueggemann (2003)

· Genesis 1-11, Claus Westermann (1976)

· How to Read the Bible & Still Be a Christian: Struggling with Divine Violence from Genesis Through Revelation, John Dominic Crossan (2015)

· How to Read the Bible: A Guide to Scripture, Then and Now, James L. Kugel (2008)

Cultural References

· Movie, Noah, dir. Darren Aronofsky (2014)

· Movie, East of Eden, dir. Elia Kazan (1955)

· Paradise Lost, Thomas Milton (1667)

· Article, How St. Augustine Invented Sex, Stephen Greenblatt (New Yorker Magazine, June, 2017)

VIOLENCE TO FORGIVENESS
Lesson 2: Patriarchs

Learning Objectives

· To see the Patriarchs as a solution to the problem of violence rather than simply folkloristic stories and carriers of God's legal covenant.

· To understand that Joseph is a type of the forgiving victim, the Messiah to come.

Core Biblical Texts

· Gen 18.1–33
· Gen 50.15–21

Key Points

· The Patriarch stories teach us the solution to the anthropological problem of violence.

· Abraham is the first figure to enter into a transformative relationship with God. This is the meaning of covenant, not a purely legal contract.

· Abraham's intercession for Sodom and Gomorrah begins to change the perceived character of God from punishment to mercy.

· Joseph, as a Wisdom figure, and forgiving victim, embodies God's anthropological solution to the problems identified in Genesis 2–11.

Key Words/Concepts

· Covenant
· Wisdom

Last lesson we saw how the prehistories describe the human problem of desire, rivalry and violence. Sin is understood as violence in its many forms. If Chapters 2–11 of Genesis lay out the problem, then the stories of the patriarchs (Abraham, Isaac, Jacob and Joseph) point the way to the solution.

Of note — just as the Christian tradition has emphasized the Garden story over the other prehistories, often the figure of Abraham (the father of faith and covenant) is seen as more important than Isaac, Jacob and Joseph. In fact more of Genesis is devoted to the Joseph saga than any of the other patriarchs:

Abraham & Isaac 12–25 (14 chapters together); Jacob 25-36 (12 chapters); Joseph 37-50 (14 chapters).

In this lesson we are going to focus mostly on the figures of Abraham and Joseph. Next lesson we will look more at Jacob.

Abraham and Joseph span the project of forgiveness which Genesis presents as the solution to the violence of the prehistories. In Abraham all the tribes of the Earth are to be blessed: Joseph fulfills this promise.

Abraham — Call and Covenant

The first thing usually connected with Abraham is the covenant (chapters 15 & 17) — but before the covenant is the call. Abraham is asked to leave his land and kindred — involving a surrender of all inherited identity and security. This becomes a pattern for his life. God has created us as mimetic and filled with desire. But it also includes the possibility of the transformation of desire into something completely new. A new space waiting to be filled. But first the space must be cleared of the old. Abraham trusts himself to this empty space and enters into a relationship with the God of the new. This is the heart of the covenant. As we read the details of Abraham's story we see how this process works in an actual human historical context. How God makes use of it to begin his project of transformation.

Blessing

Read Gen 12.1–4.

In this passage Abraham has a multitude of blessings attached to him: God will bless him, his name will be a blessing, those he blesses will be blessed, and through him all the families of the Earth will be blessed.

This theme of blessing upon Abraham and his descendants is repeated throughout the story of Abraham:

Gen 13.14–17 (his descendents will be like the grains of dust on the earth).
Gen 15.5 (his descendents will be like the stars in the heavens).
Gen 22.17–18 (his descendants will be as numerous as the stars and the sand on the seashore).
Gen 26.2–5 (all the nations will be blessed through his offspring).

Gen 28.13–15 (his offspring will spread across all the earth and be a source of blessing).
Gen 32.12 (his offspring will be as the sand of the sea).
Gen 35.11–12 (a company of nations shall come from him and kings spring from him).

The blessing of Abraham's covenant echoes the blessing of the first humans (Gen 1.28), but now found in a historical rather than a cosmic setting. The covenant is never a purely legal arrangement but a concrete source of blessing for human beings. The story of Joseph demonstrates this in a comprehensive way.

Abraham as *Hapiru*

Abraham is *Hapiru* (see Lesson 1, Story 1). His behavior reflects this social status — he will do anything to survive!

Read Gen 12.10–20.

Here he is an alien in the land; struggling to stay alive in desperate times of famine. He effectively prostitutes Sarah for the sake of survival (and again in Gen 20.1–2; and the same motifs are also repeated in the story of Isaac, at 26.1–11).

Read Gen 14.8–16

Abraham is called "the Hebrew." In this story he clearly acts as *Hapiru*. He is presented as a warlord, a mercenary or bandit, the leader of a formidable group of armed men. All this shows a man on the margins of society without established state protections. God chooses someone in this situation to establish his new project.

A Son is Promised

Read Gen 18.1–15 (God promises a son to Abraham and Sarah).

Sarah also participates in this drama. She is despised, barren — a *Hapiru* twice over. The story tells of her rivalry with Hagar, yet another instance of deadly conflict in Genesis. The theme of a barren woman blessed with a child is repeated with Rebekah and echoed in Rachel's story too. Women in highly insecure situations, on the edge of being outcast, are key female figures in the Bible (cf. Tamar, Ruth, Mary …). These women are catalysts; they are even more at risk, and yet exactly in that situation they move the project forward. Sarah's story mirrors and doubles Abraham's. Hagar's story underscores the point, even though what happens to her is in tension with the central covenant epic going through Abraham and Isaac. She is a *Hapiru* three times over, mistreated and driven out by Sarah (21.1–21) and yet God made promises to her parallel to Abraham's "multitude of offspring" (16.10). Indeed her son, Ishmael, has twelve sons parallel to Jacob's (25.13–15). Thus God works through those who are marginal, and makes and keeps promises to other such people, aside from Abraham and Isaac. The dramatic highpoint of Abraham's story is the episode of the sacrifice of Isaac (Gen 22.1–19).

Here Abraham's journey reaches its deepest, most fearful expression. Abraham is asked to surrender the supreme object of desire: his son, and with him the whole project, the pathway of all promised blessing. This is the moment in which Abraham's experience on the margins is demonstrated as an internal event of faith, of utter dependence on God. Child sacrifice was an established practice in the cultures of that time (e.g. 2 Kings 3.27). Abraham seems to be asked to repeat this, but God stays his hand, deflecting the human sacrifice onto an animal. This marks another step forward in the religious experience of the Israelites and how they perceived God. The story acts as a clear line drawn against child sacrifice in the religious practice of Israel. At the same time, Abraham's gesture of surrender within his given human context acts as a paradigm spiritual drama. He gives up the project "in his own power," in order that it be truly the new thing willed by God.

Abraham Intercedes for Sodom & Gomorrah

This story comes directly after God's promise of a son for Abraham and Sarah. It demonstrates how the Bible sees the developing spiritual experience of its people as also appearing to change the character of God. Abraham appears more merciful than God.

Read Gen 18.16–33.

The Lord said "Shall I hide from

Abraham what I am about to do, seeing that Abraham shall become a great and mighty nation, and all the nations of the earth shall be blessed in him? No, for I have chosen him, that he may charge his children and his household after him to keep the way of the Lord by doing righteousness and justice; so that the Lord may bring about for Abraham what he has promised him." (Vv 17-19.)

God has chosen Abraham for blessing, has entered into a relationship for this reason and so he now has to involve Abraham in his actions. Because of this blessing-relationship there is a new reciprocity and Abraham begins to change God. God's question to himself (how does the writer know of this?) suggests that the Lord may be providing an instance of "righteousness and justice" in punishing Sodom and Gomorrah. But the theme of "hiding" also suggests uncertainty. Does God anticipate that Abraham will try and talk him out of it, since he, Abraham, is more compassionate than avenging? Because this is exactly what happens.

The Lord answers the outcry against Sodom and Gomorrah. The city's offense is violence (intended gang rape) towards the alien/stranger (Gen 19.1–11). God is determined to destroy the city and Abraham bargains for mercy. God allows Abraham to beat his threshold against retribution down from fifty to ten righteous men in the city — though ultimately to no avail. At the beginning of the

bargaining Abraham declares to God, "Far be it from you to do such a thing, to slay the righteous with the wicked, so that the righteous fare as the wicked! Far be that from you! Shall not the judge of all the earth do what is just?" (Gen 18:25) Abraham argues against indiscriminate killing (Cain's sevenfold vengeance and Lamech's seventy-sevenfold). He stops at "ten righteous men" as the threshold at which an avenging judge should stay his hand. But the principle has been established and really Abraham could still ask the question "Would you not forgive the city for the sake of one just man?" (Abraham's argument is ultimately the inverse of substitutionary killing, one killed for all; instead all spared for one!) In effect Abraham is deconstructing the "justice" of the Flood story, and profoundly so. The story shows that Abraham's heart is filled with mercy. He is shown as exceeding God in compassion for Sodom and in fact teaching "God" the nature of true justice. In this way Abraham fulfills, in terms of a paradigm story, his role of bringing blessing to all peoples. The content of the covenant with Abraham brings about transformation both in Abraham and God. Theology changes anthropology, and anthropology changes theology. The covenant is never simply a legal contract for salvation.

Joseph

The story of Joseph is a classic of literature, the original rags-to-riches drama based in family jealousy, intended murder and abandonment. It is "Cain and Abel" with a happy outcome. The story concludes Genesis with a reversal of the themes of jealousy and murder. It becomes a paradigm of life-giving change — a second genesis at the end of the book of Genesis. Joseph's story resolves the problems of chapters 2–11 and fulfills the promise of blessing to Abraham.

Rivalry and Desire

At the beginning of the Joseph story the familiar themes of Genesis are repeated:

Read Gen 37.1–28
(the plot against Joseph who is thrown in a pit and sold into slavery because his brothers are murderously jealous).

Read Gen 39.1–20
(the story of Potiphar's wife: Joseph is the object of desire and becomes the victim).

Joseph as a Wisdom Figure

Joseph is presented as a Wisdom figure. It is his wisdom which enables him to change situations for the sake of life (41.39). His ability to interpret dreams comes from God (Gen 40.8). Even in prison he takes charge and does well (Gen 39.21–23). Later Joseph uses his gift of wisdom to prepare for famine (Gen 47.20–26).

Forgiveness

Forgiveness is Joseph's greatest gift. His brothers, schooled in the ways of violence, expect only retribution and revenge. Joseph introduces a completely new element in the story, bringing blessing to his brothers. Once

again it is a human being who demonstrates the greatest spiritual attributes and character. God remains in the background. Joseph sets the scene with great care and skill (wisdom).

Read Gen 42.1–25 (Joseph sets a test).

Read Gen 43.26–31 (the brothers return and feast with Joseph; Joseph shows great emotion).

Read Gen 44.1–13 (Benjamin is trapped with Joseph's cup).

Read Gen 44.18–34 (Judah offers himself in place of his brother, willing to take the part of the victim).

Read Gen 45.1–9 (Joseph is deeply moved and reveals himself).

Read Gen 50.15–21 (Joseph reveals a new path. He asks "Am I in the place of God?" subtly echoing Jacob's comment about Esau in Gen 33.10 — see next lesson; he forgives his brothers, teaching them about God's way, a brotherhood based on forgiveness. "Even though you intended to do harm to me, God intended it for good...").

By having them return for Benjamin Joseph leads his brothers to address their previous acts against him, so they can see things from the perspective of the victim and be transformed. Judah is willing to take on the part of the victim. This is the act that triggers the process of reconciliation. The story of the Savior-Victim becomes the greatest insight of Genesis. It parallels Job and the Suffering Servant of Isaiah. It is also the closest in narrative structure to the story of Jesus (handed over to foreigners, the victim of violence; but ultimately he is reconciled with his brothers and brings life).

Genesis is a book of radical Wisdom— an exposé and critique of victim-making violence that points towards a solution — the revelation of God in the forgiving victim. Genesis makes its points not by overtly describing God in a new way but by demonstrating human possibilities of compassion and forgiveness that then model God's deepest intentions. Anthropology shapes theology!

Genesis Before Exodus

Joseph forgives his brothers, and in a sense pre-emptively forgives the Egyptians who are the villains of Exodus. He brings a kind of sacred and utopian harmony to their society, 47.20–26. (In v. 21 of the Septuagint Joseph makes slaves of the Egyptians, but in the Hebrew text he removes them to the cities, leaving the land for Pharaoh and the priests.) In this light Genesis is a later work than Exodus, providing a transformative preface for what comes after. In the editorial construction of the Torah it is placed at the beginning in order to throw a critical light on everything that follows. Genesis chapter one, the seven day creation story, is noteworthy for the complete absence of violence in creation. This spiritual vision flows through the whole of the book and cannot be there by accident. Genesis critiques the violent anthropo-theology of Exodus and the stories that follow. Genesis is a theological meditation that implicitly reverses all the violence of Israel's history. Both violence and love are imitative and generative processes, but with very different results. Genesis tells us that God's plan is for us to choose generative nonviolence and forgiveness over generative violence.

Notes:

_____

_____

_____

_____

_____

_____

_____

_____

_____

_____

_____

_____

_____

_____

_____

_____

_____

_____

_____

_____

_____

_____

_____

_____

_____

Lesson Questions

· By reading Genesis as a seamless yet layered narrative, the message of forgiveness as the answer to the human problem of violence becomes evident. What has been your experience of hearing the Genesis stories? What has been the dominant reading and teaching of the Christian tradition drawn from the Genesis texts?

· How would reading the book of Genesis in a literal and flat way (without thinking any critique of violence is involved) change the meaning of Genesis?

· The question of creation vs. evolution has been a bone of contention in the Christian tradition. Why do you think it is so important? What theological positions hinge on this debate? Does the view advanced here fit more with an evolutionary standpoint?

· Abraham's relationship with God allows for a shift of understanding about who God is. God appears to change because of this relationship (or at least how God is presented in the text). How much (if at all) do you think our relationship with God causes God to change? Can God change? Is change and reciprocity an essential part of relationship? Is "forgiveness" the best kind of word for the change God undergoes?

Personal Reflection

· What are the stories you remember from childhood/culture? In many children's Bibles there are disproportionate chapters and illustrations of the Genesis stories. Which stories or characters were meaningful to you? Why do you think this is?

· Abraham has to surrender his security and identity in order to enter into relationship with God in the new space that opens up. Can you think of times when you have felt closer to God after having surrendered something you had previously relied upon?

· This lesson teaches that forgiveness is the solution to violence. When in your life have you truly forgiven somebody? Did you feel that the cycle of violence in that situation was broken through this act of forgiveness?

· Can you tell about a time you experienced love as imitative (or generative) to overcome violence? When in your life did love win?

Glossary

· Covenant — term for an ancient treaty or bond, protected by sanctions, which in the Bible applied to the committed relationship between God and his people.

· Wisdom — in the Bible a genre of writing specializing in rules of how to live life well; plus a personified figure, a Woman who is God's first offspring and accompanies him in the work of creation.

Resources/Background Reading

· *Love Wins: A Book About Heaven, Hell, and the Fate of Every Person Who Ever Lived*, Rob Bell (2012)

Cultural References

· Wilfred Owen poem, *Parable of the Old Man and the Young*

South Africa's *Truth and Reconciliation Commission* (TRC)

Movie, *Gran Torino*, dir. Clint Eastwood (2008)

VIOLENCE TO FORGIVENESS
Lesson 3: Prodigal Son

Learning Objectives

· To see how Jesus mined stories from his scriptural tradition to formulate his own message.

· To understand that the Jewish scriptures already contain the key message of forgiveness and how central this message is to Jesus.

Core Biblical Texts

· Gen 32.3–33.10
· Lk 15.11–32

Key Points

· The story of Jacob and Esau teaches that in forgiveness we begin to see the face of God.

· Jesus uses themes from the patriarch stories in his parables to teach about forgiveness and compassion.

· Forgiveness is the way to overcome human desire, rivalry, alienation and violence.

Key Words /Concepts

· Alienation

· Forgiveness

Genesis in the New Testament

Let's first look briefly at how Paul explains the human situation using Genesis, and how a particular reading of Romans has shaped our understanding:

Read Rom 5.12–14.

"Therefore, just as sin came into the world through one man, and death came through sin, and so death spread to all because all have sinned – sin was indeed in the world before the law, but sin is not reckoned when there is no law. Yet death exercised domination from Adam to Moses, even over those whose sins were not like the transgression of Adam, who is a type of the one who was to come."

What is Paul's primary concern?

What paradigm figure does he use?

Paul's primary concern is sin and its effect of death. Adam brings death and, in as much as everyone has sinned, all die. Paul uses Adam as a paradigm figure or model of the human situation of sin and death. Although the reasoning is muddled (how did the sins of all bring death when sin is not reckoned without law?) the model-paradigm is clear — Adam represents sin and death, Christ represents forgiveness and life.

There is a disastrous history of mistranslation of "because all have sinned" in the Romans quotation above. Augustine of Hippo did not know Greek. He relied on Latin translations of the Bible. In the one he was using the Greek phrase, rendered in most translations "because," was given as *in quo*, understood by Augustine as meaning "in whom." Thus: "Sin came into the world through one man (Adam)... in whom all have sinned..." By this translation he and others were convinced that all humans physically and legally sinned in Adam and bear responsibility for his sin and suffer its consequences. And so, "original sin." Our individual DNA is guilty!

(See article link in Resources Background Reading.)

In contrast when Jesus uses Genesis he does not look at the same themes or paradigm as Paul. He sees a different paradigm as the core of the human problem — violence. He uses a different Genesis figure to express the root problem.

Read Lk 11.49–51.

"Therefore also the Wisdom of God said, 'I will send them prophets and apostles, some of whom they will kill and persecute', so that this generation may be charged with the blood of all the prophets shed since the foundation of the world, from the blood of Abel to the blood of Zechariah ... ".

Jesus uses the figure of Abel and prophets who have been murdered. He is concerned with the human condition of violence and its generative anthropology of killing.

Read Jn 8.34–44.

Jesus identifies murder as the original sin. He is addressing those seeking to kill him and says that, though they think they are children of Abraham, their real father is the father of lies, "a murderer from the beginning." (Because Jesus is here indicting the Judean authorities, translated as "Jews," the text has been read as anti-Semitic, but it is an anthropological statement directed at those who represent a sacred order of violence.) Here in fact Jesus identifies sin with murder. The foundation of the world is built with the shedding of innocent blood, which is then covered up with lies. For Jesus it is about Abel, not Adam. Abel is the paradigm figure — the innocent victim, for whose blood all generations colluding in these murders are answerable.

When interpreting his tradition, Jesus' approach is much more anthropological — he deals with the heart of the matter from the Jewish scriptures which is bloodshed. Paul is focusing on the break with the Law represented by Jesus. Paul clearly understands that the grace of Christ brings life rather than death, but he is examining this effect in terms of the legal themes of condemnation v. righteousness (Rom 5.15–17). Paul's deployment of the terms has come to dominate.

In dealing with the core issue Jesus has a faithful yet transformative relationship with his tradition. He takes familiar themes and makes them his own, bringing things front and center which, before were marginal. In this way he takes the essential truths of the

Hebrew scriptures and reformulates them into revelations about who God is and how this changes and challenges us. His parable of the Prodigal Son is a stellar example of this. To understand it, we will look first at the patriarch story of Jacob and Esau.

The Story of Jacob & Esau

As in the other patriarch stories here are the familiar themes of rivalry (Rachel and Leah, Jacob and Esau), and the object of desire, the birthright.

Read Gen 25.22–25 (The twins rivalry starts in the womb).

Read Gen 27.27–45. (Isaac blesses Jacob; Esau's murderous anger; Jacob's flight.)

The story continues with Jacob living in fear in exile. (He marries Leah and then Rachel; incites jealousy from the sons of Laban because he has "... taken all that was our father's; he has gained all this wealth from what belonged to our father," Gen 31:1). His father-in-law, Laban, distrusts him, and he has to flee once again, this time back to Canaan.

Read Gen 32.3–23 (Jacob, still fearful, sends messages and gifts to appease Esau "... afterwards I shall see his face; perhaps he will accept me.")

Read Gen 32.24–31. (On the eve of meeting with his brother, Jacob wrestles with a mysterious man. The bout ends with Jacob declaring he has seen the face of God.)

When Jacob wrestles with the man/God, God and the human are in conflict and it is the human that prevails. Jacob is given a new name and a blessing. He says, "I have seen God face to face and yet my life is preserved." In Jacob's mind it is impossible to look on the face of God and survive. Yet God has not overpowered him in order that this might happen. He names the place "Peniel," meaning "the face of God." (Remember that Jacob wants also to see the face of Esau.)

Read Gen 33.1–10 (Jacob is forgiven by Esau).

Now Jacob is able to see the continuity between a nonviolent God and a nonviolent human. Esau receives Jacob not with revenge, but kissing and weeping. This releases in Jacob a new understanding of God. "For truly to see your face [Esau] is like seeing the face of God — since you have received me with such favor." Favor here means non-retaliation, nonviolence. Jacob recognizes God in the forgiveness, kindness and grace of Esau, and vice versa.

Parable of the Prodigal Son

Jesus' parable of the Prodigal Son (or the Two Sons) repeats and reshapes the stories of Jacob and Joseph.

Read Luke 15.11–32.

What motifs and themes does Jesus draw from the patriarch stories of Jacob and Joseph?

From Jacob

- Two sons and a father.
- The younger son seizing his

inheritance/birthright fraudulently from his father. (It was extremely disrespectful/illegal of the prodigal son to demand his inheritance while his father was still alive. Similarly Jacob completely demeans his father's honor.)
- In both cases the younger son leaves for distant lands (also present in the Joseph story).
- The character of Jacob and the prodigal son, both trying to talk and deal their way out of a deadly situation.
- Compare the stories of Jacob meeting with Esau (Gen 33.4) and Lk 15.20: here the father takes the place of Esau, repeating the very same actions. He runs, embraces, kisses — it is the same visual scene. The Greek of the Gospel even echoes the same Hebrew expression, "to hang on someone's neck" (to embrace).

Jesus sees the character of God (the Father) in the nonviolence of Esau which Genesis already signaled as "the face of God." Jesus was re-telling the truth already present in Genesis. What he adds is the explicit note of the Father "filled with compassion." He is explicitly revealing the God of compassion.

From Joseph

- Lost son found, dead son alive again.
- Elder brother/s' jealousy.
- Famine in the land.
- The best robe (coat of many colors, a sign of favor); ring on his finger (symbol of the Pharaoh's power in the Joseph story).

Key differences between the patriarch stories and the parable are:

- The role of the father. In Genesis the fathers (Isaac and Jacob) are flawed and instigate the rivalry. The father here is like Esau — because he forgives. In the Prodigal Son story Jesus makes the father the pivotal figure. He does this to teach us about the nature of God.
- The emphasis shifts from us to God. Jesus takes the anthropology of Genesis (who we are when forgiveness takes place) and makes it explicitly theology (who God is).

He takes the deeper points of the Genesis stories and creates his parables. In this way he is not abolishing the law (the Torah including the book of Genesis), but fulfilling it. For Jesus the message is about forgiveness and relationship with God and with the other.

The Older Son

As well as a commentary on violence and forgiveness, the parable becomes a characterization of the situation of the Jewish people with the Law as a privileging and separating principle.

"'For all these years I have been working like a slave for you, and I have never disobeyed your command; yet you have never given me even a young goat so that I might celebrate with my friends. But when this son of yours came back, who has devoured your property with prostitutes, you killed the fatted calf for him!' Then the father said to him, 'Son, you are always with me, and all that is mine is yours. But we had to celebrate and rejoice, because this brother of yours was dead and has come to life; he was lost and has been found.'"

The older son always obeys the law but perceives this to be like slavery. He doesn't feel the blessing of having his father with him always and everything that the father has being his. He does not recognize that the relationship with the father (and the brother) is the real treasure. His outrage about "this son of yours" is changed by the father to the loving forgiveness of "this brother of yours." Again we see how Jesus uses Genesis to meditate on the situation of his people *vis a vis* the other, including the outrageously sinful.

Jesus and Forgiveness

Read Mark 11.24–25.

"So I tell you, whatever you ask for in prayer, believe that you have received it, and it will be yours. Whenever you stand praying, forgive, if you have anything against anyone; so that your Father in heaven may also forgive you your trespasses."

Here is the key thing about Jesus: he relates divine forgiveness to human forgiveness. They are continuous for him. If we forgive, we see and understand that the nature of God is to forgive and therefore we feel his forgiveness ourselves — we are forgiven by God. This passage comes after Jesus' symbolic abolition of the temple. Prayer and forgiveness replace the temple, render it obsolete. The way of worshipping God and being with God is forgiveness rather than temple ritual.

The Parable of the Rich Man and Lazarus

This parable is often quoted as the quintessential statement of hell fire. It was frequently depicted in medieval art. Like the Prodigal Son this story is exclusive to Luke's Gospel and follows shortly after. This parable, however, can be read as an inversion of the parable of the Prodigal Son.

Read Lk 16.19–31.

Compare and contrast the two stories:

- Both the prodigal son and Lazarus find themselves in desperate situations. Both beg for scraps.
- Both are in the company of unclean animals (dogs, swine).
- Both stories have father figures: The rich man calls Abraham his "father". Lazarus leans on Abraham like the prodigal son is held by his father.
- The theme of distance — there is a great distance between the rich man and Lazarus, and between the father and his wastrel son (in "a far country"). Unlike the father who sees his son from a

long way off and runs to meet him, the rich man maintains his structural distance and indifference to the poor, so he sees Lazarus "far away" with Abraham.
- Both the prodigal son and the rich man live sumptuously, but then lose everything. But the prodigal son "comes to his senses" while the rich man does not change his way of thinking. He still treats Lazarus like an inferior wanting him to bring him water with "the tip of his finger," and then to warn his brothers. He is still thinking of his own status and social group, not of the poor.

This story is sometimes read as an attack on the Sadducees who did not believe in the afterlife. (Lazarus here shares the name of the character in John's Gospel who was raised. The five brothers may refer to the five sons of Annas, who was formerly the high priest. All five brothers served as priests and wore the priestly purple.) But the plain interpretation of rich-in-contrast-to-poor is key to Luke and the most obvious meaning.

In any case, the divide between Lazarus and the Rich Man remains the final motif. "Between you and us a great chasm has been fixed, so that those who might want to pass from here to you cannot do so, and no one can cross from there to us." The essential point is that the rich man is the one who creates the divide, so that those on Abraham's side of the chasm who "might want to pass" (i.e. act out of compassion) in fact cannot. The text clearly implies that the

rich and privileged, those with status, create the divide, not God. Thus the parable is not a picture of medieval hell but of humanly created alienation and its suffering. Again the way to the kingdom is through our relationships with others, forgiveness, and care for the poor. What we do in this world constructs the way we relate to God's kingdom.

Notes:

_____

_____

_____

_____

_____

_____

_____

_____

_____

_____

_____

_____

_____

_____

_____

_____

_____

_____

_____

_____

_____

_____

_____

_____

Lesson Questions

· What role does Esau play in the story? Is he the good guy or bad guy?

· How is Jacob described? Why do you think God chose this character to move his plan forward?

· In the parable of the Prodigal Son, the son "came to his senses." What does this mean? What happens in his mind? And what is the outcome?

Personal Reflection

· When have I been in a situation of having to "come to my senses?" How did God (the Father) respond?

· In what ways do I create chasms between myself and others?

· Tell about a person you have known who showed you "the face of God" or forgiveness.

Glossary

· Alienation — a term with a philosophical background meaning profound human separation from others and social structures of well-being.

Resources/Background Reading

· http://www.peteenns.com/paul-adam-and-salvation-maybe-augustine-really-did-screw-everything-up-and-we-should-just-move-on/

· *The Prodigal God: Recovering the Heart of the Christian Faith*, Timothy Keller (2008)

Cultural References

· Rolling Stones, "Prodigal Son" (Youtube, https://www.youtube.com/watch?v=luK1dQx5GR4)

· U2, "The First Time" (Youtube, https://www.youtube.com/watch?v=NElacDGPNws)

· Jesus telling the parable in director Franco Zeffirelli's movie, *Jesus of Nazareth* (1977)

· *Joseph and the Amazing Technicolor Dreamcoat*, musical by Andrew Lloyd Weber (1970)

· *Jacob I have Loved*, Katherine Paterson (1980)

· Animated movie, *Joseph King of Dreams*, dir. Rob LaDuca (2000)

· Song, "My son has gone away" (Saint Louis Jesuits)

3

MAGNUM
Sive
AEA INFERIOR.
Nazareth
NEPHTHALIM
MARE GENESARETH
TOPARCHIA.
Amorrhaei.
Cademoth solitudo.
Beer putrus
anah solitudo.
Nabathaei.
ARABIAE PE
IUDAEA
Daroma Interior.
VEL IDUMAEA.
Albon Diblathaim.
TRAEAE PARS
Dibon Gad.
MARE SALSUM.
MOABITIS
MERIDIES.

The Land and its Loss

Lesson Plan

· Lesson 1: Deuteronomic Worldview

· Lesson 2: Response to the
Loss of the Land

· Lesson 3: The Land and Jesus

Learning Objectives

· To see that the Deuteronomic worldview
is the dominant interpretative reading
of the Bible, but it is countered by
several alternative perspectives
of God's action in the world.

· To understand that the Deuteronomic
worldview interprets the violence
of the loss of the Kingdoms
as God's punishment for the
sinfulness of the people.

· To identify the key major responses of
the Jewish people to the crisis of the
land that emerged in the first century
and to understand how each of these
responses is rooted in Biblical tradition.

· To situate Jesus in the context of the
many movements and stressors of
his time in relation to the land and to
understand his own unique response.

Synopsis of the Story as a Whole

· Gaining the land of Israel through
exodus from Egypt was an event of grace,
but attacks by enemies were interpreted
as punishment for failure to keep the law.
This leads to a retributive understanding
of God. Nevertheless many voices in
the Old Testament are raised against
the implications of this view.

· At the time of Jesus the retributive
understanding was at crisis point,
heading toward a violent explosion.
Jesus' teaching offered a way through
and out, a completely new method of
dealing with the problem. "Be nonviolent
as your Father is nonviolent!"

Key Words/Concepts

· Biblical historical frame
story — the Exodus

· Deuteronomic worldview

· Pharisee

· Essene

· Zealot

· Sadducee

· John the Baptist

· Apocalyptic

THE LAND AND ITS LOSS
Lesson 1: Deuteronomic Worldview

Story 3: The Land and its Loss: Lesson 1

Learning Objectives

- To understand the concept of frame story, and then contrast the traditional Christian "Fall" with the Exodus as candidates for this controlling narrative of the Bible.
- To perceive that the Deuteronomic worldview is the dominant interpretative reading of the Bible, but it is countered by several alternative perspectives of God's action in the world.
- To understand that the Deuteronomic worldview interprets the violence of the loss of the Kingdoms as God's punishment for the sinfulness of the people.

Core Biblical Texts

- Dt 10.12–22
- Dt 28.1–68

Key Points

- The key historical frame story of the Bible is the Exodus. It defines the meaning of being in the land as liberation and life. (Genesis for Christians has traditionally been seen as the overall frame, i.e. the "Fall", a pivotal moment for a metaphysical problem; rather than Genesis as an exposé of human violence.)
- Deuteronomy interpreted the experience of violence against the land as punishment by God.
- Following the return from exile there was a stress on keeping the Law in order to avoid further instances of "God's wrath."

Key Words /Concepts

- Biblical historical frame story - the Exodus
- Deuteronomic worldview
- Traditional Christian Biblical frame story - the Fall

Exodus not Genesis as the Frame Story of the Bible

To understand the land we have to understand its story and its role in the Bible.

Genesis is typically seen by Christians as the frame story of the Bible. A frame story can be simply the beginning or occasion for another set of stories, or it can be the key dynamic which controls and gives shape and meaning to the rest of the text. Traditional interpretations, at least from the fourth century onwards, taught that we should understand the entire Bible from the starting point of the "Fall" of humanity in Adam. The meaning of redemption or salvation followed naturally from this catastrophic event. It was taught that the "Fall" was the end of our perfect relationship with God. As the word suggests this was a fall from on high, from a kind of heavenly state. Everything else pivots upon this event, and the whole Judeo-Christian story is one of us trying to get back to God's favor and presence "up above."

Instead, as we presented in Story 2, Genesis should be understood in a different way. It is an exposé of human violence — a primer on the dynamic that is repeated over and over in human relationships. It says that violence is our responsibility, and that the world was intended for life.

Genesis (which very probably reached its final form after the book of Exodus) is an attempt to interpret the meaning of God and humanity after and in light of the Exodus. What this means is that the experience of a personal God, and God's intention to bring life, enabled the Bible's authors to reflect deeply on what was wrong with the human condition. Unlike the peoples around them, they came to see that violence and death could not be part of God's plan. They could not possibly have come to understand this without the basic experience of the Exodus — of "a God merciful and gracious, slow to anger, and abounding in steadfast love and faithfulness" (Ex 34.6).

However, the book of Exodus is itself filled with violence, including God's. Hence, when the Torah was reaching its final form, the actual narrative of Exodus was prefaced with a profound meditation on human violence, filtered through traditions of the patriarchs and the prehistories. Chapter one of Genesis is a preface before the preface, so to speak. It shows God in definitive terms creating without violence, and thus providing the "image" according to which humans are made, i.e. nonviolent.

So what is the real frame story of the Old Testament? The story that gives meaning to the rest? The Exodus is the event that put the Hebrews and their God on the stage of history. ("God heard the cry of the people and knew their suffering;" Ex 2.24.) Exodus is the story of God's liberation of the Hebrews through the slaying of the Egyptians, one which sets the bar for the subsequent military conquest of all their enemies. It involves violence for the sake of justice. The exodus thus becomes the historical framing event of the Old Testament. This has another and different consequence from the lessons drawn in Genesis. Despite Genesis coming first, Exodus remains the real starting point. In fact this starting point is seen as so important to the meaning of the Bible that it results in a second telling of the story of the exodus at the end of the Torah — the book of Deuteronomy.

The book of Deuteronomy, reaching its final form after the exile in the 6th century BCE, retells this story from the perspective of the loss of the land, but beginning narratively at the moment when the Israelites are about to enter the land. Deuteronomy becomes the major interpretive writing at the core of the Old Testament. Genesis is in fact an outlier. Deuteronomy is central, controlling the narrative in Joshua, Judges and 1 & 2 Kings. It also has strong links to the books of Samuel and to the prophets, especially Jeremiah. Its interpretation sees the violence of the loss of the Israelite Kingdoms as God's punishment for the sinfulness of the people. It gives concrete expression to the concept of wrath as God's retributive violence. Its theological ethic gives dramatic meaning to the land and to the Temple, and their role in the life of the people. These concrete symbols become privileged markers of God's approval and then disapproval. In effect, therefore, Deuteronomy turns the story of Exodus (land as blessing) into the story of land as possibility of curse.

Land and Temple — the Shell of the New

At the same time — and this is the whole point here — the historical role of land and Temple provides a background and container for the transformative work of the whole of scripture. Without these overarching traditional, conservative symbols and institutions there would not have been the necessary continuity in the story of the people to enable new and alternative views to emerge. The whole thing could easily have blown apart. That is why our own third story puts the focus on the land (and a later one will focus on the Temple.) These two themes provide what we will call the "shell stories" which enable the pearl of the new to develop over the course of time. A "shell story" is different from a frame story, in as much as the latter is literary and interpretive, while the former provides the necessary physical and social conditions for an evolving, transformative story to emerge. The land and Temple provide the housing for the Bible's engine of revelation, ending with a nonviolent humanity and a nonviolent God. The book of Genesis is a good example of this engine at work within the traditional frame of the land.

The Meaning of the Land in the Light of the Exodus

First, to get a feeling of what the possession of land meant to the Jews, read Dt. 11:8-12. "For the land you are about to enter and occupy is not like the land of Egypt, from which you have come, where you sow your seed and irrigate by foot like a vegetable garden. But the land you are crossing over to occupy is a land of hills and valleys, watered by rain from the sky, and a land that the Lord your God looks after. The eyes of the lord your God are always on it, from the beginning of the year to the end of the year."

This is the promised land, a land flowing with milk and honey (Ex 3.17). These are all nourishing, feminine images, symbols of God's care and love for his people.

Read also Leviticus 25.8–43 for a description of the "Year of Jubilee" in which all debts, of land or person, were forgiven in the year of Jubilee.

The land is intimately connected to the people's story of liberation and to the gracious self-identity of God's people. It is the tangible evidence of God's favor and justice, and must always be understood this way. All economic violence that can build up in relation to the land is to be continually rescinded. The land in this light is essentially grace.

The Deuteronomic Worldview

Read 2 Kings 22.3 — 23.20 (a description of the reformation by King Josiah of Judah).

Josiah reigned from 641–609 BCE. The account begins with his discovery of the Book of the Law in the house of the Lord in the eighteenth year of his reign. Josiah reads the Book and repents, tearing his clothes. He is in fear of "the wrath of the Lord that is kindled against us, because our ancestors did not obey the words of this book" (22.13). These words suggest not a pure desire for reform, so much as a contextual perception of the political and military crisis that was building and a desire to avoid it. The power of Assyria was on the wane and a new imperial power of Babylon would rise and hit Judea and Jerusalem within a generation, culminating in the city's destruction and the exile of most of its inhabitants. Wrath is the unleashing of historical human violence on a world-destroying scale. Josiah makes a sweeping reformation across the land. He removes all forms of idolatrous worship — dismantling shrines and temples, deposing priests, abolishing religious cults and practices.

The scroll of Josiah is thought by many to be the basis of the book of Deuteronomy, its "first edition." A group of Yahwist reformers got the ear of the king, beginning a reform on the basis of a gathering perception of the social and political consequences of neglect of the Law. The overall Kings account is written retrospectively in the light of the fall of Jerusalem (described in chapters 24 & 25), reinforcing this viewpoint after the fact. The final editing of the book of Deuteronomy takes place in exile in Babylon, or directly after the return, solidifying the perspective of violent consequences for neglect of the Law. The blessings and curses in chapter 28 tell in terrible detail of the loss of the land and, written post-factum, they are in a very vivid way self-fulfilling prophecy.

What has happened is the translation of the blessing of the land into curse in the light of military and political disaster. Along with this goes the necessary understanding of God as vengeful and retributive. This is not to say that this viewpoint did not already exist, but that the experience of exile gave it a huge boost and classic formulation.

At the same time Deuteronomy contains the relational heart of the Law and has some of the most beautiful verses describing the covenant relationship between God and his people. Without this core relationship, paradoxically, the punitive aspect could and would not be maintained. If the people did not feel the power of this relationship they surely would not accept a God of wrath and would simply exchange Israel's God for another.

Read Dt 10.12–22 (the essence of the Law is love, and the Lord is the God of the orphan, the widow, the stranger).

However, elsewhere there comes the much more judgmental, punitive tone…

Read Dt 28.15–68 (Blessings and Curses.).

There are similar expressions in Jeremiah who lived both during the reforms of Josiah and the subsequent political crises of the Babylonian invasion and the fall of Jerusalem. Jeremiah's voice parallels the voice of Deuteronomy.

Read Jer 15.1–9 and 25.15–29 (punishment is inevitable/God's cup of wrath).

Read also Jer 5.16–17 and 6.22–23 which are very similar to Deuteronomy 28.49–52.

How is God depicted in these passages?

These readings use a violent language, a set of signs, determined by a concrete history. It is a language that reflects the historic conquest of the land and the intense violence of its loss. This violence is understood to be from God (wrath) and it becomes the interpretative key. The author is saying that all the violence done to the Israelite people in the exile came through God's hand. The loss of their promised land and the violence they experienced was because of their disobedience. The Law was broken and chaos resulted. The Deuteronomic message is a call to keep the Law at all costs, so as to hold God's wrath at bay.

Jeremiah — Struggle within the Text

As noted, Jeremiah is the prophet most closely aligned with the Deuteronomic worldview. And just as in Deuteronomy, in the text of Jeremiah there are expressions of warm relationship, and here they seek out a profound renewal of these emotions, Right in the middle of Jeremiah there are the chapters 30 — 33, the "little book of consolation".

Read Jer 30.18–22 (forgiveness and restoration).

This marks a struggle within the text of the Bible, what René Girard calls the "text in travail." There is compassion in contrast to a predominant tone of judgment and punishment.

Read Jer 31.1–20 (the exiles will return; lamentation will turn to joy).

Read 31.31–34 (the famous words of a new covenant and the law written on the human heart).

So, either God is two-faced, alternately kind and vengeful, or a deeper, more authentic meaning is emerging. A deeper truth of unbounded compassion, while wrath is a human construct. A two-faced "loving, but justly punishing" God cannot help but produce a deep emotional tension, as in a child who must continually first get a parent's approval in order to be treated well. An unstable mixture of gentleness and violence is the result, a dangerous, unhappy state of being. But if a new understanding of God is emerging it proves that the previous "two-faced" version is a human construct.

Different Biblical Voices

While the Deuteronomic worldview is the one that dominates the Old Testament, it is important to recognize that there are other voices and interpretations in the Bible which involve different responses to exile and the loss of the land, either explicitly or implicitly. In this respect the Bible is like a tree with many branches. These different voices include:

1. Isaiah's language of compassion and nonviolence — the figure of the nonviolent Servant.

2. The wisdom of Genesis: the revelation of human violence with its solution in forgiveness. What people intend for ill, God intends for good....

3. Job as innocent victim who questions the Deuteronomic deduction that because he is suffering God must be punishing him for wrongdoing.

4. The Wisdom books of Proverbs and Ecclesiastes: Proverbs declares that if a person does well their life will turn out well; conversely Ecclesiastes declares that the wicked are not punished!

5. Daniel's vision of one "like a son of man" who brings in God's kingdom nonviolently.

We have already studied Genesis, and we will be looking at these other voices in future lessons.

As we do we will see continually how Jesus in his teaching and practice opts for the nonviolent, compassionate possibilities in his Jewish scriptures. And his story goes further, revealing the codes of generative violence and their undoing in and through his crucifixion and resurrection.

Why the Deuteronomic Voice is Important

Historically, certain Christian groups have embraced the judgment and wrath contained in these texts while ignoring the other nonviolent voices. It has conversely been a tendency of "liberal" Christians to skip over these often problematic passages. It is essential to recognize that the Deuteronomic voice has its place.

In order to fully understand ourselves and to change as human beings, we have to embrace all of who we are and where we have come from. Like a recovering alcoholic who finds resolve through telling the story of who they were in their addiction, and telling that story honestly in terms of violence and suffering. Our default position is to find meaning in violence and the Deuteronomic people and writers were no different. They show us how we are quick to blame others and blame God, or see God blaming people. The "warrior-king" God of Deuteronomy is alive and well today. A retributive God fits with a very human calculus, but God's ways are not ours. We need the interpretive lens and paradigm of Jesus.

Furthermore, from the historical point of view, we can say that the Deuteronomic worldview was its own kind of "shell story." At its heart, as we have seen, there are declarations of love. The core of Deuteronomy is an unbreakable relationship. The suffering of defeat and exile was not understood as random and meaningless, precisely because the Lord was a God of total faithfulness. This is the final explanation for the unlikely combination of a "loving but violent" God. The external circumstances of violence were somehow understood as God's will because the internal experience of relationship stayed unbroken. However, the former are the contingent circumstances of human history misinterpreted as the hand of God, while the internal truth of divine nonviolent love is constant and remains the beating heart of the Deuteronomic view.

Notes:

_____

_____

_____

_____

_____

_____

_____

_____

_____

_____

_____

_____

_____

Lesson Questions

· Why do we need to study the wrathful punitive God in Deuteronomy but not follow him?

· What are the consequences of ignoring or throwing out the Deuteronomic texts?

· How crucial is the interpretative practice of Jesus for understanding how the Old Testament should be read and understood?

Personal Reflection

· What pivotal moments of loss have opened you up to new meaning in your life?

· Can you think of a time when something bad happened and you thought it was God's punishment?

Glossary

· **Key Biblical Frame Story** — the event of the Exodus and its multiple tellings and interpretations.

· **Dominant Biblical Interpretative Worldview** — Deuteronomic texts that establish a violently retributive God.

· **Traditional Christian Biblical Frame Story** — the Fall, a metaphysical change from the presence of God to alienation from God.

· **Shell Stories** —term used in the *Seven Stories* for the Land and the Temple, institutions providing the physical-social background and necessary continuity for transformative meaning over time.

Resources/Background Reading

· *The Jesus Driven Life*, Michael Hardin (2010)

· *A New Kind of Christianity*, Brian McLaren (2010)

Cultural References

· Movie, *True Grit*, dir. Joel & Ethan Coen (2010): "You must pay for everything in this world, one way or another. There is nothin' free except the grace of God."

THE LAND AND ITS LOSS
Lesson 2: Response to the Loss of the Land

The exodus and the exile were the cardinal events that formed the Jewish identity and sense of self. The exile occurred in 587 BCE with the return happening under the Persian king Cyrus (his decree was 539 BCE, and the first group of exiles returned in 538/7 BCE).

We are going to look at how four different groups of Jews at the time of Jesus responded to the loss of the land, the return of the Israelites to the land after the exile, and then its virtual loss once more under the Romans. Paying attention to these four responses teaches us more about the nature of the land in the Jewish experience. It sets the scene for Jesus' mold-breaking freedom from the land as a sacred legacy.

Josephus (37 CE — c.100 CE) is a major historical source on the Jewish War, which started in 66 CE. He was a general with the Jewish rebels. He was defeated by Vespasian, and later became a sycophant historian for Rome, telling the Jewish story in a way that was acceptable to his imperial audience. He describes in his histories four different philosophies in Judea at the time of Jesus: the Pharisees, Essenes, Sadducees, and Zealots. We will be looking at these groups, and add one more, John the Baptist and his followers. It is important to recognize that there was a lot of overlap between the groups.

The Pharisees

To understand the Pharisees you have to have in mind the background of the Deuteronomic viewpoint we described in the previous lesson. The loss of the land was perceived as a punishment and warning — the act of God as the result of unfaithfulness and a threat of future similar punishment should sinfulness reappear. On the return from exile there emerged an overriding concern to maintain the land at all cost. It went hand in hand with realizing the spiritual and legal uniqueness of Judaism and taking measures to preserve it. The people could not hold the land through military strength but they could do so by embracing their exclusive cultural identity in the sight of God, and then relying on God to protect them.

We will start by reading from the books of Nehemiah and Ezra which describe events after the exile, from the middle to end of 5th century BCE (exact dates are disputed). Nehemiah was the governor, Ezra a priest.

Read Neh 13.15–22.

(" … What is this evil thing that you are doing, profaning the sabbath day? Did not your ancestors act in this way, and did not our God bring all this disaster on us and on this city? Yet you bring more wrath on Israel by profaning the sabbath.")

Read Neh 8.13–18 (the Festival of Booths restored).

Read Ezra 9.5–15 (Ezra's prayer forbidding intermarriage; exclusivity results).

From the late 4th century BCE this focus on strict observance of the Law was dramatically heightened with the rise of the Greeks.

The Hellenistic Crisis

Alexander the Great, son of Philip II of Macedon, conquered most of the known world in a nonstop campaign from 334 to 323 BCE when he died. Judea fell under the power of his successor generals and their dynasties, first from Egypt and then from Syria. But things did not get critical until the 2nd century and the arrival of Antiochus Epiphanes (a Hellenic Syrian ruler, 215-164 BCE). With the support of an assimilationist group of Jews in Jerusalem, Antiochus tried to impose Greek culture upon the Jewish people. The Greek way of life, with gymnasium, theater, hippodrome etc., was intensely seductive (think BCE "consumer lifestyle"). Up until then invaders had allowed the Jews to do their own thing as long as they paid tribute and bowed to the might of the foreign power. This was very different. Encouraged by the Hellenizing Jews (a group in Jerusalem wishing to adopt Greek culture), Antiochus Epiphanes tried to wipe out Jewish religious practice and belief. His campaign included erecting a statue of Zeus above the Temple altar. A resistance movement known as the Maccabees defeated Antiochus' forces in fairly short order, rededicating the Temple in 164 BCE. But the experience of religious persecution and its violence was traumatic.

To grasp the historical emergence of the Pharisees (and in fact all of the groups) we have to understand this context as clearly as possible. The two deutero-canonical books of Maccabees contain invaluable background to help us.

Read 1 Macc 1.1–8 (Alexander the Great).

Read 1 Macc 1.10–15 (Antiochus Epiphanes becomes king of Judea).

Read 1 Macc 1.41–64 (desecration of the Temple).

Read 1 Macc 2.15–48 (Mattathias, father to a family of sons, refuses to worship pagan gods; his violent response, alongside a reference to nonviolent responses).

The sons of Mattathias led the resistance and became known as the Maccabees. They were not of Davidic or Zadokite (High Priest at time of David) descent, but took over the political and Temple leadership as the Hasmonean dynasty. The Romans eventually replaced the Hasmonean Temple high priests with their own appointees. Herod was the the last of the Hasmonean rulers, having married the last Hasmonean princess, Mariamne. He was a corrupt puppet of the Romans. His son, Herod Antipas (by another wife) continued his rule in Galilee, which brought him into direct confrontation with Jesus. Antipas built the Galilean capital Tiberius in 17 CE in honor of his Roman overlord — not only was it Hellenistic, but it was built on a graveyard so at first no pious Jew would live there.

Read Lk 13.31–33.

(Herod Antipas is described by Jesus as a "fox" — referring very probably to his interloper and foreigner status, both an Idumean (not Judean) and a monarch without Davidic credentials. The Salome story and his execution of John the Baptist further exemplify Herod Antipas' unrighteousness and corruption.)

Pharisees

The Pharisees represent a spiritual rebellion against the corruption of political Jewish leadership resulting from this Hellenistic crisis. They would have had the same basic reaction to Herod as Jesus, but they coalesced over heightened practice of the Law. The Mishna is a book of interpretation and codification of oral laws rooted in the world of the Pharisees. It was published after their time, around 200 CE, providing the basis of rabbinic discussion from then on. The rules of the Law are traditionally numbered at 613 and then there are interpretations and rulings. One overall purpose of the compendium is to build "a hedge around the Law," preserving it from even unintentional infraction. It is clear that at the time of Jesus there was a strict form of legal interpretation — Pharisaism — and we can understand some of its character from the intense discussions of the later rabbis.

New Testament Saul before his conversion is an example of someone who zealously embraced the Pharisee philosophy.

Jesus and the Pharisees

Throughout the Gospels there are many recorded instances of conflict. It seems that Jesus was so close to the Pharisees that he — and later the Gospel writers — had to emphasize the difference very sharply. In Matthew's Gospel we hear that "unless your righteousness exceeds that of the scribe and Pharisees, you will never enter the kingdom of heaven" (5.20). This suggests that both the Pharisees and Jesus were aiming for an exceptional degree of righteousness, but the method Jesus proposed stood at a very great variance from theirs. In the overall context of the *Seven Stories* we would say that the core of the difference was Jesus' abandonment of purity and separation and their roots in generative violence. In their place he proposes a radical change in the engine of human meaning and action, one generated out of forgiveness and nonviolence. As we saw in the 1st cycle lesson, on the Sermon on the Mount, this would itself result in the fulfilment of the Law's core purpose.

Read Mt 15.10–20. (Jesus reinterprets the Law, about what defiles and what does not.)

Read Mt 23.1–36. (Jesus denounces the Pharisees as hypocrites and murderers.)

The Essenes

The Essenes can be understood as perhaps an even more extreme form of this philosophy of "spiritual rebellion." They were known to the ancient world (Pliny, Josephus) as a group who lived an admirably ascetic and pious life. While their existence was known, there was no archeological or major written evidence until the discovery of the Dead Sea Scrolls in 1946, in cliff caves on the western edge of the Dead Sea. The discovery of the scrolls prompted the excavation of nearby community dwellings known as "*Qumran.*" This massive find is generally believed by scholars to represent the Essene movement referenced by Josephus and others. From the internal evidence of their writing we can see they were strictly purist and removed themselves entirely from the inhabited land and Temple, awaiting at its very edge for God's decisive intervention. They looked forward to a tremendous final battle against evil, including the Romans, followed by the complete purification of land and Temple from corruption. Essentially they had the same motivation as the Pharisees — to reclaim the purity of the land, but they were much stricter and more radical in their approach. In a way the Essenes can be seen as a cult, while the Pharisees were an internal reform movement. If we read 1 Macc 2.29–38 we are perhaps being given a snapshot of the "seeking (for) righteousness and justice" that birthed both these movements. Modes of separation from a corrupted land, in order ultimately to reclaim it, lie at the heart of both. In both cases the background is a negotiation with the possibility of wrath or divine violence.

The Zealots

These were the freedom fighters who were actual killers. They looked for a violent rebellion to rid the land of the invading Romans. Their goal was a restoration of national independence, with the Davidic kingdom as their ideal. They drew inspiration from the Maccabean revolt of the 2nd century when the Maccabees overthrew the Hellenizing Antiochus Epiphanes.

The Romans took direct control of Judea in 6 CE, installing a prefect or procurator in Jerusalem together with a garrison of soldiers. They also carried out a census, including Galilee, which led to a rebellion by someone called Judas the Galilean. According to Josephus, this Judas was the founder of the Zealots. There is dispute about the accuracy of that designation, but there is no doubt that Judas the Galilean represented the style of revolt that we associate with nationalist "zeal" (see again 1 Macc. 2.24–27). What seems to have been an earlier revolt, just after the death of Herod (4 BCE), brought brutal retaliation from Rome: the Roman commander, Varus, crucified 2000 rebels on the roads of Judea. This kind of violence only stored up future revenge in the hearts of observers. The sight of these crucifixions would have been living memory during Jesus' boyhood. It is noteworthy that Jesus had a disciple called Simon the Zealot (Lk 6.15).

The ever increasing tension and unrest culminated in mass rebellion of the Jews about 30 years after Jesus died. This was the First Jewish War, 66-70 CE. During this war the Zealots had a major role. Very many Jews were killed in the war (Josephus placed it at over a million), others were sold into slavery, and the Temple was destroyed. Yet another revolt happened at the beginning of the 2nd century (the Bar Kokhbah Revolt, 132-36 CE), resulting again in an enormous number of deaths. Judea was severely depopulated, the name Judea deleted from the maps, and the Temple sanctuary replaced with one dedicated to Jupiter. The Jews did not fully regain the land until after World War Two in 1945.

In the Gospels Jesus refers to the coming crisis:

Read Mt 23.37 — 24.2 (Jesus' lament over Jerusalem).

Read Mt 24.15–28 ("the desolating sacrilege... there the vultures gather").

Other translations, such as King James version, give "eagles" which is the original Greek and would refer to the standards of the Roman legions. Jesus' advice is to flee not fight.

There is no way that Jesus would not be aware of the intense contemporary dangers connected to violent nationalism. And it is likely he saw the Temple as the spiritual and physical stronghold of this viewpoint. He consistently advocated a way of nonviolence and warned of the coming catastrophe.

The Sadducees

The Sadducees represented Temple Judaism. They were theologically conservative and believed they would be protected through sacrificial practice and the observance of religious feasts. In this they differed from the Pharisees who found purity through observance of the minutiae of the Law. The prophetic exemplar of the Temple tradition is Ezekiel (prophecy written during the Babylonian exile). Ezekiel proposed an idealized vision for the rebuilding of the Temple. The new Temple, built according to the plan and design of God, would bring purity and please God. These themes are explored in more detail in Story Six.

The Books 1 & 2 Chronicles are a retelling of the story of 1 & 2 Kings and one of their major accents is the Temple. Almost a third of 1 Chronicles is dedicated to David minutely planning the Temple, and handing the plans over to Solomon. 2 Chronicles returns to the Temple again and again, and ends with the words of Cyrus, the Persian king: "The Lord, the God of heaven... has charged me to build him a house at Jerusalem.... Whoever is among you of all his people, may the Lord his God be with him! Let him go up." Chronicles forms the last writing in the Jewish Tanakh, and it expresses the absolutely central role of Temple in the post-exilic era. The Sadducees stand atop this tradition.

By the time of Jesus the Temple was corrupt, its leadership working hand in glove with the Roman invaders. The high priests kept order for the Romans in order to preserve their privileges. They were politically astute, conservative nationalists.

Read Jn 11.48.

The High Priest argues that "if we let (Jesus) go on like this, everyone will believe in him, and the Romans will come and destroy both our holy place and our nation."

John the Baptist

Read Lk 3.1–14 (John the Baptist in the wilderness, baptizing in the Jordan).

John emerged from the apocalyptic tradition. This was a mindset, a set of ideas, that included a breaking in of heavenly power into the world, the final coming of the Lord on the great "Day of the Lord." This day would defeat evil, and vindicate the good. At the time of Jesus the coming of Elijah was seen as the necessary precursor to the Day of the Lord (Malachi 4.5). The apocalyptic mindset can be found in parts of Isaiah, Ezekiel, the end of Zechariah and parts of Joel. It is a visionary literature and viewpoint. Its vision often expands beyond Jerusalem and Israel to embrace the whole Earth. The greatest of the apocalyptic prophets was Daniel. Daniel was the last of the four great prophets. The book of Daniel was written in the 2nd century BCE, though the narrative is set at the time of the exile. Its late date is also suggested by the fact that it is the only Old Testament book with parts originally written in Aramaic rather than Hebrew. It is in Daniel that we find the figure of "one like a Son of Man," a figure that Jesus appropriated. (We will return to Daniel in Story Seven.)

John the Baptist preached repentance as preparation for the coming of the Lord and he seemed to have been awaiting the figure of Elijah as precursor to the Day of the Lord.

Read Lk 7.18–23. John asks Jesus whether he is "the one who is to come," referring to Malachi's messenger who will be sent and is "coming" (Malachi 3.1–2). This clearly connects to Elijah at Malachi 4.5. But Jesus returns the compliment and says John is the one who was sent, i.e. Elijah (Lk 7.27 & Mk 9.13).

John made his base at the River Jordan, a geography which represented a re-entrance to the promised land, a new beginning echoing the return from exile. This was where God's true return and in-breaking would begin, in repentance, and then, expectedly, with the coming of Elijah. There is a clear non-Temple theology in John's approach: purification is achieved by immersion in the Jordan, not Temple ritual. Other groups shared elements of his apocalyptic viewpoint: for example, the Pharisees believed in the resurrection; the Essenes believed in the imminent final battle between the forces of evil and good. John had a powerful ministry, in which Jesus shared for a period, and then broke away from (John 3.22–23; 4.1–3). John opened the door for Jesus, setting the stage of intense expectation which Jesus fulfilled, but in a very different pattern from the violent model of Elijah (e.g. 1 Kings 19.20–40). Jesus lays out the difference at Lk 7.22–28. We will examine this in detail in the next lesson.

Where Jesus Stood

All these groups and figures help us both to set the scene for Jesus and identify how different he was. He shares the apocalyptic background and sense of expectation, and he experiences, at first hand, the enormous tensions generated by the Romans in the land. His response and solution are meaningful within these conditions and yet exceed them in a new and unique way. Again, we will look at this in the next class.

Lesson Questions

· This course argues that Jesus' message was of God's nonviolence and in this he introduces something new. How are each of the responses to the loss of the Land that we have explored still grounded in violence?

· How were the Romans perceived by each of these groups? What was the impact of the Roman occupation?

· Do the religious attitudes of 1st century Judea represented by these groups show us how the Jesus movement offered something both recognizable and strikingly new?

Personal Reflection

· Jesus lived at a time of intense stress and increasing violence. How can feeling hopeless or helpless in the face of external forces sometimes lead to internal spiritual growth, enhancing our perception of God's hidden power and presence?

· How do I usually respond to crisis? How do I see God at work in those times?

Glossary

· Pharisee — a group originating in the two centuries before Jesus, who sought to resolve the tensions of military occupation and corrupt government by increased and detailed attention to purity boundaries and rule keeping.

· Essene — a group originating in the second century BCE, who found a solution to military occupation and corrupt government by complete separation, both spatially and in terms of mindset and lifestyle.

· Sadducee — the priestly class representing a conservative set of beliefs and the need to preserve the Temple as the last remaining independent symbol of Judaism.

· Hellenization — the cultural movement throughout the Mediterranean, from the time of Alexander the Great onward, promoting and adopting Greek practice and thought. It deeply impacted the Jewish world at the turn of the millenium.

· Hasmonean — the name for the dynasty of kings (non-Davidic) resulting from the Maccabean revolt and ruling through the 2nd and 1st centuries BCE.

· Maccabee — the nickname (meaning "hammer") given to Mattathias and his sons who led the revolt against the persecuting king Antiochus Epiphanes IV.

· Zealot — a general term for a rebel against Rome in the 1st century CE, but then referring to a specific group of militants during the Roman-Jewish war, 66-70 CE.

· Qumran — an archeological site on the shore of the Dead Sea thought to be home to the community which produced the Dead Sea Scrolls and associated by many scholars with the Essenes.

· Dead Sea Scrolls — a treasure trove of ancient Jewish manuscripts discovered in 1946 in clay jars in caves above the western shore of the Dead Sea, their contents covering all the books of the Old Testament except Esther, and including deuterocanonical works and other unique writings proper to the sectarian community at their source.

· Apocalyptic — a term meaning "unconcealing, withdrawal of a veil," referring to a "heavenly" understanding of earthly events, here interpreted as in-breaking of divine nonviolence. Also a genre of writing representing heavenly visions.

· Mishna — a book of Pharisaic interpretation and codification of the laws of the Torah (traditionally numbered at 613) published around 200 CE, but developing from the beginning of the Common Era.

· Zadok — High Priest at the time of David, important in the Dead Sea Scrolls as true priestly ancestor.

Resources/Background Reading

· *Bandits, Prophets, and Messiahs: Popular Movements at the Time of Jesus,* Richard A. Horsley (1999)

· *The New Testament and The People of God,* N.T. Wright (1992)

· *Jesus and the Victory of God,* N.T. Wright (1997)

· *Jesus Risen in Our Midst,* Sandra Schneiders (2013)

Cultural References

· Movie, *Risen,* dir. Kevin Reynolds (2016)

· Movie, *Ben Hur,* dir. Sam Zimbalist (1959)

THE LAND AND ITS LOSS
Lesson 3: The Land and Jesus

Learning Objectives

- To situate Jesus in the context of the many movements and stressors of his time in relation to the land.
- To understand some of the context in First Century Judea that led progressively to the Jewish-Roman war of 66-70 CE.
- To place Jesus in distinction from his closest mentor, John the Baptist.

Core Biblical Texts

- Lk 4.16–30
- Lk 7.18–35

Key Points

- There were multiple Jewish movements in the first century offering their solution to the problem of the land.
- To distinguish Jesus from these movements the critical factor is always his nonviolence and the nonviolence of the God he preached.
- John the Baptist was for a while Jesus' mentor but Jesus broke from him on the issue of violence.

Key Words /Concepts

- Blessed is he who is not scandalized in me!
- The least in the kingdom of heaven is greater than he!
- Beware the leaven of the Pharisees!

If the overall vision of the Seven Stories *is right — that there are a series of revolutionary shifts in meaning in the Bible leading to human transformation — then the land (and Temple) provide the protective layer, allowing the seed time to grow. These two elements are vital: the seed and the husk or shell. Without the shell there would not have been enough continuity of time and identity to build up to the profound shifts of meaning we have discussed. Biological evolution takes time, even more so does meaning evolution. They both depend on an "ecological niche" for a life form to thrive in. The land of Israel was the ecological niche for the emergence of new humanity, one of forgiveness. But it could only come at a moment of intense crisis for the land itself. The shell was about to burst!*

Our last two studies show how the loss of the land became a pivotal factor in the understanding of God: it was seen in the Deuteronomic tradition as a demonstration of God's wrath. The groups covered in the last lesson — Pharisees, Essenes, Zealots, Sadducees, John the Baptist — all had a core relationship to the land. All of them understood its current crisis in terms of wrath/violence, present and/or threatened.

Jesus presents a unique response to the land, one that empties out the anthropology of wrath. He thus brings the transformative springtime that the long history of Israel had always been nurturing and preparing.

Jesus' Relationship to the Land.

Jesus locates himself on the edge of the land. Initially a disciple of John the Baptist at the River Jordan, Jesus moves instead to the Sea of Galilee. The sea in Jewish mythology was the place of primordial chaos, a place of demons and violence (cf. the Book of Jonah). He calls his disciples from fishermen who live in this space. It is likely that the fishermen were displaced peasantry who had lost their land and were forced to make a living from the sea.

Jesus starts his ministry preaching within the borders of Israel.

See Mt 10.5.

("These twelve Jesus sent out with the following instructions: 'Go nowhere among the Gentiles, and enter no town of the Samaritans, but go rather to the lost sheep of the house of Israel.'") However, in John 4.1-42 he enters into conversation with the woman at the well of Sychar in Samaria, a non-Jew. He appears to journey deliberately outside the boundaries of the land, opening up to the non-Jews he meets.

Read Mt 15.21–28.

In this story of the Canaanite woman, Jesus journeys to the district of Tyre and Sidon echoing the journey Elijah made to Zarephath in the region of Sidon where he raised a widow's son. Did Jesus go there intentionally to repeat this pattern from Elijah? He seems to endorse this pattern in his sermon in Nazareth in chapter 4 of Luke. Here Jesus heals the Canaanite woman's daughter after Jesus is impressed by her faith and wit — another example of how Jesus' ministry breaks its own boundaries. This can also be seen as an extension of "eating and drinking with sinners." Once the boundary with the impure and sinful is breached what is there to exclude the foreigner?

Jesus lets go of identification with the land as a way of framing relationship with God. He thus moves beyond the possibility of loss of the land as experience of wrath.

Jesus Contradicts the Retributive Deuteronomic Worldview

The language of relationship between Israel and God in the Deuteronomic texts was retributive. We saw that an alternative language of compassion arrives alongside this in Jeremiah — "Is Ephraim my dear son? Is he the child I delight in? As often as I speak against him, I still remember him. Therefore I am deeply moved for him; I will surely have mercy on him, says the Lord" (Jer 31.20) — but it is mixed up with the other kind and runs risk, in psychological terms, of feeling like push-pull abuse.

How does Jesus deal with the Deuteronomic worldview?

Read Mt 5.17–48 (the Antitheses from the Sermon on the Mount).

In the 1st, 2nd and 4th antitheses Jesus directly quotes the Decalogue. But he cites it as "it was said," rather than "it is written." In other words he is declaring these laws are already interpretations. He then proceeds to set out a new authoritative interpretation. At the 5th and 6th he directly contradicts the retributive model. Compare Deut 19.21, "Show no pity: life for life, eye for eye, tooth for tooth, hand for hand, foot for foot." And while "hate your enemy" is nowhere said as such, it is formally implied in Dt 7.1–6.

The 3rd antithesis can appear like a law added to Moses, one excluding divorce. But reading Mt 5.31 we can see that the permission of divorce was a male-privilege ("let him give her a certificate of divorce"), forcing the woman to seek another man as protector. Jesus' words frees the woman from the overlordship, requiring the male to undertake the same power-surrender or commitment as the woman.

Therefore, in the Sermon on the Mount Jesus systematically overturns the legal models found in Deuteronomy, while radically undermining the retributive function which makes the laws work.

This is made definitive in the final antithesis, where human beings are required to love their enemies and so be perfect as the Father is perfect. The new code of behavior is based on the new theological model of God's nonviolence. If nonviolence and non-retaliation are expected of Jesus' followers, it is because this is the character of God. Thus Jesus rejects Deuteronomic retribution both by word and implication.

Jesus' Response to the Pharisees and Essenes

In the same spirit Jesus' response to Pharisees (and by extension Essenes) offers no purity regime, no "hedge around the Law." Jesus is free of the need for purity as an anthropological principle.

Read Mt 15.16–20 "... to eat with unwashed hands does not defile."

Read Lk 10.29–36 (the parable of the Good Samaritan).

We can note that the Cynic philosophers of Greece also advocated along these lines. Diogenes stated, "I am a citizen of the world." Jesus has been called a Palestinian Cynic. Common features are his rejection of convention and critique of greed which may possibly reflect cultural cross currents. However, Jesus could not have defied "the story of the land" tradition (along with the sacredness of Temple), without something much stronger than abstract philosophy. What is it? For Jesus it is Wisdom.

Jesus as Wisdom

Wisdom literature is a distinct form of writing in the Old Testament, including Proverbs, Ecclesiastes, and Job. The Book of Job is a masterpiece of the Bible which already begins to question the dominant Deuteronomic formula. It declares innocent the one whose suffering seems to have proven him guilty. Proverbs contains the picture of personified Wisdom.

Read Prov 8.22–36

Read Lk 7.33–35.

In the Luke passage Jesus adopts Wisdom's persona, a figure which has no weight of retributive violence. He calls a class of people to himself, the "simple" or ignorant who are considered sinners. These

are closely allied to the poor and afflicted, who could also be dismissed as "cursed." (See John 7.49 where the chief priests and the Pharisees describe Jesus' audience as "this crowd, which does not know the law - they are accursed.") Instead Jesus says, "Wisdom is vindicated by her children"... i.e. those born of the kingdom of God, unlike John born of a woman! This appears to be an astonishing claim on the part of Jesus to represent/be identified with Biblical Wisdom. In which case, Jesus has an unrivalled peaceful intimacy with God which allows him to overturn purity practice.

We will be further developing the theme of Wisdom in Story Seven.

Jesus' Response to the Zealots

In response to the Zealots, Jesus teaches to "love your enemy."

Read Mt 5.43–45 (from the Sermon on the Mount).

Jesus never says there is wrath in the Father. Rather the Father "makes the sun to rise on the evil and the good" (v. 45).

Read Lk 4.16–30 (Jesus preaches in Nazareth).

Here Jesus quotes from Isaiah 61.1-2 but omits Isaiah's final words after "to proclaim the year of the Lord's favor," i.e. "and the day of vengeance for our God." This nonviolent motif is reiterated in Lk 7.18-27 when he tells John the Baptist's messengers to report to him what they have seen: "the blind receive their sight, the lame walk, the lepers are cleansed, the deaf hear, and the dead are raised, the poor have good news brought to them." In other words, he presents the fulfilment of the Isaiah prophecy, but without judgment or Elijah-style violence. (See below on John the Baptist.)

Jesus Response to the Sadducees

In response to the Sadducees, Jesus declares and enacts the end of Temple.

Read Mk 11.12–25. (The judgment and abolition of the Temple. Mark interweaves Jesus' action in the Temple with the enacted parable of the withering of the fig tree.)

Read Dan 7.9–27. (Dominion is given to one like a Son of Man in an apocalyptic throne scene, which trumps the authority of Temple.)

Read Mt. 26.59–66. (Jesus quotes from the Daniel passage when he is interrogated by the High Priest, implicitly declaring his authority to abolish the Temple.)

Jesus saw the redundancy of the Temple. Also its violence. In John, Jesus accuses the Temple authorities of being thieves, murderers and killers (John 10.10). Jesus as the "true shepherd" sets humanity free from the sacrificial system. (We will reflect more on the Temple in Story Six.)

Jesus' Response to John the Baptist and his Followers

In response to John the Baptist, Jesus declares the dawn of Wisdom's children — those who are birthed out of a new generative principle, one of non-boundaries, nonviolence.

Read Lk 7.28; 33-35.

Of those born of women no one is greater than John the Baptist, but the least in the kingdom is greater, i.e. those born of Wisdom. She is vindicated by her children who are nonviolent. See the same passage in Matthew 11.11–15 where violence is explicitly seen as the generative principle now displaced by Jesus Wisdom: "From the days of John the Baptist until now the kingdom of heaven has been taken over by violence, and the violent have hijacked it" (*Seven Stories* translation).

Read Jn 4.1–3.

Jesus separates from John, i.e. he seems to have been his disciple up to this point, but breaks away from him to begin his own ministry centered on Galilee and its Sea.

How did Jesus differ from John?

John still saw repentance in terms of purity and wrath. So in this he retains the Deuteronomic or retributive mindset. Jesus ate and drank with sinners, abolishing the purity boundaries.

John understood the intervention of God would be a violent overthrow of the present world order. Jesus renounced violence and embraced the cross, which changes the mainspring of the human heart and human society.

Read Mt 11.2–15.

John's question to Jesus from jail ("Are you the one who is to come?") shows that John expects an Elijah-like figure. (Cf. Malachi 4.5 for Elijah sent before the day of the Lord, and 3.1–2 for the messenger of the covenant: "indeed he is coming… but who can endure the day of his coming…?) This Matthew passage has Jesus explicitly identify John with this prophecy, and as Elijah: "if you are willing to accept it, he is Elijah who is to come" (v.14). Jesus

replies to John at 11.6, "Blessed is anyone who takes no offense in me;" i.e. blessed is the one who is not placed in contradiction to Jesus because violence remains their generative principle.

Notes:

_____
_____
_____
_____
_____
_____
_____
_____
_____
_____
_____
_____
_____
_____
_____
_____
_____
_____
_____
_____
_____
_____
_____
_____
_____
_____
_____

Lesson Questions

· What is the purpose of situating Jesus amongst his contemporaries and their different responses to the loss of the Land?

· How does Jesus identify with the landless or those outside the Land? Why is this important in the light of rejecting violence?

· Why does land always seem to provoke violence?

Personal Reflection

· Jesus ate and drank with people outside the law and beyond the boundaries of his land. How does love break boundaries? When have you experienced this in your life?

· John Lennon in his song "Imagine" argues for " ... no countries ... nothing to kill or die for ...." Are land, patriotism and national identity inherently connected to violence in our world?

Glossary

· Purification — primarily a temple ritual to prepare priests and people for offering sacrifice, but extended progressively to cover many other situations. John's baptism at the Jordan could be seen as purification, for the sake of a life without sin in the land, and to preserve the people from wrath. (It was also a marvelous semiotic code for a completely fresh beginning as an Israelite.)

Resources/Background Reading

· *Bandits, Prophets, and Messiahs: Popular Movements at the Time of Jesus*, Richard A. Horsley (1999).

· *The Library of Qumran: On the Essenes, Qumran, John the Baptist, and Jesus*, Hartmut Stegemann (1998)

Cultural References

· John Lennon, "Imagine"

· *Rome and Jerusalem at War* (66-70 AD): https://www.youtube.com/watch?v=GTxDcif-XT4

· *Pascale's Wager*, Anthony Bartlett (2014) — Pascale's transformation of Heaven's outcasts into a community of love.

Wrath to Compassion

Lesson Plan

- Lesson 1: Suffering Servant
- Lesson 2: Compassion in Isaiah
- Lesson 3: The Cup of Wrath

Learning Objectives

- To understand the massive shift in human meaning that arises with Second Isaiah through his figure of the Servant and the language of compassion.

- To recognize that this shift is so radical that it remains historically unfulfilled until Jesus.

- To see the profound influence of Second Isaiah on the New Testament.

- To see that the interpretation of the "cup of wrath" as God's personal violence has distorted the meaning of Jesus' death.

Synopsis of the Story as a Whole

- Second Isaiah introduces a dramatically new set of motifs — compassion, nonviolence and non-retaliatory suffering

- The Suffering Servant is the Nonviolent Servant and a new revelation of God.

- Second Isaiah's development of revelation is signaled in highly personal communication.

- The cup of wrath is a symbol of human violence

- Jesus as the answer to the human system of violence, the cup of the nonviolent New Covenant.

Key Words/Concepts

- Biblical historical frame story — the exodus
- Suffering/nonviolent Servant
- Compassion
- Cup of wrath; cup of the new covenant
- The violence of the nations

WRATH TO COMPASSION
Lesson 1: Suffering Servant

Learning Objectives

· To grasp the dramatic change that takes place in the prophecy of Second Isaiah.

· To see the shift in human meaning from generative violence to generative nonviolence.

· To understand how the New Testament reflects this shift in its framing of Jesus as the Servant.

· To understand that this reading reverses the distortions of a violent God requiring Jesus' death.

Core Biblical Texts

· Is 52.13 — 53.12
· 1 Pet 2.21–24

Key Points

· Second Isaiah introduces a shift in the understanding of God's action and character.

· Compassion, nonviolence and non-retaliatory suffering become key motifs.

· The Suffering Servant is the Nonviolent Servant and a new revelation of God.

Key Words /Concepts

· Suffering Servant
· Nonviolent Servant
· Nonviolent atonement

In this lesson we are going to talk about a change in the language and perception of God. This is another of the semiotic shifts that we mentioned during the introduction classes. We are reminded that "semiotics" is the study of signs and elements of communicative behavior. So a semiotic shift is when a symbol takes on a new meaning within a culture, or an entirely new symbol arises.

The symbolism we are looking at here relates to the meaning of suffering. The semiotic shift is found in the middle part of the book of Isaiah (chapters 40-55) known as "Second" or "Deutero" Isaiah. It is very likely the biggest of the shifts we are describing throughout this course. The whole body of writing in the prophecy of Isaiah spans two hundred years and has at least three different authors. Descriptions within the Second Isaiah material show it was written around 540 BCE, just before the end of the exile. In this part of the book Isaiah's audience is a devastated, impoverished and powerless people. Out of this situation the prophet finds new meaning for the suffering experienced by his people. He changes the semiotics of suffering. It becomes a revelation of nonviolence and a new understanding of righteousness.

Ahab and Elijah

To understand this change in perception more clearly let us look at the story of Ahab and Elijah for contrast. The background to this story is the divided kingdom. After the reigns of David and Solomon, the kingdom divided into Judah in the south and Israel in the north. Ahab is a king who ruled over the northern kingdom of Israel from 885–850 BCE. He married Jezebel, the daughter of the king of Tyre, to cement a political alliance. Under her influence, Ahab abandons Yahweh and sets up places of worship for other gods — specifically the Phoenician god Ba'al (the word means "Lord") and the goddess figure Asherah. Elijah, the prophet, is sent to warn the Israelites of the consequences of their actions. Elijah challenges the priests of Ba'al to a demonstration of power. Elijah sets the scene … the priests of Ba'al will get one bull and he another. They are to call on Ba'al for the fire to consume their sacrifice, then he will call upon the God of Israel for fire for his. The God who answers wins the hearts of the people.

Read 1 Kings 18.26–29 (the priests of Ba'al call on their god to no avail).

Elijah has his servants pour water on the altar to increase the dramatic tension ...

Read 1 Kings 18.36–40 (Yahweh consumes the burnt offering; Elijah kills the priests of Ba'al).

Elijah, fleeing from Jezebel's wrath, meets God on mount Horeb and pleads for protection.

Read 1 Kings 19.15–18 (God announces further violence, ordering the destruction of the house of Ahab).

How is Yahweh depicted? What is the character of Elijah?

This story is an example of how God was perceived in a core part of the tradition. It shows why what follows in Second Isaiah is so radical. We go from a God of fire and violence against his enemies, to a God who exalts a nonviolent, suffering Servant. Elijah as a prophet engages in holy war and instigates a palace massacre. Anthropologically speaking there could not be a greater contrast than with the figure of the Nonviolent Servant.

The Songs of the Servant in Second Isaiah

There are four "songs" (poetic accounts) of the Suffering Servant in Second Isaiah. To get a full picture of the Servant we need to take quick glance at all four songs. It is these songs together that best express the change in perception about violence.

Read Is 42.1–4 (the First Song of the Servant).

This first song states that the Servant will bring justice. His voice is gentle. His action is expressly nonviolent. His justice will not come through the sword, but rather through his teaching.

Read Is 49.1–7 (the Second Song of the Servant).

"He made my mouth like a sharp sword." Again a reference to the Servant's teaching. His fighting is done by means of his teaching. He will serve to gather together not only the scattered tribes of Israel and Judah, but all of the nations.

What would make kings bow down?

God chooses one who is "deeply despised, abhorred by the nations." What is despised more than weakness, lack of power? And yet the kings bow down. It is the Servant's nonviolence which paradoxically penetrates the human situation like "a sword."

Read Is 50.4–9 (the Third Song of the Servant).

Again the Servant is described as a teacher. "The Lord God has given me the tongue of a teacher." Here the non-retaliatory suffering of the Servant is evident — he is struck and the object of insult, but does not hide his face.

Read Is 52.13 — 53.12 (the Fourth Song of the Servant).

Now things get more challenging. This is the most important of the songs, certainly the one most employed by Christians, beginning in the New Testament. It is from here that the penal interpretation of Christ's death is commonly derived, having a reverse effect from the nonviolence of the Servant. The Servant is seen to suffer a punitive violence from God, a reading that has settled the text's interpretation in common opinion. Such is the power of this interpretation, it is very difficult to read Isaiah 53 and not think of penal atonement. So in order to read it more authentically we begin with some general reflections and then we'll offer a more authentic translation.

If we look at Is 52.15 we see that what the Servant communicates is something startlingly new, repeating and expanding on Is 49.7. This is a revelation of a shocking alternative to the favorite perspective of kings, always that of triumphant violence. In contrast, that which they had not previously seen or heard they now understand!

The Servant communicates a new knowledge, but this has

not been accented because of previous phrasing choices. There are no punctuation marks in the original Hebrew so it is entirely possible to translate Is 53.11 as follows: "through his knowledge, the righteous one, my Servant, shall make many righteous..." The Servant communicates new human knowledge — a new way of being human.

Sometime around the first century BCE an Aramaic translation of Isaiah was produced known as the "Jonathan Targum." In reality it is much more of a midrash or reinterpretation of Isaiah than a translation. It is instructive to quote some verses of its version of Isaiah 53. It is hard to be precise about the final date of this redaction, but for our purposes it does not matter: the text demonstrates how conflicted and tendentious a reading of this passage from Isaiah can be. In this version the suffering of the Servant is turned upside down and becomes violent victory over the nations and the wicked. (From *The Isaiah Targum*, Bruce D. Chilton, 1987.)

53:7 *He beseeches, and he is answered, and before he opens his mouth he is accepted; the strong ones of the peoples he will hand over like a lamb to the sacrifice, and like a ewe which before its shearers is dumb, so there is not before him one who opens his mouth or speaks a saying.*
53:8 *From bonds and retribution he will bring our exiles near, the wonders which will be done for us in his days, who will be able to recount? For he will take away the rule of the Gentiles from the land of Israel; the sins which my people sinned he will cast on them.* **53:9** *And he will hand over the wicked to Gehenna and those rich in possessions which they robbed, to the death of the corruption, lest those who commit sin be established and speak of possessions with their mouth.*

So, it is clearly a struggle to get a handle on what this passage is really saying.

Before we now get to our own version, there are a couple of further points to underline. Between the end of chapter 52 and the beginning of 53 the speaker or voice changes from the third-person Lord to a first-person "we." The change indicates that we are here dealing with a human interpretation of a victim — "yet we accounted him stricken, struck down by God ... " (v 4) — and any interpretation must give full prominence to this human (scapegoating) perspective shown up by the text.

Finally, 53.10 is a crucial verse in supporting the penal understanding. However, the Hebrew word normally translated "pain" is uncertain, and can be rendered "disease" or "grief." Generally we must not read God's will here as vindictive (the knee-jerk popular understanding), but as a function of the overall purpose of instruction and human transformation. The Hebrew word used here is "sin-offering." However, the Servant's life should not be seen as a temple sacrifice. The word is used because that was the standard way of understanding an action that takes away sin. It is simply a metaphor for the effect of his death.

So now, here is the *Seven Stories* translation of the key verses 53.4-11. It attempts a faithful translation of the Hebrew while acknowledging there is also reading at work. (Capitals and comments in brackets and italics are used to highlight meaning.)

4. Surely he has borne our griefs and carried our diseases; yet WE accounted him stricken, struck down by God, and afflicted.

5. BUT [*in other words the previous opinion is not correct, the following is*] he was wounded by reason of our ill deeds and broken by reason of our wrong ways.

[*In other words, the causative relation of sin to the Servant's suffering is not God's punitive wrath but the human system of violence played out and revealed in the Servant's suffering. It is both the wrongs and their revelation that are the reason for the suffering. So...*] UPON HIM WAS THE INSTRUCTION THAT WAS FOR OUR WHOLENESS, AND BY HIS BRUISES WE ARE HEALED.

6. All we like sheep have gone astray; we have all turned to our own way, and the Lord brought it about that the wrong ways of us all fell on him.

[How this revelatory event actually happened is now described, i.e. *through the nonviolence of the Servant.*]

7. He was oppressed, and he was afflicted, yet he did not open his mouth; like a lamb that is led to the slaughter, and like a sheep that before its shearers is silent, so he did not open his mouth.

8. Who of his generation shall reflect that by a perversion of justice he was taken away? He was cut off out of the land of the living through my people's offense, to whom the stroke was due.

9. They made his grave with the wicked and his tomb with the rich, although he had done no violence [exactly!] and there was no deceit in his mouth [no imitation of violence].

10. Yet it was the will of the Lord that he be brought down by grief, as you make his life an event that takes away sins, thus he shall see his offspring, and shall prolong his days; through him the will of the Lord shall prosper.

11. Out of his anguish he shall see; he shall find satisfaction. Through his knowledge the

righteous one, my servant, shall make many righteous, and he shall bear their wrong ways.

The Meaning of the Servant's Suffering

God's active will is for the Servant to suffer nonviolently and so to reveal a new righteousness. God is not in mimetic opposition to the Servant, as a stand-in for humanity's sins, but his will through the Servant is demonstrative and transformative. At v. 10 there is no implication of "offering satisfaction" to God. Remember ancient humanity had no theory of sacrifice; the action simply produced the required effect. Thus, as we have noted, to describe the Servant using sacrificial terminology simply puts to use available language without specifying an actual mechanism. Loading this passage with sacrificial interpretation then is a circular process, one that skews the meaning toward vindictive attitudes and purposes of God. In reality, however, what is being understood is that it is the Servant's nonviolence which opens up a new space in human experience, and mimetically drains an observer of his/her violence and thus unrighteousness.

The Suffering Servant texts are profound because their symbolism is entirely new. Not to see this is to miss their value and reduce them to a transaction with God, something derived not from the Bible but Christian legal thinking, especially the Middle Ages. The enormity of the text is also often missed because we all "know" the story of Jesus. This text in fact reveals a God who approves a nonviolent figure before Jesus. In this connection the Servant is often seen as Israel itself because of the suffering of the exile. This is entirely possible. But a Biblical figure can be both individual and corporate (e.g. Jacob; or prophets like Jeremiah who take on the destiny of the people). The Second Isaiah prophet almost certainly experienced the suffering at first hand either in himself or in a companion. (Compare Psalm 22 as a first person record of victim suffering.) The descriptions are too vividly nonviolent to be otherwise. The prophet then also extended this experience to the whole people.

The Nonviolent Servant and the New Testament

The early church quickly identified Jesus with the Servant, and the Gospels and New Testament letters clearly reference the figure, in particular the 4th Song. There follows a list of quotations which show its pervasive presence. We can see in the quotations (highlighted) that there is nowhere any hint of penal substitution. Rather it is the relational nonviolence of the Servant that stands out.

Read Mt 8.16–17.

"That evening they brought to him many who were possessed

with demons; and he cast out the spirits with a word, and cured all who were sick. This was to fulfill what had been spoken through the prophet Isaiah, "He took our infirmities and bore our diseases." (Is 53. 4.)

Read Mt 12.14–2.1.

The Pharisees conspire against Jesus, about how to destroy him. When Jesus became aware of this, he departs, but the crowds follow .... "Many crowds followed him, and he cured all of them, and he ordered them not to make him known. This was to fulfill what had been spoken through the prophet Isaiah: 'Here is my servant, whom I have chosen, my beloved, with whom my soul is well pleased. I will put my Spirit upon him, and he will proclaim justice to the Gentiles. He will not wrangle or cry aloud, nor will anyone hear his voice in the streets. He will not break a bruised reed or quench a smoldering wick until he brings justice to victory. And in his name the Gentiles will hope.'" (Is 42.1–4.)

Read Jn 12.38.

The people do not believe in Jesus even though he performs signs in their presence "This was to fulfill the word spoken by the prophet Isaiah: 'Lord, who has believed our message, and to whom has the arm of the Lord been revealed?'" (Is 53.1.)

Read Gal 2.20.

"It is no longer I who live, but it is Christ who lives in me. And the life I now live in the flesh I live by faith in the Son of God, who loved me and gave himself for me." (Is 53.12.)

Read Rm 4.24–25

"It will be reckoned to us who believe in him who raised Jesus our Lord from the dead, who was handed over to death for our trespasses and was raised for our justification." (Is 53.12.)

Read Romans 8.32.

"He who did not withhold his own Son, but gave him up for all of us ..." (Is 53.12)

Read 1 Peter 2.21–24.

"For to this you have been called, because Christ also suffered for you, leaving you an example, so that you should follow in his steps. 'He committed no sin, and no deceit was found in his mouth.' When he was abused, he did not return abuse; when he suffered, he did not threaten; but he entrusted himself to the one who judges justly. He himself bore our sins in his body on the cross, so that, free from sins, we might live for righteousness; by his wounds you have been healed." (Is 53.9; 53 10–11; 53.4.)

Read Mark 10.45.

Here Jesus identifies himself with the Servant: "... the Son of Man came not to be served but to serve, and to give his life a ransom for many." (Is. 43.3–4.)

Lesson Questions

- Church tradition has stressed the passive suffering of the Servant as necessary payment to God. We have presented the Servant as a figure who teaches and exemplifies nonviolence. What do you think about this change in meaning?

- Before Jesus, and even after, why do you think the Servant texts were so difficult for people to interpret?

- Why did the New Testament embrace the Servant figure as a type for Jesus?

- How much does the God of Elijah still prevail in popular spirituality and theology today?

Personal Reflection

- Culture (movies, TV) glamorizes violence and the violent hero. The Servant and Jesus give a different witness, to nonviolence. In my life which type do I seek to emulate?

- Nonviolence is not just a political or social action, but firstly the nature of God. Does this change the way I am in relationship to God? How I feel about God?

Glossary

- Deutero-Isaiah (Second Isaiah) — second part of the Book of Isaiah comprising chapters 40-55, written by a different author from the previous chapters towards the end of the exile and in the early days of the return.

- Exile — the captivity of the Jerusalem population in Babylon from 597–538 BCE after the the fall of the Southern Kingdom of Judah. It ended when the king of Persia, Cyrus the Great, decreed that they could return to their land.

- Targum — an Aramaic version of the Hebrew Scriptures, often a very loose translation of the original text.

Resources/Background Reading

- Anthony Bartlett's chapter on 2nd Isaiah in *The Jesus Driven Life, Reconnecting Jesus With Humanity*, Michael Hardin (2015); also at http://www.preachingpeace.org/about/recommendations/33-worship-resources/bible-studies/294-bible-study-of-isaiah-40-53.html

- *Cross Purposes, The Violent Grammar of Christian Atonement*, Anthony Bartlett (2001)

- *The Nonviolent Atonement*, Denny Weaver (2nd Ed. 2011)

- *The Isaiah Targum*, Bruce D. Chilton (1987)

Cultural References

- Movie, *The Last Temptation of Christ,* dir. Martin Scorsese (1988)

- Movie, *The Passion of the Christ,* dir. Mel Gibson (2004)

WRATH TO COMPASSION
Lesson 2: Compassion in Isaiah

Learning Objectives

- To understand the qualitative shift in Second Isaiah's viewpoint and language from the Deuteronomic worldview.
- To grasp how this perspective is crucial for the figure of Jesus and his ministry.
- To see how God is presented as intensely personal and relational in Second Isaiah.

Core Biblical Texts

- Is 54.7–8
- Is 49.14–16
- Is 51.12

Key Points

- Second Isaiah's response to the exile is a dramatically new revelation of the compassionate nature of God.
- He expresses this in terms of highly personal language.
- His repetitive use of personal pronouns accentuates this personal address.
- The Gospels are heavily influenced by the vision of Second Isaiah.

Key Words /Concepts

- Compassion
- Personal Pronouns

Shift to a Personal, Compassionate Understanding of God

In 597 BCE Nebuchadnezzar of Babylon began the deportation into exile of the peoples of Judea. He carried off the king, royal family, officials, administrators, military officers, soldiers, craftsmen, smiths and leading families of Jerusalem. In 587 BCE, after a rebellion of those left behind, the city was destroyed, as well as fortifications, the palace, and large buildings throughout Judea. It was an absolute trauma: the apparent taking back of the gifts of the Lord and rejection by him.

Read Lam1.1–5. "How lonely sits the city that was once full of people! How like a widow she has become ... "

The exile is a key moment of transformation in the Old Testament. All four major prophets (Isaiah, Jeremiah, Ezekiel and Daniel) are associated with that time. (Daniel was written later, but is set during the exile.) There were two major responses to this crisis, represented in the books of Ezekiel and Second Isaiah:

Ezekiel's Response to the exile

Ezekiel is called the father of Judaism, because of his focus on the holiness and transcendence of God. He emphasizes the role of the restored Temple — a priestly rather than a political Israel. Ezekiel's fantastic visions (chariots and divine beings) demonstrate the trauma, the altered consciousness brought on by the exile. The sacred is shown as semi-monstrous. God is both splendid and monstrous: see chapter one with its living creatures, fire and wheels. The vision of the living creatures returns in chapter ten at the violent destruction of the city.

Read Ez 43.1–9. (God's glory returning to reside in the new Temple; the glory is "like the vision which I saw when he came to destroy the city," v.3.)

Ezekiel's response is to create a strong new purity with a new Temple. We will be returning to Ezekiel in more depth at a later time when we study the Temple.

Deutero-Isaiah's Response

In contrast Second Isaiah is full of gentleness and compassion. It marks a major shift from the tone of the Deuteronomic God toward a Compassionate God. It is a very different response to loss, violence and suffering.

Read Is 40.1–11.

("Comfort, O comfort my people, says your God. Speak tenderly to Jerusalem, and cry to her that she has served her term, that her penalty is paid, that she has received from the Lord's hand double for all her sins. A voice cries out: 'In the wilderness prepare the way of the Lord, make straight in the desert a highway for our God ...'")

Read Is 54.7–8.

A key synopsis or summary of the prophet's overall vision — "For a brief moment I abandoned you, but with great compassion I will gather you. In overflowing wrath for a moment I hid my face from you, but with everlasting love I will have compassion on you, says the Lord, your Redeemer."

Wrath is seen here as a momentary aberration, an excess. Compassion and love are forever.

Read Is 49.14–16.

("But Zion said, 'The Lord has forsaken me, my Lord has forgotten me.' Can a woman forget her nursing child, or show no compassion for the child of her womb? Even these may forget, yet I will not forget you ...")

There is a shift to an intensely feminine imagery, and its keynote of compassion. God's very character is perceived as compassion — he does not just decide to act compassionately for the moment. Compassion implies and creates relationship. Because of this change in God's character, his people are now welcomed into a relationship of love. For the first time relationship as such becomes revelation. (Note this kind of relationship is already present in Hosea, but it is not yet a fully developed theme as in Isaiah where it is expressed centrally and in multiple ways.)

Second Isaiah's Language of Compassion

Second Isaiah is noteworthy for a new and remarkable manner of address by God. God's first-person language here is almost unique. It signifies an explicitly personal address — where God is accenting his selfhood in relation to Israel. It is an opening up of self which cannot occur when there is violence. In Second Isaiah God often uses two first-person pronouns and one third-person pronoun, in place of the usual first-person singular "I". He says, "I, myself, he" or "Me, myself, he." This sounds strange to our ears, but it is the literal translation of the Hebrew. The Greek, and later the English translators, have changed this language to more comprehensible expressions which also fit with the self-revelation of God in Ex 3.13-14. So "I, myself" became translated as "I am," or "I, myself, myself" becomes "I, I am he". The original, Hebrew however, by multiplying the use of personal pronouns, has the effect of making God more personal and accessible. It is the use of language to express a new meaning.

Read Is 41.4. ("Who has performed and done this, calling the generations from the beginning? I, the Lord, am first, and will be with the last.")

Here the literal translation of the verse is "The last, I, he, who has worked and done it, calling the generations from the beginning, I, the Lord, the first." A glance at an interlinear version of the text shows the pronouns in English transliteration on the line above the Hebrew (ani, hu, ani).

See Table 5.1.

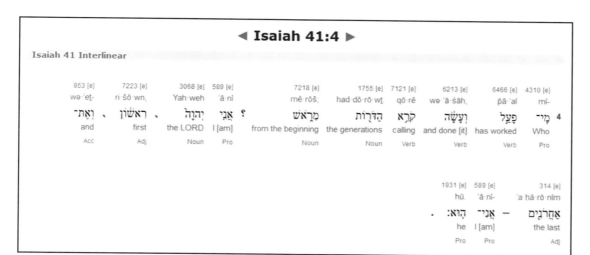

Isaiah 41 Interlinear

853 [e]	7223 [e]	3068 [e]	589 [e]	7218 [e]	1755 [e]	7121 [e]	6213 [e]	6466 [e]	4310 [e]
wə·'eṯ-	ri·šō·wn,	Yah·weh	'ă·nî	mê·rōš,	had·dō·rō·wṯ	qō·rê	wə·'ā·śāh,	pā·'al	mî-
וְאֵת־	רִאשׁוֹן	יְהוָה	אֲנִי	מֵרֹאשׁ	הַדֹּרוֹת	קֹרֵא	וְעָשָׂה	פָּעַל	מִי־ 4
and	first	the LORD	I [am]	from the beginning	the generations	calling	and done [it]	has worked	Who
Acc	Adj	Noun	Pro	Noun	Noun	Verb	Verb	Verb	Pro

1931 [e]	589 [e]	314 [e]
hū.	'ă·nî-	'a·ḥă·rō·nîm
הוּא׃	אֲנִי־ —	אַחֲרֹנִים
he	I [am]	the last
Pro	Pro	Adj

Table 5.1

The tripled pronouns become the name God gives himself. They signify a deeply personal address. The same style of address is repeated several times.

Read Is 43.10.

("You are my witnesses, says the Lord, and my servant whom I have chosen, so that you may know and believe me and understand that I am he.")

The original Hebrew is literally "understand he, I" (hu ani).
The Greek (LXX) translates this as "understand I am."
The English translation becomes "understand I am he."

Read Is 41.13–14.

("For I, the Lord your God, hold your right hand; it is I who say to you, 'Do not fear, I will help you'. Do not fear, you worm Jacob, you insect Israel! I will help you, says the Lord.")

A literal translation of the Hebrew here includes the pronoun "ani"

repeated on three separate places, meaning "myself" or "I". Apart from these pronouns there are in addition three first person verbs that also imply the first person pronoun, "hold" and "help" twice. These verbs are like, for example, Italian where the word parlo means "I speak" without a necessary pronoun. All this is an example of how often in Second Isaiah God speaks in the first person and refers to himself.

Read Is 43.25. ("I, I am he who blots out your transgressions.")

In the Hebrew this is "he, myself, myself" (another form of the first person pronoun, anoki, anoki). In the Greek it is "I am I am who blots out your transgressions."

Read Is 48.12. ("I am he, I am the first, and I am the last.")

In Hebrew this is literally "I, he, I, the first, I, and the last."

See Table 5.2.

◄ Isaiah 48:12 ►

Isaiah 48 Interlinear

314 [e]	589 [e]	637 [e]	7223 [e]	589 [e]	1931 [e]	589 [e]	7121 [e]	3478 [e]	3290 [e]	413 [e]	8085 [e]	
'a·ḥă·rō·wn.	'ă·nî	'ap̄	ri·šō·wn,	'ă·nî	hū	'ă·nî-	me·qō·rā·'î,	wə·yiś·rā·'êl	ya·'ă·qōḇ,	'ê·lay	šə·ma'	
אַחֲרֽוֹן׃	אֲנִי	אַף	רִאשׁוֹן	אֲנִי	הוּא	אֲנִי־	מְקֹרָאִי	וְיִשְׂרָאֵל	יַעֲקֹב	אֵלַי	שְׁמַע	12
the last	I [am]	also	the first	I [am]	he	I [am]	my called	and Israel	O Jacob	unto me	Listen	
Adj	Pro	Conj	Adj	Pro	Pro	Pro	Verb	Noun	Noun	Prep	Verb	

Table 5.2

You can see how the poetry of the writer multiplies the first person address, unmistakably accenting relationship.

Read Is 51.12. ("I, I am he who comforts you.")

This is literally "Myself, myself, he who comforts you" (*anoki, anoki, hu*).

In all of these passages that speak of God's compassion the language is intensely personal. The personal address is doubled, tripled to emphasize it. It is like the very heart of God is a relationship, his very identity.

There is only one other place in the Bible where this kind of language is attributed to God. It is a single verse in the book of Deuteronomy.

Read Dt 32.39–41.

("See now that I, even I, am he [literally I, I, he — *ani, ani, hu*]; there is no god beside me. I kill and I make alive; I wound and I heal; and no-one can deliver from my hand. For I lift up my hand to heaven, and swear: As I live forever, when I whet my flashing sword, and my hand takes hold on judgment; I will take vengeance on my adversaries, and will repay those who hate me.")

Here there is an extremely different tone and message. Both books reached their final form at about the same time. Is Second Isaiah a commentary about this verse in Deuteronomy? Or is Deuteronomy (more likely) offering an orthodox "balancing" of Second Isaiah's dramatic new language and identity for God?

Second Isaiah as Revelation of the Compassionate God

Putting together Second Isaiah's focus on compassion and consolation, the very personal relational language of God, and the Songs of the Servant, make Second Isaiah the major source of transformative semiotics before Jesus. Second Isaiah is a laboratory for dealing with the violence and loss of the exile, producing something wonderfully new.

The Gospels Deeply Influenced by Second Isaiah:

We have shown the presence of the Suffering Servant in the Gospels. But there are other connections too, including the following.

Read Lk 3.4–6.

("... as it is written in the book of the words of the prophet Isaiah, 'The voice of one crying out in the wilderness: 'Prepare the way of the Lord ... '")

The voice in the wilderness is a headline of Second Isaiah (Is 40.3) and it is referenced in respect of John the Baptist at the opening of Jesus' ministry in all the Gospels. It is one of the few expressions common to all four. Thus starting from John the Baptist, Jesus continues and fulfills the vision of Second Isaiah.

Read Mt 23.37–39 (Jesus' lament over Jerusalem).

Here Jesus, like a mother hen, and like Zion's motherly God described in Isaiah, wants to shelter and protect the chicks, Jerusalem's children.

Notes:

_____

_____

_____

_____

_____

_____

_____

_____

_____

_____

_____

_____

_____

_____

_____

_____

_____

_____

_____

_____

_____

_____

_____

Lesson Questions

· Why do you think Isaiah sees compassion as the response to the exile?

· What does the change in language in Second Isaiah mean for Biblical revelation? Has the meaning of God changed, from violence to compassion? Can God somehow be both?

· Is this a semiotic shift? Is God different, or have our tools for understanding God changed?

· Is violence such a core issue for human beings that we can see the move to compassion as a core change?

Personal Reflection

· When have you experienced God as compassion? Non-judging?

· The compassionate language in Isaiah is at times feminine. Have you been touched by the feminine, nonviolent character of God?

Glossary

· Return from exile — the physical return of a group of Judean exiles from Babylon to Jerusalem; also the spiritual return — led by God — that was still in process in Gospel times.

of-isaiah-40-53.html

· *Second Isaiah* (The Anchor Bible, Vol. 20), John L. McKenzie (Editor, Translator, Introduction)

· *The Secret Life of Pronouns: What Our Words Say About Us*, James W. Pennebaker (2013)

· English Interlinear of the Hebrew Bible is taken from biblehub.com

Cultural References

· Spiritual Awareness groups use the words ani hu as basis of chants, e.g. https://www.youtube.com/watch?v=JN28dRP0E1w&t=826s

· Leonard Cohen's Hallelujah, with lyrics ("It doesn't matter which you heard, the holy or the broken Hallelujah"): https://www.youtube.com/watch?v=a4WgaSKN9c4

Resources/Background Reading

· http://www.preachingpeace.org/news/33-worship-resources/bible-studies/294-bible-study-

WRATH TO COMPASSION
Lesson 3: Cup of Wrath

Learning Objectives

· To see the "the cup of wrath" as an anthropological reality which became a theological construct, one which Jesus transformed into nonviolence.

To read the Old Testament metaphor of the cup along its developmental pathway, all the way to Jesus and his revolutionary intervention.

To understand how an imaginative trope (the cup of wrath) became transformed in Christian tradition into an eternal attribute of God. In reality Jesus empties wrath from humans and God, and breaks the cycle of violence.

Core Biblical Texts

· Hab 2.6–17
· Lk 22.39–42.
· Mk 15.33–37
· Lk 22.14–20
· Jn 18.10–11

Key Points

· The cup of wrath is a symbol of human violence.

· Jesus is the answer to the human system of violence.

· Jesus transforms the symbolism of the cup into the cup of the nonviolent New Covenant.

Key Words /Concepts

· Cup of wrath
· The violence of the nations
· Cup of the New Covenant

Violence as the Cup of Wrath or Cup of Staggering

Throughout the Hebrew Scriptures the cup is used as a symbol of judgment. It is found in earlier writings such as the Psalms and Habakkuk, but also in later works like the major prophets, Second Isaiah and Ezekiel. Because the experience of an invading army is utterly overwhelming it is described as something that makes the victim nation drunk, to the point of staggering, falling down, being stripped naked. The cup then becomes a symbol of the devastation and violence that falls on the nations. It becomes something administered by God, as a kind of impartial umpire, in a basic distributive justice: you have done this to others, so the cup will be returned to you. It fits with the Deuteronomic view that judgment comes from God, it applies to all the nations, and is distributive and retributive. Subsequently it becomes directed towards Judah or Jerusalem because of their sins, and that is when it takes on a more personal note, because of the personal relationship between God and Israel. But we must never forget the basic anthropological and distributive character of the cup. "What goes around comes around!"

We will start by looking at some of the relevant passages.

Read Hab 2.15–17.

" ... Alas for you who make your neighbors drink, pouring out your wrath until they are drunk, in order to gaze on their nakedness!' You will be sated with contempt instead of glory. Drink yourself and stagger! The cup in the Lord's right hand will come around to you, and shame will come upon your glory! For the violence done to Lebanon will overwhelm you; the destruction of the animals will terrify you — because of human bloodshed and violence to the earth, to cities and all who live in them."

Read Jer 25.15–29.

"For thus the Lord, the God of Israel, said to me: Take from my hand this cup of the wine of wrath, and make all the nations to whom I send you drink it. They shall drink and stagger and go out of their minds because of the sword that I am sending among them ..."

Read Jer 49.12 (judgment on Edom).

"For thus says the Lord: 'If those who do not deserve to drink the cup still have to drink it, shall you be the one to go unpunished? You shall not go unpunished; you must drink it.'"

Read Lam 4.21.

"Rejoice and be glad, O daughter of Edom, you that live in the land of Uz; but to you also the cup shall pass; you shall become drunk and strip yourself bare."

The cup is a human event which includes the violence and shame of being stripped bare, i.e. the devastation of violence as a personal humiliation and loss of human standing.

Read Zech 12.2.

"See, I am about to make Jerusalem a cup of reeling for all the surrounding peoples; it will be against Judah also in the siege against Jerusalem. On that day I will make Jerusalem a heavy stone for all the peoples ..." According to this image Jerusalem in its turn becomes a cup of wrath for its enemies.

Read Ez 23.32–33.

"Thus says the Lord God: 'You shall drink your sister's cup, deep and wide; you shall be scorned and derided, it holds so much. You shall be filled with drunkenness and sorrow. A cup of horror and desolation is the cup of your sister Samaria; you shall drink it and drain it out, and gnaw its shards, and tear out your breasts.'"

Read Ps 60.3.

"You have made your people suffer hard things; you have given us wine to drink that made us reel."

In all of these passages there are common themes:

The people stagger; they are drunk, out of their minds, as a result of the violence.

They experience also a stripping bare: nakedness, humiliation, dehumanization.

The cup is always passed on — from one nation to another. The violence does not end, it is simply displaced from one nation to the next. It has to go somewhere. God is seen as the final administrator of this brutal form of justice.

Now read Is 51.17–23

"Rouse yourself, rouse yourself! Stand up, O Jerusalem, you who have drunk at the hand of the Lord the cup of his wrath, who have drunk to the dregs the bowl of staggering .... Therefore hear this, you who are wounded, who are drunk, but not with wine: thus says your Sovereign, the Lord, your God who pleads the cause of his people: 'see I have taken from your hand the cup of staggering; you shall drink no more from the bowl of my wrath. And I will put it into the hand of your tormentors ...'"

Here the effect is different — God positively removes the cup of wrath, because Israel's time of punishment is over. Here the personal relationship outlasts the cup; in the meantime it is passed on to others. Paradoxically it is this personal relationship which makes people see the cup of wrath as a personal emotional state of God. But the cup is an anthropological reality of historical violence and should not be identified with the character God. It is rather the enduring relationship that is God's character. The text of Isaiah struggles with the reality of historical violence understood as under God's jurisdiction. Essentially the prophet explains it as a temporary aberration in regard to Jerusalem and Judea — God's wrath lasted only for a moment, but his compassion and love are forever.

Again read Is 54.7–8.

"For a brief moment I abandoned you, but with great compassion I will gather you. In overflowing wrath for a moment I hid my face from you, but with everlasting love I will have compassion on you, says the Lord, your Redeemer."

Gethsemane: Jesus Reconciles Himself to Drink the Cup of Wrath

If we see Jesus as drinking up this historical human cup, rather than a cup of God's personal wrath, it becomes a huge shift in meaning. It was very easy for human beings to attribute the cup personally to God — both because of the personal relationship of Israel with the Lord, and generally because of the "sacred/divine" (Girardian) meaning of violence. But if we follow the text of the Gospels that is not the meaning: in one concerted action Jesus exhausts the cup of human violence and undoes the theological construct of God's character as wrath.

Read Mk 14.35–36.

"And going a little farther, he threw himself on the ground and prayed that, if it were possible, the hour might pass from him. He said, 'Abba, Father, for you all things are possible; remove this cup from me; yet not what I want, but what you want.'"

These are words of intimacy and trust, not of alienation from an angry God. And the sense is not of necessity but of possibility. It is God's desire that something possible should happen, rather than Jesus' action be the fulfillment of an implacable legal will. In other words, the Father's desire is that Jesus consume the cup of human wrath/violence. We may also look at it from the dimension of John's Gospel where Jesus does "only what he sees the Father doing" (5.19). If Jesus is to drink the cup it is because, mysteriously, the Father first drinks the cup.

Read Mk 10.37–39.

The request of James and John to sit in positions of power next to Jesus in glory. Jesus replies: "Are you able to drink the cup that I drink?" Then he adds, "The cup that I drink you will drink …"

This strongly suggests first that he is to do something which is extremely difficult, but still within the human sphere, and second that his disciples will in fact drink the cup — something impossible if this is a deal with God that only Jesus the Savior can make. It makes much more sense that the cup is the cup of human violence, which Jesus is draining. After him it becomes possible for others to drain it too.

Read Jn 18.10–11 (Peter draws his sword and cuts off the ear of the High Priest's servant).

Jesus stops him saying, "Am I not to drink the cup the Father has given me?" We can read this as Jesus asserting a lofty metaphysical goal, which in this instance precludes fighting; or, much more organically, as Jesus directly identifying the cup with all human violence that he must drain nonviolently to its dregs.

Jesus on the Cross

The crucifixion narrative is loaded with references to Old Testament texts/themes — Psalm 22, the Songs of the Servant, and the Cup of Wrath.

In this connection it is important first to reference the Suffering Servant as it links us to the converse of the cup of wrath which we will see below in the eucharistic passages. In the Fourth Song of the Servant, Isaiah 53.12, we read, "Because he poured out himself to death." Literally this is "poured out his nephesh/soul to death" (or, in the Hebrew, was "made naked/laid bare," reminiscent of the victims of the cup of violence above).

Jesus Drinks Wine on the Cross

In all the Gospels except Luke Jesus' death occurs after he is offered the bitter wine (Mk 15.36–37; Mt 27.48–50; John 19.28–30). John makes a point of saying he drank the wine and then said "It is finished." Jesus drinks the bitter wine of the world's violence until the last drop, and then his job is done.

The Passover Cup

The understanding of this cup provides a counterpoint to the cup of wrath and underlines the centrality of the motif of the cup. If Jesus leaves us a cup to drink, it is the opposite of the cup of wrath — a cup of nonviolence and forgiveness.

By the time Jesus observed the Passover, drinking a cup during the meal was a standard part of the observance. The Mishna instructs those celebrating Passover to drink from the cup four times during the seder meal. Each time the cup is filled it has a different name. Most agree the first is the Kiddush, which means "sanctification" and begins the seder. The second cup is the cup of plagues. The third is the cup of redemption or the cup of blessing. The fourth is often called the cup of *hallel* which means praise. It is also known as the cup of Elijah. All four use red wine to recall the blood of the passover lamb. Both judgment and redemption are themes of the Passover. Judgment on the Egyptians; redemption through the Red Sea. God poured out his judgment on the Egyptians, but spared the Israelites who placed the blood of the lamb on their doorposts.

Read Lk 22. 4–20.

This now becomes a crucial passage. It strongly suggests that Jesus opted out of eating the Passover the night before he died, and vows not to eat it "until it is fulfilled in the kingdom of God." (This would explain why Luke does not mention the final offer of bitter wine on the cross, possibly understanding the gesture as contradicting Jesus' vow.) Jesus had previously called a halt to the sacrificial practices in the Temple. Now he was giving a radical new meaning to the Passover ritual. His personal nonviolent self-giving, including fasting from the old Passover, brings in this new meaning.

The Cup of the New Covenant

The cup after supper is usually understood as the third cup (the cup of blessing or redemption). Paul calls the Eucharistic cup "the cup of blessing that we bless" and "the cup of the Lord" (1 Cor 10.16 & 21). In Luke, Jesus calls this cup, "The cup that is poured out for you is the new covenant in my blood" (Lk 22.20). The seder cup of blessing/redemption recalled the escape of the Hebrews from Egypt, but also the blood of the Egyptians who were killed when the angel of death passed over. Jesus takes this cup of blessing and uses it to reinterpret God's plan and purpose in an entirely nonviolent way. The cup which is the new covenant in Jesus' blood evokes Isaiah 53.12 and the Servant whose soul or life is "poured out." It also

makes a direct reference to Jer 31.31–34. The old covenant is abrogated. Jesus' new covenant will be written instead on our hearts through the direct embracing of Jesus' personal nonviolence and non-retaliation. So all sin (violence/alienation) is overcome and forgiven in immediate personal relationship. (In this light there is no difference between the forgiveness of Jesus and that, for example, offered to the paralytic at Mk 2.5, "Son, your sins are forgiven.")

The Eucharistic cup enacts both God's new covenant with humans through Jesus, as well as the "price" paid to end the violence of the world – Jesus' blood spilled to break the cycle of violence. But violence is not "paid off," it is simply exhausted as a phenomenon in the human heart by Jesus' astonishing witness. The Eucharist also resonates with symbolism associated with the coming feast of God's kingdom. For example, in Isaiah where a wonderful feast is prophesied at 25.6–9. It is worth noting that an alternative translation of the Lord's prayer is: "Give us today the bread of tomorrow (epiousios)."

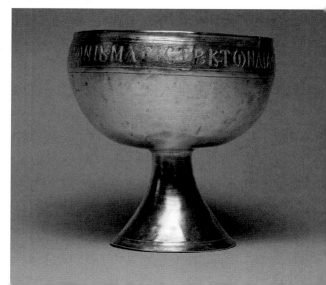

Notes:

_____

_____

_____

_____

_____

_____

_____

_____

_____

_____

_____

_____

_____

_____

_____

_____

_____

_____

_____

_____

_____

_____

_____

_____

_____

_____

Lesson Questions

· If the cup of wrath is seen as the violence of the world, how does Jesus turn the system of violence on its head on the cross?

· Does the Biblical pathway (from Habakkuk through Isaiah) demonstrate that the cup of wrath is a human phenomenon attributed to God?

· How is the eucharistic cup understood in the church tradition? Is it understood as the nonviolent cup of the New Covenant or a re-play of the old sacrificial system?

Personal Reflection

· What does the eucharist (communion) mean to you? Is it God's transformative nonviolence displayed to humankind? Do you think we can grow as communities in this meaning and in its practice?

· The Cup of Wrath symbolizes the violence in the world that always has to be discharged somewhere. If Jesus drinks this cup, he has changed our human situation. How do you feel about violence in the world today? How has Jesus changed things?

· Jesus reveals a nonviolent God. Do you still feel any violence in God? If the answer is yes, then where does this come from?

Glossary

· Wrath — the human attribute of anger and violence that becomes an attribute of God both because of its "sacred" power and because the prophets saw it as cyclical and retributive. Jesus subverts this interpretation in every sense.

Resources/Background Reading

· *The Eucharistic Words of Jesus,* Joachim Jeremias (2012)

· https://leonardooh.wordpress. com/2011/09/07/what-of-the-cup-on-penal-substitutionary-atonement/ — giving the traditional penal point of view.

Cultural References

· *Harry Potter and the Half-Blood Prince,* J.K. Rowling (2005) — Dumbledore drinking the cursed goblet to its dregs in order to retrieve the locket from the basin.

Victim to Vindication

Lesson Plan

Lesson 1: Job

Lesson 2: The *go'el*

Lesson 3: Jesus and Jonah

Learning Objectives

· To understand various ways in which the figure of the victim is central to the Old Testament narrative.

· To see how the actual social and historical victim was of central concern to the Israelites.

· To grasp how the Bible began to see the collective scapegoat as a foundational instance of the victim: the book of Job is the paradigm example.

· To see how Jesus takes on the role of the scapegoat in order to subvert it from within, filling it with nonviolence.

Synopsis of the Story as a Whole

· The victim by definition is lost to history. The Bible always seeks to reverse this fact and thus ultimately reveals a different way of being human.

· Paradigm stories of Job and Jonah are semiotic shifts of the highest order.

Key Words/Concepts

· *go'el*

· Job's innocence

· Sign of Jonah

VICTIM TO VINDICATION
Lesson 1: Job

Learning Objectives

· To see the book of Job as a complex literary composition examining the problem of the suffering victim, blame and vindication.

· To understand Job as a reply to the Deuteronomic penal worldview — that if you suffer it is because you have sinned.

· To appreciate the enormous breakthrough of Job that sees the suffering of the victim, the victim's innocence, and the way in which the victim's vindication leads to forgiveness.

Core Biblical Texts

· Job 11.1–6
· Job 19.1–27
· Job 42.2–9

Key Points

· The literary construction of Job as revelation.
· Job's consistent defense of his innocence before God.
· The role of the satan as accuser.
· The Book of Job separates God from the mechanism of the scapegoat.

Key Words /Concepts

· *Ha'satan*
· Ransom

Job as Literature not History

Job is the indisputable case, the locus classicus, of the innocent victim who is vindicated. Because it is such a magnificent piece it has universal appeal. It is the textbook example of theological humanism — God is real, but humanity has cause for complaint. Tennyson described the work as the greatest poem of ancient and modern times. In this Biblical writing there is a significant movement in understanding and emphasis, from a narrative of election for life/salvation, to a diagnosis of the problem from which our life might be saved. In a way, the Bible goes from a history class, about patriarchs, territories, and kings, to a psychology class, about guilt, blame, and innocence. This is itself a profound semiotic shift, leading the Bible away from its narrative solution toward humanity's deepest problem.

Job represents the deep anthropology of the Bible — an incisive description of the human predicament. This story of Job is a story about our human problem of suffering and the way we traditionally use blame to make sense of it.

There is a lack of historical context — concrete events and markers which could tell us clearly when and by whom it was written. Therefore literalists/conservatives date the text to 2000 BCE. Historical-critical scholars date it to somewhere between 6th – 4th centuries BCE, because of the sophistication in the writing and the content of the argument.

How the Book of Job is Structured

Job 1–2: The Book of Job begins with a frame story set in the court of heaven. The satan is charged with testing the righteous and blameless Job who loses everything except his life.

Job 3: Job curses the day he was born.

There follows eight speeches of condemnation of Job by his three friends (Eliphaz, Bildad, and Zophar) to which Job replies each time. (The last of these speeches seems to have Job replying twice, possibly indicating a missing third speech by Zophar.) There then follows another argument made by a new figure, Elihu, to whom Job does not reply. Then God himself intervenes, with two speeches against Job. Job makes a short reply in the middle, and then a final, highly ambivalent reply suggesting that he still maintains his innocence.

Job 4–7 (Eliphaz & Job's reply); Job 8–10 (Bildad & reply); Job 11–14 (Zophar & reply); Job 15–17 (Eliphaz & reply); Job 18–19 (Bildad & reply); Job 20–21 (Zophar & reply); Job 22–24 (Eliphaz & reply); Job 25–27 (Bildad & reply); Job 28 (An Interlude on Wisdom); Job 29–31(Job's reply to Bildad continued).

Job 32–37 (Elihu's speech); Job 38–40.2 (the Lord's first speech); Job 40.3–5 (Job's first reply to the Lord); Job 40.6–41.34 (the Lord's second speech); Job 42.1–6 (Job's final reply to the Lord).

The book concludes with a final judgment by God which comprises the second part of the original frame story:

Job 42.7–9 (Job's friends are rebuked); Job 42.10–17 (Job's fortune is restored).

This complex, layered structure demonstrates a powerful, difficult argument is taking place, one without a totally clear outcome — and yet with enough ironic hints to point a way forward. There is ambivalence in some of the statements, indicating that perhaps there is a totally different way of looking at the question. This character of the text cannot be ignored. It points to the huge problem of why someone should suffer. The final outcome of the work (God rebuking the friends) suggests Job won the argument, that he is in fact innocent. At this point — and suddenly this takes the whole thing to a totally new level — the role of the innocent victim becomes pivotal in its own right, as an intercessor for the friends.

God in Job

This text is also controversial because of the way it depicts the Lord as capricious and violent. It seems foreign to our modern, post-Jesus way of looking at God. Is this deliberate, to make us question our received understandings of God?

Read Job 1 – 2.10.

This sets the scene and introduces the Lord in the story. He allows *ha'satan* (the satan) to afflict Job with all sorts of ailments. Hence the immediate question: how could God possibly be an initiator in this kind of game played with the life of his servant?

The Satan (*ha'satan*)

It is important to be clear about the meaning of this figure. "The satan" is not God's cosmic opponent, as he appears to be in the New Testament. In fact, the word satan occurs 26 times in the Old Testament, in both verb and noun forms, where it always means an adversary, or accuser, but is never a proper name. Here in Job, *ha'satan* refers to a role or office in God's court, a figure with the role of testing an individual's honesty. He is essentially a police inspector or attorney general, acting within the power and permission of God.

Read 1 Sam 29.4 .

David and his men plan to fight with the Philistines against Saul, but the Philistine commanders object, "Send the man back, so that he may return to the place you have assigned to him; he shall not go down with us to battle, or else he may become an adversary to us in the battle." The word here is (a) satan, without definite article.

Read 2 Sam 19.22.

Another instance of satan in the sense of an adversary/opponent — David argues against his adversary/satan, Abishai, for mercy for Shimei.

Read 1 Chr 21.1.

"Satan stood up against Israel and incited David to count the people of Israel." Here (a) satan incites David to take a census.

There is a tendency in Biblical translators to see this as "Satan" of popular imagination, but now compare this verse to its earlier form at 2 Samuel 24.1: "again the anger of the Lord was kindled against Israel, and he incited David against them, saying, 'Go, count the people of Israel and Judah.'" If we recognize both these versions as inspired, how could the Lord be his own metaphysical opponent? Rather we can see the Chronicles author recognizing a problem in the Lord acting like this toward his servant David, and so shifting the provocation to an unspecified agent acting as adversary. It is much more reasonable then to understand the

Biblical account as first viewing everything under God's final agency (a Wisdom viewpoint) but slowly separating out the function of mimetic rivalry. Anthropologically speaking, the "accuser" here is simply within David's head, presumably an internal rivalry with kings of other nations.

Read Zech 3.1.

The satan — with definite article — stands as accuser of the high priest, Joshua. Here the accuser has a formal role, as in Job, but it is not shown as an enemy of God.

Remember that in the New Testament "Satan" is a function of the apocalyptic showdown between Jesus and the forces of evil/violence. The figure is personified because it is all about a final crisis of mimetic personhood — human being as a creature of rivalry and moving always to crisis point. If we analyze Jesus' temptations by Satan we see they are all instances of suggested rivalry, in terms of status and power (material, political, semiotic). Jesus triumphs over this rivalry in unity with his Father.

After the first two chapters of Job, the Satan disappears from the narrative. His place, as accuser and adversary, is taken instead by the three friends and then by Elihu.

Read Job 8.1–7 and Job 11.1–6 as examples of their accusations.

The Character of Job

Read Job 29.1–17 to get a sense of Job's voice (he is presented as a seeker of justice, a friend to the oppressed).

Read Job 24.1–22 (Job complains against violence on the earth).

Read also Job 21.7–26.

This is an incredible complaint for it implies the only final reckoning is death, not God. There is no justice, because God as understood to this point does not deal with these issues. Yet Job hopes in the ultimate justice of God.

Read Job 23.1–7 (Job wants to bring his case to God, he believes in the justice of God).

Read Job 19.27 (he cries out for a redeemer — a go'el).

Elihu at Job 33.22–28 fleshes out this idea of a redeemer in a surprising way. He speaks of one who will pay the ransom — almost as if he is foreshadowing, despite himself, the solution to the whole enigma: there is one who takes the side of the victim! We will examine the role of the *go'el* in the next lesson.

God's Response

Read Job 38–39 (the Lord speaks and declares his majesty in arranging the wonders of creation).

Then the Lord appears in the whirlwind:

Read Job 40.6 – 41.34 (God says essentially only he can deal with violent monsters, like Behemoth and Leviathan).

God's responses are noteworthy

for their "sound and fury" but they are hollow. They do not answer the actual question!

Job's Response to God

At the end of God's blustering speech against him, Job makes an ambiguous response.

Read Job 42.2–6.

Job repeats the Lord's words back to him at 42.3 and 4 which could appear to be submission, but also as putting the words straight back to God. As in, "Your own words could be applied to you, and I will use them to question you!"

"I know that you can do all things, and that no purpose of yours can be thwarted. 'Who is this that hides counsel without knowledge?' [See 38.2] Therefore I have uttered what I did not understand, things too wonderful for me, which I did not know. 'Hear and I will speak; I will question you, and you declare to me' [See 38.3b & 40.7b]."

Finally he says, "I had heard of you by the hearing of the ear, but now my eye sees you; therefore I despise myself, and repent in dust and ashes."

These final words may seem like repentance, but the Hebrew can be better translated, "I reject and regret dust and ashes ..." Or, "I reject and regret about dust and ashes ..."

The verb "despise" can be translated as "reject" and is in multiple places (for example 1 Sam 8.7, "Listen to the voice of the people in all that they say to you; for they have not rejected you, but they have rejected me ... "). Moreover it is not a reflexive form, so it does not describe the person speaking. If it is translated non-reflexively, as it should be, it would read not "I despise/reject myself" but simply "I reject."

Similarly the word translated here as "repent" is translated elsewhere as "regret," "rue," "lament."

The whole meaning of the book hinges on the translator's choice at this point. If Job's words are shoehorned to mean self-loathing and repentance, then the literary labor of twenty plus speeches becomes redundant and serves only to illustrate Job's sinful arrogance. But if they are read with their built-in ambiguity then they affirm everything Job has said to this point.

At this final climactic moment Job subtly restates his position, despite the bombast the Lord has directed at him. Translators fall for the ruse, siding with the traditional language of submission to God. But the story is not over yet. The frame narrative returns and clearly supports this alternative reading, vindicating everything Job has said.

Job as Redeemer

Read Job 42.7–9.

Job is vindicated by the Lord. The Lord rebukes the friends and commends Job: "for you have not spoken of me what is right, as my servant Job has" (v.7). In this little note (twice repeated, see v. 8) all Job's words are vindicated. He is suffering unjustly, and meanwhile his so-called friends have piled on him as scapegoaters, sensing with the certainty of collective violence that he must be guilty. In consequence the Lord's wrath is kindled against them! However, they are exhorted to ask for Job's prayers. Job becomes now a mediator of forgiveness, signaled by the accompaniment of a required sacrifice.

There are parallels between the figure of Job at this point and the Suffering Servant of Isaiah 52–53 (Story 4). Both suffer horribly, both are vindicated and restored by the Lord, and both have the effect of making others righteous. The new sensibility (of the revealed innocent victim changing people's situation before God) has come in the context of the Babylonian exile, and this feature is another marker dating Job to around this period.

What is the way in which Job becomes a mediator, or even a redeemer (*go'el* – see next lesson)? It is not a matter of Job's suffering paying a ransom to God. It is the fact that he spoke right about God; i.e. he declares that the victim is innocent and God is on his side; and that he maintained this position with integrity. The book of Job is a critique of Deuteronomic orthodoxy. It is a revelation of God on the side of the victim and nonviolence.

At the end of the book of Job, God lets go of his "might makes right" and appeals only to Job's words. Redemption is the revelation of the nonviolent victim as one who is approved by God. The friend's scapegoating arguments are "folly." Job's words are wisdom. Note that the Deuteronomic name for God — YHWH or "Lord" — is used in God's speeches at the end and also in the frame story. In the speeches made by the friends the term for God is different (the more traditional and generic names "El," or "Elohim"). The Book of Job thus takes on the issue of the nature of the Lord. In the final reckoning the story shows the Lord allowing the accuser/satan to wreak havoc in order, finally, to reveal redemption through the nonviolent innocent victim.

Lesson Questions

- How is God portrayed in the Book of Job? And, even more important, why?

- How is the satan in Job different to the Satan of popular culture?

- How does Job respond to God's long harangue against him?

- How does Job argue against the Deuteronomic worldview?

- If Job is an essay on the problem of innocent suffering what is its conclusion?

- Job calls out for a redeemer in chapter 19 — how is he himself portrayed as redeemer to his friends?

- How does Job point forward to the figure of Jesus?

Personal Reflection

- How have I reconciled innocent suffering with belief in a just God?

- Have there been times in my life where I have felt suffering as punishment?

- There is a human tendency to rejoice in the troubles of others (*schadenfreude*): why does this happen? Do I recognize this tendency in myself?

- What messages did I receive growing up about whom to blame when things go wrong? Do I blame myself? A particular individual or group? What would it feel like not to blame anyone?

Glossary

- *ha' satan* — the accuser or adversary, a social category and role in Hebrew culture, not a metaphysical enemy of God. In the New Testament "Satan" is the name for rivalry and violence as a constant "cosmic" force in opposition to Jesus.

- Sons of God — the gathering of companions or heavenly court around God, sometimes understood as angels (e.g. Job 1:6).

Resources/Background Reading

- *Job: The Victim of His People*, René Girard (1987)

- *On Job (God-Talk and the Suffering of the Innocent),* Gustavo Gutierrez and Matthew O'Connell (1987)

- *The Suffering of Innocents*, Marc Zirogiannis (2015)

- *The Archive and the Repertoire: Performing Cultural Memory in the Americas,* Diana Taylor (2003) — Latin American drama theory revealing the victim

Cultural References

- George Handel's use of Job 19.25 ("I know that my redeemer liveth") as an aria in his 1741 oratorio Messiah.

- Broadway production, Fiddler on the Roof, from basis in Yiddish short stories by Sholem Aleichem from 1894.

- Movie, A Serious Man, dir. Coen Brothers (2009), has strong elements of the Job story.

- Movie, *Willy Wonka and the Chocolate Factory*, dir. Mel Stuart (1971), where the children are tempted by an employee of Wonka's (the satan) and Charlie passes the test.

VICTIM TO VINDICATION
Lesson 2: The *go'el*

Learning Objectives

- To understand the ancient Israelite figure of *go'el* and how it functioned in a society without a centralized justice system.
- To see how the *go'el* functions to restore life that has been taken away.
- To understand how God takes on this role in the circumstances of the exile.
- To grasp how Biblical redemption is rooted in this need to restore the life of the victim.

Core Biblical Texts

- Num 35.9–34
- Ruth 3.9–13
- Is 59.20

Key Words /Concepts

- *go'el*
- Avenger of Blood
- Cities of Refuge
- Redeemer

Key Points

- The *go'el* is the avenger of blood.
- The *go'el* redeems lost land.
- The *go'el* is next-of-kin to raise up descendants.
- Ruth functions as the *go'el* in the Biblical story.
- God becomes the *go'el* of his people.

In this lesson we talk about the meaning of "redeemer," the go'el. If we dig down to the root Hebrew meaning of this term it will show us concern for the victim at the most primary levels of the Biblical experience. And it allows us to understand in a very human (anthropological) sense the meaning of Jesus' work as "redeemer," in contrast with a traditional church "salvation-from-hell" reading.

The noun form *go'el* belongs to a word group with root *gaal*, meaning to "to redeem/to act as kinsman." It denotes a person who is the nearest relative, next-of-kin, the one given the duty of restoring a kinsman's alienated rights to liberty or life. It is also translated "avenger of blood," meaning it is this person's job to redeem, act as kinsman-redeemer, avenge, buy back, in respect of the relative's lost or disappearing life. The fact that this task is carried out by shedding life-blood in compensation (killing the killer) shows the visceral demand that life not be lost without equivalent payment. It exposes the human gut sense of the sacred quality of blood, to which only further extreme shedding of blood is a proportionate response.

The figure of *go'el* belongs to a semi-desert tribal setting where there was no institutional justice, no police force or law courts. The *go'el* afforded a minimal assurance to a victim that his/her existence would not be allowed to vanish without trace at the hands of violence, whether criminal or happenstance. As such the *go'el* is concerned with the vindication of the victim in a very fundamental sense — i.e. in respect of the disasters that can happen to people when there are little or no institutional or social protections.

When the term is applied to God it comes to mean God's personal intervention on the side of his people who are in a condition of loss or elimination of life. It strongly suggests that God becomes the kinsman of his people.

It is only by grasping the primitive social background that we get an idea of how raw and real the role of *go'el* is.

Go'el as Redeemer of Property

The concept can be seen playing out in the following circumstances.

Read Lev 25.47–49.

"If resident aliens among you prosper, and if any of your kin fall into difficulty with one of them and sell themselves to an alien, or to a branch of the alien's family, after they have sold themselves they shall have the right of redemption; one of their brothers may redeem them, or their uncle or their uncle's son may redeem them, or any one of their family who is of their own flesh may redeem them; or if they prosper they may redeem themselves."

Read Lev 25.25–26.

"If anyone of your kin falls into difficulty and sells a piece of property, then the next-of-kin shall come and redeem what the relative has sold. If the person has no one to redeem it … "

Go'el as avenger of blood
Read Num 35.9–34.

The references here are to the *go'el* in respect of a murder or manslaughter that has occurred, and to the institution of "cities of refuge" as places someone who kills accidentally may flee for protection from the *go'el*: " … or anyone who strikes another with a weapon of wood in hand that could cause death, and death ensues, is a murderer; the murderer shall be put to death. The avenger of blood (*go'el*) is the one who shall put the murderer to death; when they meet, the avenger of blood shall execute the sentence ..."

Read 2 Sam 14.4–11.

The context is a parable with reference to David's son, Absalom, and it neatly illustrates both the role of *go'el* and how its reciprocal violence may indeed not bring life: here a higher wisdom is required, not to exact vengeance: "'please, may the king keep the Lord your God in mind, so that the avenger of blood (*go'el*) may kill no more …'"

But the intense sensibility to spilled blood remains. We could even call it the visual power of blood immediately to signal violence. (Today surgeons' gowns are green, on which a bloodstain turns black — in this way the visual cue of blood is not given.) In Deuteronomy there is an example of random blood needing to be purged, otherwise bloodguilt falls automatically upon all the people.

Read Dt 21.1–9.

If a body is found out in the open and it is unknown who killed that person then a heifer must be sacrificed to counter the blood guilt, together with this prayer: "'… absolve, O Lord, your people Israel, whom you redeemed; do not let the guilt of innocent blood remain in the midst of your people Israel.' … Then they will be absolved of bloodguilt. So you shall purge the guilt of innocent blood from your midst, because you must do what is right in the sight of the Lord."

The legislation for cities of refuge recognizes the power of the avenger of blood. They are safe spaces for those who have caused accidental death. Beyond the city the avenger is entitled to kill even those who caused death unintentionally. Not only in Numbers, but also in Deuteronomy and Joshua this legislation is present.

Read Dt 19.1–13 (go'el at vv. 6 & 12).

Read Josh 20.1–9 (the same account, but naming the cities).

The spilled blood/life of a person had an effect almost like gravity, demanding satisfactory blood poured on it. This brings us inescapably to Jesus' death and how it has been interpreted. In the eleventh century the Christian tradition in some way regressed to this point of view: Anselm's satisfaction theory effectively made God the victim for whom Jesus' blood had to be poured out. But see Hebrews 12.24, Jesus' blood "speaks a better word than the blood of Abel." This is because it is a nonviolent blood of forgiveness which God has raised up physically and historically, fulfilling the root goal of *go'el* which is to restore life! To understand this better we have to read further uses of the term.

Boaz as *go'el* to Ruth and Naomi; and Ruth as implied *go'el* in the story

It is useful to read the whole story to see how everything pivots on Ruth. She is a Moabite woman and so a foreigner, formerly married to an Israelite. Her mother-in-law, Naomi, journeyed to Moab, with her husband and two sons, one of whom married Ruth. In the course of time both Naomi's husband and her sons die, leaving her without support or protection. She returns to the homeland of Judah, and Ruth insists on staying with her when she could have by rights sought another husband in Moab. Thus Ruth exercises covenant loyalty to Naomi (*hesed*, 1.8) and sets up her role as redeemer. Ruth gathers food in the fields of a kinsman to Naomi, a man named Boaz. At 2.20 Naomi says he is the next-of-kin, *go'el*. When the harvest is in Ruth goes to the threshing floor and lies down next to Boaz. There then follows a passage dense with the theme of redemption: Boaz is again named as *go'el*; and if the term *go'el* is not used directly in respect of Ruth the description of her covenant loyalty mirrors it.

Read Ruth 3.9–13.

"He said, 'Who are you?' And she answered, 'I am Ruth, your servant; spread your cloak over your servant, for you are my next-of-kin (*go'el*).' He said, 'May you be blessed by the Lord, my daughter; this last instance of your loyalty is better than the first; you have not gone after young men, whether poor or rich. And now, my daughter, do not be afraid, I will do for you all that you ask, for all the assembly of my people know that you are a worthy woman. But now, though it is true that I am a near kinsman (*go'el*), there is another kinsman

(*go'el*) more closely related than I. Remain this night, and in the morning, if he will act as next-of-kin for you, good; let him do it. If he is not willing to act as next-of-kin for you, then, as the Lord lives, I will act as next-of-kin for you. Lie down until the morning.'"

Read Ruth 4.1–6.

Boaz connects Naomi's parcel of land, something that should be redeemed by next-of-kin, with Ruth whom he will take as wife. In this way he ensures that Naomi — through him and Ruth — will have a child for her dead husband's line who will inherit the property. For this reason the nearer next-of-kin forfeits his rights — not wishing to raise a child for another man's property: " … at this, the next-of-kin (*go'el*) said, 'I cannot redeem it for myself without damaging my own inheritance. Take my right of redemption yourself, for I cannot redeem it.'"

Read Ruth 4.14. "Then the women said to Naomi, 'Blessed be the Lord, who has not left you this day without next-of-kin (go'el)...'"

Read Ruth 4.11–12.

Ruth is connected in prestige with three matriarchs of Israel, Rachel, Leah, Tamar, the last of whom was also a foreigner and joined Israel in similar "disreputable" circumstances.

The whole story riffs on the existential demand that "the name of the dead may not be cut off from his kindred and from the gate of his native place" (4.10). The rules of the *go'el* go through the male figures but the effective agent of redemptive life is Ruth, carrying Naomi's hope from beginning to end. Thus the thought of redemption is widened here from buying back, or reciprocal killing, to one of faithfulness. Ruth's name is strikingly included in the Gospel of Matthew's genealogy of Jesus, along with Tamar, Rahab, Bathsheba, and Mary (Mt 1.1–16). Matthew signals another, feminine kind of redemption-of-life, one which does not operate through violence.

The Lord as *go'el*

Already in Exodus the function of the redeemer is assigned to the Lord.

Read Ex 6.6.

"Say therefore to the Israelites, 'I am the Lord, and I will free you from the burdens of the Egyptians and deliver you from your slavery to them. I will redeem you with an outstretched arm and with mighty acts of judgment.'"

However, it is in Second and Third Isaiah that the role of God as *go'el* receives the greatest emphasis. The Lord is called Redeemer ten times in chapters 40–66. Why? Second Isaiah is written at the end of the exile. In the exile the people of Israel have had their life stolen and destroyed. Land, city, temple, army and king have all been taken.

Humanly speaking their lifeblood is draining away. Second Isaiah calls them a "worm," an "insect" (41.14). But in the selfsame verse the Lord speaks precisely in the name of Redeemer. "I will help you, says the Lord; your Redeemer is the Holy One of Israel." Now, in such desperate circumstances, only God is able to act as kinsman. He alone can restore Israel in circumstances of near extinction, to bring back to life out of an experience of death. It is also of huge significance then that the restoration of life takes place without violence. There is a divine act of redemption that does not involve force, nature miracles, or armies. The victim is vindicated by means other than reciprocal violence, than retaliatory blood-letting. It is the relationship itself which then becomes the key.

Read Is 43.14. "Thus says the Lord, your Redeemer, the Holy One of Israel: For your sake I will send to Babylon and break down all the bars ..."

Read Is 44.24. "Thus says the Lord, your Redeemer, who formed you in the womb: I am the Lord, who made all things ..."

Read Is 49.7. "Thus says the Lord, the Redeemer of Israel and his Holy One, to one deeply despised, abhorred by the nations, the slave of rulers ..." (It is noteworthy this also comes in the context of the second of the Servant Songs.)

Read Is 59.20. "And he will come to Zion as Redeemer ..."

Finally *go'el* is presented in an exceptional way at Job 19.25: " ... for I know that my Redeemer lives, and that at the last he will stand upon the earth; and after my skin has been thus destroyed, then in my flesh I shall see God, whom

I shall see on my side …" The exact translation of some of this is questioned but the general sense of Job having a Redeemer (whether before God, or God himself) is not disputed. The supreme Old Testament example of the innocent victim claims for himself a go'el. Then, as we said before, at the end of the book Job himself becomes a type of redeemer, praying for the friends and saving them from "God's anger," in a similar pattern to the Servant.

How does all this work? It has to be because the truth of the nonviolent victim is established before God, and in the very same moment the victim becomes a source of forgiveness and is restored by God. There are only hints given us and they are muddled at best. But the Bible is striving toward a new meaning of redeemer and vindication. It is moving from the victim demanding vengeance through a reciprocal murder, to the victim bringing life through the truth of nonviolence and forgiveness. The Bible is, therefore, not simply about recognizing the victim. In the end it is about the nonviolence of the victim and the victim's restoration by divine means other than violence. In this way the character of God too is changed, from the use of violence, to one who vindicates nonviolence.

In the New Testament Jesus himself acts as redeemer in the Old Testament sense (all the healings are examples, but see especially the raising of the dead son of the widow of Nain in Lk 7.11–17). Then in his own life he dramatically fulfills the Biblical arc of the victim, in the cross and resurrection. He becomes a forgiving victim raised up physically and historically by the power of God. In this sense he becomes the definitive go'el. Through his resurrection and its vindication of nonviolence all are redeemed.

Notes:

Lesson Questions

· Do you think the classic Old Testament *go'el* (as avenger of blood) helped prevent an escalation of violence?

· Redemption has been understood by the church in terms of Jesus' blood offered to God for sin. In the scriptures the *go'el* has a wider function — restoring human life. How do you interpret Jesus' role as redeemer in light of this scriptural understanding of the *go'el*?

· In the story of Ruth, who is the *go'el*, Boaz or Ruth?

Personal Reflection

· Has anyone acted like a *go'el* in my life?

· Do I understand Jesus as my redeemer? What does that mean to me?

· Can God's character change when human beings attain new understandings about themselves? Does God change or do we change the way we see God?

Glossary

· *go'el* — denotes a person who is the nearest relative, next-of-kin, the one given the duty of restoring his or her kinsman's alienated rights to liberty or life.

· Avenger of Blood — one of the meanings of *go'el*, a kinsperson whose job is to execute the one who killed a family member.

· Cities of Refuge — designated cities (named in the Book of Joshua) where someone who has killed accidentally may flee and be protected from the automatic vengeance of the *go'el*.

· Redeemer — the English translation associated with the root *gaal*, a term applied to Christ but needing its full anthropological content in order to see its meaning.

Resources/Background Reading

· See ACLU report on debtors' prisons in the U.S., demonstrating the basic anthropology of debt in need of redemption: https://www.aclu.org/sites/default/files/field_document/InForAPenny_web.pdf

· *The Levirate and Goel Institutions in the Old Testament With Special Attention to the Book of Ruth*, Donald A. Leggett (1974): http://faculty.gordon.edu/hu/bi/ted_hildebrandt/OTeSources/08-Ruth/Texts/Books/Leggett-GoelRuth/Leggett-GoelRuth.pdf

Cultural References

· Movie, *Fried Green Tomatoes*, dir Jon Avnet (1991) — based on the book *Fried Green Tomatoes at the Whistle Stop Cafe* by Fannie Flagg. Has elements that are a retelling of the Book of Ruth.

· Songs by Bob Dylan, "Quinn the Eskimo," "I Shall Be Released:" https://www.youtube.com/watch?v=MjtPBjEz-BA

· Movie, *Saving Private Ryan*, dir. Steven Spielberg (1988)

· Movie, *Bringing Out The Dead*, dir. Martin Scorsese (1999)

VICTIM TO VINDICATION
Lesson 3: Jesus and Jonah

Learning Objectives

· To understand Jesus' use of the figure of Jonah as a crucial metaphor for the meaning of his death.

· To see that the "sign of Jonah" is a subversion of the generative violence which constructs human culture.

· To understand how Jesus used the story of Jonah, embracing Jonah's destiny but refusing Jonah's anger and violence, thus making the forgiving victim the source of transformation.

Core Biblical Texts

·Lk 11.29–32
· The Book of Jonah (Chapters 1-4)

Key Points

· The book of Jonah as a nonhistorical parable but with revelatory meaning.

· Jesus' choice of Jonah refers to the whole of the book and its various levels of meaning.

· Jesus chooses Jonah as a model but transcends him.

Key Words /Concepts

· Sign of Jonah
· *ra'ah*
· Something greater than Jonah

The Question of a Sign

The figure of Jonah in the Gospels allows us a good entry point to the mindset of Jesus regarding the victim. For Jesus the victim becomes the pathway to a whole new way of being human.

Gospel texts featuring the Son of Man and/or referencing the Servant from Isaiah provide a template for understanding Jesus' suffering and death. There is a huge amount of literature and discussion about these themes, and rightly so, because they provide a major framework in the New Testament. However, exactly because of their formal importance they may lack immediacy and remain abstract.

The figure of Jonah, on the other hand, has a roughness and rawness which perhaps brings us close to actual conversation and debate in first century Palestine. Jonah is a scandalous runaway prophet and very poor role-model by comparison with the Servant or Son of Man. It is at once striking that Jesus should choose him as his prophetic sign.

Read Lk 11.29.

"When the crowds were increasing, he began to say, 'This generation is an evil generation; it asks for a sign, but no sign will be given to it except the sign of Jonah.'"

The mere fact that the Gospel reports this statement tends to warrant its authenticity. Would anyone make up a story where Jesus' chosen prophet-sign is a scapegrace who not only runs away from God's command to preach, but then when he finally agrees, and the Ninevites repent, he is absolutely furious with God and his attitude of mercy? (We will look at these details shortly.)

In contrast, it might be argued that the sign of Jonah has only to do with the part of the story where Jonah is three days in the belly of the fish. And that the sign is put retrospectively in Jesus' mouth by the evangelists, because they see that bit of the story as a useful figure or type by which to understand Jesus' death and resurrection. Indeed this is exactly how Matthew seems to use the saying.

Read Mt 12.38–40.

"Then some of the scribes and Pharisees said to him, 'Teacher, we wish to see a sign from you.' But he answered them, 'An evil and adulterous generation asks for a sign, but no sign will be given to it except the sign of the prophet Jonah. For just as Jonah was three days and three nights in the belly of the sea monster, so for three days and three nights the Son of Man will be in the heart of the earth.'"

But Luke's version of the saying does not do this. It simply leaves the question of the sign — of what it might mean — hanging. Generally speaking in an instance where Luke and Matthew share the same saying scholars take Luke's version as more original. In this case it certainly makes sense. The context is a credible real-life challenge to Jesus to give a sign authenticating his ministry, and that is the issue.

Matthew puts in a helpful post-Easter explanation. (Incidentally Jesus was not in the tomb for three days and three nights, suggesting Matthew is forcing the interpretation somewhat.) However, if we stick with Luke's version we see Jesus is dealing with this urgent present-tense question: of the asking for a sign. His reply is that only an "evil generation" asks for a sign. In other words there is something fundamentally wrong with the people's asking for a sign. It is the wrong approach, involving an evil mind frame. In which case we must assume that if Jesus responds with "the sign of Jonah" he is volunteering an anti-sign. This is a sign that works against the dominant system of meaning by which people wish to be convinced. It is not about power and the violent evidence of power, but something else.

If "the sign of Jonah" is simply Matthew's pattern of Jesus-dead-in-the-earth-followed-by-resurrection it looks like a pretty straightforward case of "Here's something marvelous — be convinced by it!" It is not an anti-sign and it actually gives the crowds/scribes/Pharisees what they want (at least retrospectively).

No, "the sign of Jonah" refers to the whole Jonah story and it can only be understood by paying attention to that entire story. In doing that we see that "the sign of Jonah" refers to letting go of violence as the way to see God and his dealings with humanity. At the heart of the story is a declaration of the nonviolence of God, and the image of a victim of violence who is lifted up by God from the violence in which he has been submerged. It is this overturning of violence by God — Jonah delivered from the belly of the fish — that acts as the persuasive witness to the Ninevites, that moves them to give up their own violence.

In other words, it is not the simple "fact" of Jesus' death and resurrection which is the issue. It is the way in which Jesus' pathway through death abolishes the power of violence to shape our world and replaces it with another power altogether. The "sign of Jonah" is a semiotics of nonviolence. That is why it is an alternative sign to the one desired by the crowd. And that is what Jesus meant.

Story of Jonah

Read the Book of Jonah (chapters 1-4).

If we pay attention to the story and text of Jonah we can see how the whole thing revolves around

the problem of violence. We meet Jonah as he runs away from God rather than obey his command to preach against the wickedness of Nineveh. No reason is given, but later we find out why. When God changes his mind about destroying Nineveh because its citizens repented, Jonah bursts out in exasperation, "That is why I fled to Tarshish at the beginning; for I knew that you are a gracious God and merciful, slow to anger, and abounding in steadfast love, and ready to relent from punishing. And now, O Lord, please take my life from me, for it is better for me to die than to live" (Jon 4.2–3).

Despite this being a classic description of the character of Israel's God (Ex 34.6–7) Jonah wants no part of it; he does not want this mercy or nonviolence to apply to the Ninevites. (Note how the writer of Jonah leaves out the harsher language following at Ex 34.7b. The accent is purely on the Lord's mercy.)

Now, we have to understand that there is no chance that this is an actual historical intervention by God in the story of the Ninevites. By the time the story of Jonah was written, probably no earlier than 4th century BCE (http://www.jewishencyclopedia.com/articles/8751-jonah-book-of), the city of Nineveh was a very distant historical memory with no contemporary connection or relevance. It was purely a mental symbol of an oppressive foreign power hated by Israelites. Similarly

Jonah is purely a symbol of a national prophet (the one mention of an historical Jonah at 2 Kings 14.25 contains no reference to Nineveh; it simply shows Jonah to be a successful court prophet). In other words, the book of Jonah is fantasy literature, and intended to be recognized as such. The reason it is included among the prophets is because of the exceptional prophetic/teaching value of the story. (In this respect it is somewhat like the Book of Ruth, which has a parallel message to Jonah and is roughly contemporary. But Ruth instead is included in the Writings/Ketuvim.) There can be no doubt that Jesus recognizes and appropriates this teaching value.

Let's return to the story. As well as running from God Jonah displays a constant desire to die, suggesting a terminal case of passive aggression. He readily admits that he is the cause of the great storm and tells the pagan sailors to throw him in and that way the sea will quiet down (1.12). Jonah's state of mind mirrors the violence of the storm and he has no problem in seeing himself merged with it, making himself its bitter victim. The descriptive language used in the text backs up this identification. The storm is described as *ra'ah*, a Hebrew word meaning evil/calamity/destruction (1.8). A form of this word is used to describe Jonah's state of mind at 4.1 when he sees that God is not destroying Nineveh. The violence that surrounds Jonah like a storm is not mirrored in

God, and when he understands this he is more than ever consumed by destructive anger.

Jonah thus becomes a pattern of the resentful victim. He recognizes God's mercy and nonviolence but, because he has been infected by the violence of his enemies, he wants only violence from God. In contrast, the king of the Ninevites tells his citizens (including the animals!) to "turn from their evil ways (*ra'ah*) and from the violence (*hamas*) that is in their hands" (3.8). The violence which the prophet internalizes the Ninevites are told to get rid of! And when in fact they do, turning "from their evil ways (*ra'ah*)" (3.10), then "God changed his mind about the calamity (*ra'ah*) that he said he would bring upon them" (3.10). The Ninevites get a nonviolent God when they turn from their violence. This sounds a lot like the wisdom Jesus teaches in the Lord's prayer: "Forgive us our sins, for we ourselves forgive everyone indebted to us" (Lk 11.4). The only difference is that Jesus makes it explicitly a matter of forgiveness, not just letting go of violence. But in both cases we get the kind of God we give out.

If we think about the sea monster which swallowed Jonah we can see that such a beast is a further manifestation of violence. In Hebrew thought sea monsters are symbols of immense power and destructiveness. (See Job 41, a whole chapter devoted to the violence of Leviathan.) Jonah goes to the very symbolic belly of violence and yet God orders the great fish to spit Jonah out safe on the shore. The God of this book of prophecy will not allow violence to have the last word, including the angry prophet's identification with its mechanism. He transforms the mythical symbol of violence into a means of rescue or redemption.

So, when we read the story in these ways we can appreciate what Jesus meant by "the sign of Jonah." He meant the whole chain of meaning it presented regarding violence, something that would be apparent for anyone listening to it in Hebrew and being sensitive to its many spiritual ironies. Above all Jesus means his own identification with the Jonah pathway — not in terms of resentment but now fully owning the nonviolent meaning and promise of God which the book teaches.

Jesus' Remarks about Jonah

How do we know this? How do we know that Jesus identified with this meaning?

Jesus' relationship to Jonah does not depend simply on "the sign of Jonah" saying. This saying is in fact linked to a different saying, the verbal subject of which is the Ninevites, not Jonah.

Read Lk 11.31–32.

"The people of Nineveh will rise up at the judgment with this generation and condemn it, because they repented at the proclamation of Jonah, and see, something greater than Jonah is here."

This other saying is itself accompanied by a parallel statement about "the queen of the South" and Solomon (Lk 11.31). This further statement actually comes first, before the one about the Ninevites. But in front of the two statements Luke (or his tradition) puts in an explanatory verse referring forward to the Ninevites. "For just as Jonah became a sign to the people of Nineveh, so the Son of Man will be to this generation" (Lk. 11.30). The verse is obviously out of place in the sequence of themes — coming before the "queen of the South" verse. This awkward structure (along with the fact Matthew has a different but parallel explanatory comment, Mt.12.40) suggests that the evangelists glued together two different sayings related to Jonah: one about the sign, and one about significant Bible figures whom Jesus used to validate his ministry. Jesus chooses Solomon and Jonah as role models in the way they impacted their contemporaries. And then he gives the all-important conclusion, "But, see, something greater than Solomon/Jonah is here!" (Lk. 11.31–32).

Jesus is greater than Solomon in terms of Wisdom (which at Mt 11.11–19 is shown as to do with eating and drinking with sinners and renouncing violence). And he is greater than Jonah. Why? He has to be greater in some aspect which Jonah already foreshadows. Jonah is a victim of the abyss of violence: he ends up in the belly of the great fish. Jesus is adopting Jonah's situation in the belly of violence, but without Jonah's resentment. Jesus chooses to be a nonviolent victim, in imitation of the nonviolent God of Jonah, and in order that he might be vindicated with God's life-beyond-violence. In this way he revolutionizes the role of the victim, introducing a radical forgiveness and a completely different way of being human on earth. Jesus goes beyond the other victims we have studied, including Job. He does not simply reveal the innocence of the victim as a point of reference and truth. He lets go of all angry violence in relation to the victim, trusting in the new nonviolent life that will come from his Father.

Notes:

_____

_____

_____

_____

_____

_____

_____

_____

_____

_____

_____

_____

_____

_____

_____

_____

_____

_____

_____

_____

_____

_____

_____

_____

_____

_____

_____

_____

Lesson Questions

· Who is Jonah? Is he historical? Does it matter?

· Why does Jesus invoke this figure? Is it credible that he did so?

· If so what was his purpose?

· What does asking for a "sign" mean, and why does Jesus consider it "evil?"

Personal Reflection

· Jonah demonstrates passive aggression, adopting the role of victim and using it to justify and prolong his anger. Do I ever use the "victim card" in this way?

· In what ways do I understand that Jesus is greater than Jonah? What does this mean for me in terms of the world's violence? My own violence?

· In the world's crisis of violence (Nineveh?) can I see the signs of redemptive love, the signs of the forgiving victim in the world?

Glossary

· *ra'ah* — Hebrew for "destruction," "evil," "violence," "disaster."

· Sign — a manifestation of divine power. For a violent mindset this implicitly involves some form of violence. In Jesus' mind it is God's vindication of nonviolence by means other than violence.

Resources/Background Reading

· *Virtually Christian*, Anthony Bartlett (2011)

· *Racism, Politics and the Gospel*, Rev. Jim Wallis and Rev. Dr. William J. Barber II: https://www.youtube.com/watch?v=8nvi2U1ahU4

· *The Third Reconstruction: How a Moral Movement Is Overcoming the Politics of Division and Fear*, Rev. Dr. William J. Barber II and Jonathan Wilson-Hartgrove (2016)

Cultural References

· Movie, *Jonah: A VeggieTales Movie*, dir. Phil Vischer (2002)

· Movie, *Animated Pinocchio*, dir. Walt Disney (1940)

· *The Book of Jonas*, Stephen Dau (2012)

· Movie, *ParaNorman*, dir. Sam Fell, Chris Butler (2012)

The Temple and its Deconstruction

Lesson Plan

· **Lesson 1:** Temple Theology

· **Lesson 2:** Prophetic Critique of the Temple

· **Lesson 3:** Jesus and Temple Deconstruction

Learning Objectives

· To gain an understanding of the social and religious role of the Temple in ancient Israel, especially in the post-exilic period.

· To grasp the objections and underlying intuition of the many prophets who spoke against the Temple.

· To understand the meaning and consequences of Jesus' action in the Temple.

· To see how Jesus' death completes the deconstruction of the Temple through forgiveness.

Synopsis of the Story as a Whole

· "Temple" is a worldwide human institution which produces the holy through killing/sacrifice.

· The Jewish Temple was no different, except that it acted as a marker of identity for a covenant people.

· The prophets sensed the tension in this reality. Jesus drove the contradiction to its term.

Key Words/Concepts

· "My eyes and my heart will be there for all time" (the Temple as promise of everlasting presence)

· "My house shall be called a house of prayer for all the nations. But you have made it a den of robbers."

· "Something greater than the temple is here."

THE TEMPLE AND ITS DECONSTRUCTION
Lesson 1: Temple Theology

Learning Objectives

- To understand the crucial role of the Temple in post-exilic Israel.
- To see how the Temple developed from a simple religious function and extension of the king's power to a vital identity marker for the people.
- To see how the Book of Chronicles massages the story in 2 Samuel and 1 Kings so there will be no gap between David and the Temple.

Core Biblical Texts

- 2 Sam 7.1–13
- 2 Chr 7.15–16
- Ezek 43.1–7

Key Points

- The Temple grows immensely in importance in post-exilic Israel.
- In the absence of a king or army the Temple becomes repository for the national imagination.
- The prophecy of Ezekiel constructs a purified "virtual" Temple, as an ideal of holiness for the land.
- We keep in mind the Girardian anthropology of sacrifice presented in Method, lesson 3.

Key Words /Concepts

- Temple Theology
- Temple Holiness
- Tabernacle

We earlier looked at the story of the Land and its Loss, now we are looking at the Temple. We remember how the topics of these two stories have a crucial role in the overall "Seven Stories" scheme. Without the stabilizing, conserving function of these institutions (of land and Temple) the experience of the people could not have had the longevity needed to fully develop the other, subversive stories. Forgiveness and compassion, for example, are so fragile — non-foundational and directly relational — in comparison to violence, that it needs a sustained journey to develop them into strong self-standing stories and teachings. Thus the land and the Temple act as "shells," robust containers in which to grow the precious pearl of a more intangible vision. They endure over time, building and maintaining the people's identity. Within their boundaries, however, little by little something new is emerging, something that will burst through the boundaries entirely.

Temple

The Bible has given us two different accounts of the founding of the Jerusalem Temple, one in the First Book of Kings and the other in the Book of Chronicles. Why should a single compendium of reported events (the Bible) contain two different accounts of something as important as the Temple (and, following that, the history of the kings)? Because ... the Bible is all about interpretation, about value and meaning, and Temple is a classic example of disputed value and meaning. (To underline this see especially the next lesson, the critical viewpoint of the prophets.)

Read 2 Sam 7.1–13.

We remember that in 2 Samuel David desired to build a temple for the ark. But the Lord replied to him through the prophet, Nathan: "Are you the one to build me a house to live in? I have not lived in a house since the day I brought up the people of Israel from Egypt to this day, but I have been moving about in a tent and a tabernacle" (2 Sam 7.5–6).

Then God says, "When your days are fulfilled and you lie down with your ancestors, I will raise up your offspring after you ... He shall build a house for my name ... " (2 Sam. 7.12–13).

This leaves a critical gap, a space in which a suspicion about the Temple might linger. The Lord recalls the youthful experience of Israel when he accompanied them in their wanderings and "lived rough" like they did. It suggests a special value to this kind of relationship. David as king is associated with this ideal time, one of insecurity, trust, and immediacy. Instead, it is his son, Solomon, who will establish the imperial focus of a temple, along with heavy taxation and forced labor needed to build it (1 Kings 5.13, 10.14, 9.15ff). The Temple will represent glory, stability and national power.

In contrast to the more ambivalent approach of 2 Samuel and 1 Kings the Book of Chronicles goes to great lengths to establish the full continuity and symbolic identity between David and the Temple, without nuance. It shows how David conceived, designed and organized the temple.

Read 1 Chr 21.28 — 22.6.

"Then David said, 'Here shall be the house of the Lord God and here the altar of burnt offering for Israel.' ... Then he called for his son Solomon and charged him to build a house for the Lord, the God of Israel."

Read 1 Chr 22.14.

"With great pains I have provided for the house of the Lord one hundred thousand talents of gold, one million talents of silver, and bronze and iron beyond weighing, for there is so much of it; timber and stone too I have provided. To these you must add more."

Read 1 Chr 23.2–32.

(David assembles Levites for service in the Temple, musicians, officers, cleaners etc..

Read 1 Chr 28.11–13.

"Then David gave his son Solomon the plan of the vestibule of the Temple, and of its houses, its treasuries, its upper rooms, and its inner chambers, and of the room for the mercy seat; and the plan of all that he had in mind: for the courts of the house of the Lord, all the surrounding chambers, the treasuries of the house of God, and the treasuries for dedicated gifts; for the divisions of the priests and of the Levites, and all the work of the service in the house of the Lord, for all the vessels in the service of the house of the Lord .... "

David is the planner, the financier, the architect and organizer of the Temple, responsible for its location, materials, staffing, and economic support. Solomon is simply his delegate. The Temple becomes a monument to David, a shrine to his memory as Israel's ideal king, favored of God.

First Chronicles also makes David the center of the extensive genealogy running through the first nine chapters. There then follows the personal story of David continuing to the end of the first book. Second Chronicles then picks up with Solomon's actual building of the Temple. It is almost as if the story of David and his founding of the Temple become the single story of Israel's history before and after the exile.

The context of Chronicles is the return from exile. The Book of Chronicles was written in this period, also known as the Persian period. (This is illustrated by internal evidence within the text, for example 1 Chr 29.1 & 19 where a Persian loanword for temple is used, which actually means "citadel" or "fortress." Also at the end of the book, 2 Chr 36.23, where "Cyrus the Persian" is mentioned.)

The situation of exile and loss of national sovereignty under a foreign power makes the Temple the last functioning symbol of Israel's independence and national identity including its ideal king, David. The people may be under the control of a foreign ruler and army but in the Temple they celebrate an idealized history, they serve their God alone and this God is the guarantor of their eventual freedom. There is a merging of national identity and Temple holiness.

Read 2 Chr 6.37–39.

God is asked by Solomon to hear the people's prayer directed toward the Temple even from the land of exile. "If they sin against you ... and you are angry with them ... then if they ... repent and plead with you in the land of their captivity ... and pray toward ... the house that I have built for your name ... then hear from heaven your dwelling place their prayer ...."

Read 2 Chr 7.15–16.

God then promises. "Now my eyes will be open and my ears attentive to the prayer that is made in this place. For now I have chosen and consecrated this house so that my name may be there forever; my eyes and my heart will be there for all time."

Chronicles is a reconstructive response to the trauma of exile, very much in sympathy with the worldview of Nehemiah and Ezra. Like these other books, Chronicles is filled with names of the authentic Israelite lineages, giving the pedigree of those who return. It is a document which legitimizes the group of those who return and the Temple is the engine of these people's identity and legitimacy. It is the institutional identity marker of post-exilic Judaism.

Compare 2 Kings 25, a factual account of destruction of Judea and its leadership, with 2 Chr 36.15–23, a very different (non-Deuteronomic) ending. Chronicles ends with the return and rebuilding of the Temple, providing a continuity between David's Temple and the post-exilic Second Temple. Now it is Cyrus of Persia who will "build [God] a house at Jerusalem."

Temple Holiness

The symbolic importance of the Temple necessarily revolves around its actual sacrificial function. The Book of Leviticus gives detailed legislation for this practice, without ever describing why sacrifice is religiously necessary. This course book began with the Girardian understanding of sacrifice — as a repetition of a founding murder. A couple of passages in the Bible give us some sense of the terror and violence at the heart of sacrifice.

Read Gen 15.12–20.

This is not strictly a sacrifice, rather a covenant ceremony — the slaughtered animals are an anticipatory curse self-inflicted by God should he not maintain his covenant. But the ceremony in its own context uses the original terror of sacrifice to sanction against any possible breaking of the deal. It thus displays the underlying power of the holy, its source in brutal violence against the victim, something that creates the man-made sacred. Holiness in this sense implies the "presence of God," a fearful power on my side and against my enemies. Once it is unleashed it is very easy to kill in its name. War is an explosion of the "holy" in this primitive sense.

Read Ezek 9.1 — 10.22.

Ezekiel is the prophet of divine and Temple holiness expressed in disturbing, violent imagery. Chapter 9 describes the annihilation of the citizens of Jerusalem by divine command, parallel to the departure of the divine glory from the city. The slaughter of Jerusalem's inhabitants (barring those bearing a privileging mark) reflects the actual slaughter of the invading Babylonians. But here it is divine agents who are carrying it out. The passage indicates the deep ambivalence of the holy: on the one hand it seeks peace (9.9), on the other it unleashes wrath and destruction. The chariot of God's glory is a visual depiction of this double valence.

Ezekiel then looks forward to an ideal reconstructed Temple. This is part of the background of Jesus' time and the worldview of those around him.

Read Ezek chapter 40 — 43.

The temple is described in detail

and the divine glory returns at 43.1– 7. "... this is the place of my throne and the place for the soles of my feet, where I will reside among the people of Israel forever ...."

Read Ezek 48.

A picture of an idealized spatial Israel, with a holy area for the Temple and then twelve equal strips of land for the tribes stretching to the north and south. This is never intended as actual. It is a symbol of Israel reconstituted around the Temple and its holiness.

Lesson Questions

- Why do you think the Temple became so important in terms of Israelite self-identity after the exile?
- Why was there ambiguity about the initial building of the Temple with David?
- Why does Chronicles go to such length to smooth over this ambiguity?
- Why do you think Ezekiel had an idealized vision of the Temple? What is its relationship to Israel?
- How do you understand Temple holiness? How does this affect how God is perceived?

Personal Reflection

- How do I understand "holiness?"
- How important is "holiness" to me? Why?
- Do I associate certain physical spaces/places with "holiness?"
- How important have temples been through culture and history?
- What are our modern temples/sacred spaces?
- Is there another kind of the "sacred," which does not require violence or exclusion?

Glossary

- Ark of the Covenant — a box containing the stone tablets with the ten commandments and acting as a sacred force in the vanguard of the people. Later it was kept in Solomon's Temple.
- Tabernacle — an elaborate transportable tent acting as a sanctuary during the wilderness wanderings and housing the Ark (perhaps non-historical).
- Levite — a member of the tribe of Levi which was set apart for sacred duties in the land, eventually exclusively in the Temple.
- Temple Theology — an understanding of the Temple, chosen by God as his house, (strictly speaking a place where his name would dwell), a space where he may be encountered by his people.
- Temple Holiness — a sense of purity and proximity to God constructed by means of animal sacrifice. In the case of the Jerusalem Temple this was overlaid with the national and spiritual history of Israel.

Resources/Background Reading

- *Mysterium Tremendum et Fascinans*, Rudolph Otto (1958)

Cultural References

- *Till We Have Faces, A Myth Retold*, C.S. Lewis (1956) — for descriptions of the terror and power of the sacrificial holy.

THE TEMPLE AND ITS DECONSTRUCTION
Lesson 2: Prophetic Critique of the Temple

Learning Objectives

· To understand the intimate connection between kings and temples, twin pillars of power.

· To recap the Girardian understanding of sacrifice as the repetition of original violence and its benefits — primary organization of group, including boundaries and hierarchy.

· To see how the prophetic critique of temple ritual runs in parallel to Girard and intuits its essential violence.

Core Biblical Texts

· Am 5.21–25
· Jer 7.1–15
· Is 66.1–3

Key Points

· Temple religion is the product of sacrifice, where the killing of an animal awakens the original experience of the sacred/the god.

· The Biblical record contains a fierce critique of the violence in Temple religion, one often overlooked or downplayed.

· Israel as a religious community inevitably developed sacrificial practice. It was as "natural" to Israelites as to the rest of humanity. At the same time a profound tension begins to develop when sacrifice is institutionalized in association with royal power and its claimants. The prophets are the great witnesses to this tension.

Key Words /Concepts

· Scapegoat
· Sacrifice
· *Parisim*

The prophets rail against the Temple, and understandably so. Temples and sacrifice are embedded in every human culture and their religious function is indifferent to social justice or the lack of it. Kings, tyrants, women, men, reformers, and oppressors may all use the authority of a temple without any critical commentary from the temple. On the contrary, the temple will always act as endorsement to a ruling power. The instances where a priest conspires against a king (e.g. 1 Sam 22.11–19, Ahimelech against Saul, or 1 Kings 1.7, Abiathar against David) are the exception that proves the rule: you have to have temple on your side if you're going to rule.

Read Judg 6.11–27.

The story takes us back to the earliest days of Israel. We see Gideon is called as "judge" — a charismatic leader emerging spontaneously from the people. His first act is to build an altar and sacrifice to the Lord. Later he defeats the Midianites and then, despite the fact that he had refused the people's offer to make him king, he creates an "ephod" (Judg 8.22–27). This is a symbolic piece of temple apparatus which focuses sacred power on the wearer. The High Priest in the later Temple had one as part of his vestments. Yet we read here "all Israel prostituted [submitted] themselves to it …" (Judg 8.27), meaning Gideon effectively finds a back-door to personal authority through the sacred power of the ephod. Gideon is a good example of the unity of kingly and sacred power.

Read 1 Kings 8.14–66.

Solomon fully demonstrates this unity. He is the builder and first priest in the Temple, offering prayer and sacrifice.

Read also 1 Kings 12.25–33.

This passage illustrates the necessary alliance of Temple and king: Jeroboam rebels against Solomon's successor, Rehoboam, and at once feels the need to set up ritual centers or temples under his control.

Brief Recap of Girardian theory

Primitive humanity emerged in the context of the killing of a scapegoat who was blamed for the ills of the group, and then suddenly became the source of the group's newfound peace and prosperity through discharge of group violence. These sacrificial benefits were enormous and they were constantly in demand. New crises of mimetic desire and rivalry constantly afflicted the group: some produced externally — through things like food shortage, drought, plague; others internally, through competition for status, women, food etc. Every time a crisis boiled over there would be a new victim — providing the only way to resolve things at this primitive level and go forward as a group. Along the way it is possible many groups succumbed to chaotic violence and did not find the surrogate victim. In other cases the group spontaneously discovered that killing an animal would have many of the benefits of the human victim and was of course much less dangerous to the group. The killing was mimetically linked to the sacred character of earlier human victims.

Because these first victims produced such enormous effects experienced as transcendence (the feeling of a force greater than the known world) the victim was sensed as a divine being — a god. Killing the animal could easily be felt as part of the same primitive violence involved with the first victim, and so experienced as a repetition of the transcendent feelings associated with it. The animal is thus a sacer-facere, a "making (of the) sacred" alongside and reawakening the first act of killing. The animal is an "offering" to the god — the violence of the later killing is experienced as "offered up," and so united, to the violence of the first. Of course, none of this is apparent to the temple worshipper, caught up in the function of the sacred, and of the myths (stories of the gods) that overlay and obscure it.

Here is the origin of temples and their sacrifices. A regular practice of sacrifice obviously serves to maintain the social order, working to keep everybody and everything in their place and role. In the Biblical material there are various forms of sacrifice, indicating a very developed religious system. All the developments (including, for example, where the priest or offerer share in the meat of the animal) are possible and intelligible from this first origin and basis.

The Prophets

Many of these exceptional individuals show a deep sense that somehow this "sacrifice" is not essential to Israel, and does not even fit with it. They stand against the self-reinforcing system of state and its temple which is blind to justice.

Read Am 5.21–25.

"I hate, I despise your festivals, and I take no delight in your solemn assemblies. Even though you offer me your burnt offerings and grain offerings, I will not accept them; and the offerings of well-being of your fatted animals I will not look upon. Take away from me the noise of your songs; I will not listen to the melody of your harps. But let justice roll down like waters, and righteousness like an ever-flowing stream. Did you bring to me sacrifices and offerings the forty years in the wilderness, O house of Israel?"

Amos sees how Temple religion diverts concern from the covenant and its injunctions against oppression and injustice. He implies sacrifice was not part of the original founding experience in the desert.

Read Hos 6.6–9.

"For I desire steadfast love and not sacrifice, the knowledge of God rather than burnt offerings. But at Adam they transgressed the covenant; there they dealt faithlessly with me. Gilead is a city of evildoers, tracked with blood. As robbers lie in wait for someone, so the priests are banded together; they murder on the road to Shechem, they commit a monstrous crime."

This passage is twice quoted by Jesus in the Gospel of Matthew, at 9.13 and 12.7. It directly relates priestly activity to murder.

Read Is 1.12–17.

"When you come to appear before me, who asked this from your hand? Trample my courts no more; bringing offerings is futile; incense is an abomination to me. New moon and sabbath and calling of convocation — I cannot endure solemn assemblies with iniquity. Your new moons and your appointed festivals my soul hates; they have become a burden to me, I am weary of bearing them. When you stretch out your hands, I will hide my eyes from you; even though you make many prayers, I will not listen; your hands are full of blood. Wash yourselves; make yourselves clean; remove the evil of your doings from before my eyes; cease to do evil, learn to do good; seek justice, rescue the oppressed, defend the orphan, plead for the widow."

It is noteworthy how sensitive the prophets are to the question of actual violence on the part of those who partake in temple worship. The latter appears as a cover for the former. Note also that the psalms echo parallel sentiments from the point of view of the individual at prayer (see Pss 40.6-8 and 51.15–17).

Perhaps Jeremiah is most explicit.

Read Jer 7.1–15 .

The pivotal line at v. 11 is quoted by Jesus in all three synoptic gospels during his action in the Temple: "Has this house, which is called by my name, become a den of robbers in your sight?" The word for "robbers" here is *parisim,* whose root form in Strong's Concordance is *parats*, the violent one, the destroyer, the violent (cf. Ps 17.4 where the word is translated as "the violent"). Jesus would have understood it in its full violent sense, not softened as "robbers." (Although, the modern legal definition of robbery is in fact theft with violence.) In other words: "My house shall be called a house of prayer; but you are making it a den of violent men" (Mt 21.13).

Violence and injustice are naturally at home with the the violence and injustice of sacrifice and Jesus says this in so many words.

In a stunning finale to the prophetic critique of temple sacrifice Third Isaiah simply identifies sacrifice with brutal violence, depicted in several of its "unholy" forms. The force of this passage should not be minimized, either in translation or interpretation.

Read Is 66.1–3.

"... what is the house that you would build for me, and what is my resting place? ... Whoever slaughters an ox is (like) one who kills a human being; whoever sacrifices a lamb (like) one who breaks a dog's neck ..." (In the Hebrew there is no word "like," instead it is simple identification.)

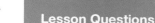

Lesson Questions

· We have argued that sacrifice is at the root of all human culture. What role do you think sacrifice (as a means of bringing order and the experience of transcendence) continues to have in the world today? In the church?

· Who are the sacrificial victims/scapegoats today? Where do we dump our group violence?

· Why would the prophets have a problem with sacrifice?

· What do you think of Isaiah equating sacrifice with murder? Is it the same?

· The discharge of violence from the killing of the victim is experienced as transcendent power/peace. Girard argues this was the birth of "the god." The Bible reveals a different God beginning with the Exodus. Why is it important that the Bible reveals both expressions of the divine, sacrificial and relational? Can they be reconciled?

· How is violence in entertainment part of the sacrificial system?

· Can we see the sacrificial role of lynching in the U.S.?

Personal Reflection

· When in your life (at work, at home, in your social groups) have you experienced situations when the group has discharged their violence/stress onto an individual? How did you feel?

· When have you experienced or witnessed violence as a way of discharging tension?

· Have there been times when you felt led to speak out against scapegoating? Why was this?

· Have you experienced the power of the crowd? Why does this feel so dangerous?

Glossary

· Sacrifice — the act of killing or destruction that evokes the original violence against a surrogate victim and renews its benefits.

· Temple — a sacred space created and defined by formal use of sacrifice.

· *parisim* — the violent men, in Jeremiah and Jesus' denunciation, who make the Temple their headquarters.

Resources/Background Reading

· *Violence and the Sacred,* René Girard (1979)

· *The Bible, Violence and the Sacred,* James Williams (1991)

· *Strength to Love*, Martin Luther King Jr. (1994)

· *The Cross and the Lynching Tree*, James H. Cone (2013)

· *The New Jim Crow: Mass Incarceration in the Age of Colorblindness*, Michelle Alexander and Cornel West (2012)

Cultural References

· Movie, *To Kill a Mockingbird,* dir. Robert Mulligan (1962)

· Movie, *Apocalypse Now,* dir. Francis Coppola (1979)

· *The Lord of the Flies,* William Golding (1954)

· Movie, *12 Years a Slave*, dir. Steve Mcqueen (2013)

THE TEMPLE AND ITS DECONSTRUCTION
Lesson 3: Jesus and Temple Deconstruction

Learning Objectives

· To gain a clear view of Jesus' revolutionary prophetic action in the Temple.

· To understand the cumulative significance of overturning the moneychangers tables, driving out the animals, and stopping through-traffic in the Temple.

· To see how Jesus abolishes the Temple by replacing it with person-to-person forgiveness made transcendent through his own nonviolent death and resurrection.

Core Biblical Texts

· Jn 2.13–17
· Mk 11.12–25

Key Points

· Jesus' action in the Temple is not a "cleansing" but an abolition.

· The action is given its full effect as deconstruction (i.e. undoing Temple meaning) through Jesus' death and resurrection as transcendent event of forgiveness.

Key Words /Concepts

· Deconstruction
· Tyrian coin
· Temple "vessel"
· Temple Mount
· Enacted Parable

Jesus has a revolutionary relationship with the Temple. In his time the community behind the Dead Sea scrolls looked toward a completely new Temple, one characterized by an intense purity (see the "Temple Scroll," https://en.wikipedia.org/wiki/Temple_Scroll). It is very possible that the group living at Qumran on the Dead Sea (near where the scrolls were discovered) embraced this view, practising a complete separation from the Jerusalem Temple. John the Baptist carried out his ministry "in the wilderness" and offered a religious renewal pointedly separate from the Temple. In other words the corruption and failure of the Jerusalem Temple was a live issue in Jesus' time. However, Jesus did not practice separation. Rather, he "set his face" toward Jerusalem (Luke 9.51) looking toward a showdown with the institution of the Temple, one which would render its existence — and that of any comparable sacrificial institution — obsolete.

It is the final actions of Jesus' life in relation to the Temple which unleash the fatal judgments against him and at the same time deliver Jesus' radical critique and temple-shattering alternative. There was something very definitive about what Jesus did in relation to the Temple. He dramatically undermined the authority of the priests and showed himself a claimant to Messianic authority. It was impossible that he would be left to carry on his ministry once he did these things.

In which case the Gospel of John's depiction of those actions taking place at the beginning of Jesus' ministry, in John chapter two, cannot be historical. (His ministry would have been all over before it began!) Instead, just as the prologue ("In the beginning was the Word") already shows Jesus to be with God "from the beginning," so his action in the Temple shows him, right at the start of his work, to be the undoing and replacement of the Temple. What Jesus did in the Temple was so absolutely significant John makes it the first public thing he does.

Read Jn 2.13–17.

"The Passover of the Jews was near, and Jesus went up to Jerusalem. In the temple he found people selling cattle, sheep and doves, and the money changers seated at their tables. Making a whip of cords, he drove all of them out of the temple, both the sheep and the cattle. He also poured out the coins of the money changers and overturned their tables. He told those who were selling the doves, 'Take these things out of here! Stop making my Father's house a marketplace!' His disciples remembered that it was written, 'Zeal for your house will consume me.'"

Overturning the Tables of the Money Changers

John's description highlights both the expulsion of the animals and the money changers. What is going on? In both cases Jesus is bringing the actual operation of the Temple to a halt. Jesus is not simply "clearing" the Temple, or "cleansing" it, he is rendering sacrifice impossible. If there are no animals, there are no sacrifices. If there is no money to buy the animals, again no sacrifice.

Tyrian coin was used in the Temple for the purchase of sacrificial animals: the Jewish shekel had to be exchanged for it. Unlike the Jewish coinage, which was not a major currency, the Tyrian currency was financially valuable (rather like "the dollar"). Exchange was therefore a profitable, money-making enterprise. Previous interpretations have always put the emphasis on the moneychangers, focusing on greed and exploitation in a sacred space. This is certainly true ("... do not make my Father's house a marketplace!"). However, it masks the deeper focus. Jesus' action is directed at abolishing the sacrificial mechanism entirely.

Jesus Interrupts the Sacrificial Process

Read Mk 11.15–17.

"Then they came to Jerusalem. And he entered the temple and began to drive out those who were selling and those who were buying in the temple, and he overturned the tables of the money changers and the seats of those who sold doves; and he would not allow anyone to carry anything through the temple. He was teaching and saying, 'Is it not written, "My house shall be called a house of prayer for all the nations?" But you have made it a den of robbers.'" (Note: the Greek for "robbers" is *lestes*, a term implying violence.)

See Mk 11.16. "And he would not allow anyone to carry anything through the temple."

This simple statement — which on the surface can be interpreted again as a "cleansing" of impure "stuff" from the Temple — carries a much more revolutionary meaning. The word translated "anything" is skeuos which means "vessel." It actually has a technical meaning in the context of Temple. See, for example, the LXX for 1 Kings 7.45–51 where the form, skeue, is used repeatedly for the sacred vessels and implements provided by David and Solomon for the Temple. The passage at 1 Chr 28.13, quoted in the previous lesson, uses the same Hebrew word that stands behind the Greek of the Kings verses. Jesus stops the transport of temple implements and vessels, which carry the fuel or cinders of the altar fire, or sacrificial meat to be consumed by a worshipper, through the area. This goes along with driving the animals out. If you can't keep the machinery working there can be no sacrifice.

Prophetic Witness

Jesus' clearing of the temple was a symbolic act not a random fit of anger. People sometimes refer to Jesus use of a whip as his "getting angry" or "using violence." They are missing the point entirely. What Jesus is doing is producing a forceful enacted parable changing the meaning and reference of a situation. (Compare, for example, Jeremiah at Jer 19.1–13, smashing the clay pot in front of the people, as an image of the destruction of the city.)

As anyone who has dealt with animals knows, there is nothing like the crack of a whip to get them moving. Thus Jesus creates a stampede of animals and people, signifying a powerful, definitive break. Jesus is not simply quoting Jeremiah 7.11, "Is it not written 'My house shall be called a house of prayer for all the nations? But you have made it a den of robbers [or violent men],'" he is bringing this situation to an end. It is because the authorities recognized the revolutionary implication of his action that at this very point they decide to put him to death. See Mk 11.18 where the people are "spellbound" by this "teaching" and the chief priests look for a way to kill him. They fear they are about to lose control over the crowd, which is their reason for existence. Because their Temple understanding is that humans only work in and through sacrificial violence, once they are gone they can conceive of no other result than a huge crisis of violence. "If we let him go on like this, everyone will believe in him, and the Romans will come and destroy both our holy place and our nation" (Jn 11.48).

The Cursing of the Fig Tree

Something else that proves Jesus' intention to bring the Temple to an end is the cursing of the fig tree recorded in Mark. The episode at Mk 11.12–14 and 20–21 comes on either side of Jesus' action in the Temple and clearly frames and interprets the Temple event. Jesus seeks out a fig tree for fruit to eat and finding none he curses the tree. The next day, directly following the enacted closing down of the Temple, Peter remarks on the tree, confirming that it has indeed withered. Again this could be interpreted as a violent act on Jesus' part if it were not recognized as another action parable, complementary to the one in the Temple. Jesus has come to the Temple seeking fruit of mercy, and finding none he physically demonstrates its end. It is a powerful sign of an irreversible break.

If we continue in the Markan passage we see how the prophetic critique is extended.

Read Mk 11.20–25.

The context is that Jesus and the disciples are making the trip from the Mount of Olives, where they have spent the night, back to Jerusalem and the Temple. (The custom of doing this during that time is described in a parenthetical remark by Luke, at Lk 21.37–38.) This means that as Jesus is speaking he is facing directly toward the Temple Mount. He really can have no other mountain in mind to be delivered to the abyss of non-existence other than the one right in front of him. In which case, he is talking about his own faithful project of abolishing the Temple and its citadel of violence! The fact that he then turns directly to the theme of forgiveness reinforces the interpretation. What renders the Temple redundant is forgiveness: if we humans forgive, i.e. respond nonviolently, then necessarily there will be no need for Temple and we will be one with the forgiveness/nonviolence of the Father. Forgiveness deconstructs and replaces sacrifice.

John 10 Reinforces the Critique of the Temple

Read Jn 10.1–42.

The passage known as "the Good Shepherd" (it could be also translated as "the True Shepherd") can be taken in a sentimental fashion as Jesus caring for the helplessness of sheep. But we remember that the previous mention of sheep was Jesus driving them out of the Temple at 2.15. The very same verb (to drive, ekbale) is used at 10.4 (here it is usually translated as "brought," losing the connection to the sacrificial animals). We then hear that all who came before the true shepherd are "thieves and bandits" (the violent, *lestes*, as in Mark 11.17). And then, "The thief comes only to steal and kill and destroy." This makes clear the question of violence, but the word "kill" is *thuo* whose proper meaning is "to kill as a sacrifice and offer on an altar." Thus those who come before the True Shepherd are Temple sacrificers, coming to "steal, sacrifice and destroy!" The True Shepherd leads the sheep out of the Temple to where they will find pasture. He does this by laying down his life nonviolently, disabling the violent mechanism of the sacrificial system.

Jesus Replaces the Temple

Read Mt 12.6–8.

"I tell you, something greater than the temple is here. But if you had known what this means, 'I desire mercy and not sacrifice,' you would not have condemned the guiltless. For the Son of Man is lord of the sabbath."

Jesus claims status greater than the Temple while citing Hosea's critique of sacrifice. How is Jesus greater than the Temple? Everything that Jesus said and did in relation to the Temple takes on its final meaning in his death. Jesus

could not drive the sheep out of the Temple unless he had something to lead them to. They would simply be rounded up and brought back in. (As in fact has happened in history many times.) By his death Jesus gives a world-shifting transcendent example of forgiveness, and it is this which establishes the anthropology of forgiveness in the world and completely deconstructs the Temple. The Lord's supper, or the eucharist, is the perennial symbol of this world-shifting event.

The Eucharist Displaces Sacrifice

The Temple was clean and pure space. Outside the Temple and the city gate everything is progressively unclean. Jesus is crucified at the place of the skull and his body cleared away so as not to desecrate the Sabbath. Before his death Jesus tells his followers to celebrate the meal of bread and wine as a sign of the absolute reversal he brings to this situation, and thus the new way of being human. The eucharist can occur anywhere — outside the Temple and its precincts. It is boundary breaking, no longer needing a sacred space. Instead it works to transform the ordinary and unclean into a space where God gives himself in love. The whole earth is transformed. There is no more clean and unclean; nowhere where God is not.

Jesus replaces the ritual of the sacrifice with this symbol of his life and death. He replaces the sacrificed animal with bread and wine, as a constantly-to-be-enacted parable of his nonviolent self-giving death. Nothing is hidden here. There is no secret agenda of discharging the group's violence, or, even more terribly, a theory of God's violence. What is disclosed is pure and simple nonviolence and forgiveness. The eucharist is the supreme semiotic shift — or rather it is a semiotic event rolling all the previous shifts into one.

It is a light so bright it can certainly dazzle, being translated back into sacrifice by church tradition in order that we all can see it with our old human eyes. But looking on it with the "single" eye of mercy and love we catch a glimpse of the transformative power of the cross and resurrection, changing the old world of death into the new creation of peace and life.

Notes:

_____
_____
_____
_____
_____
_____
_____
_____
_____
_____
_____
_____
_____
_____
_____
_____
_____
_____
_____
_____
_____
_____
_____
_____
_____

Lesson Questions

- The church has traditionally taught that Jesus "cleansed" rather than abolished the Temple. How does this change the significance of his actions? Why would this be the preferred explanation?

- How does Jesus draw from the prophetic tradition?

- In what way is what he said and did so radically new?

- According to Girard, sacrifice fulfils a deep human need by providing a mechanism for the discharge of violence. How does the eucharist (and what it symbolises) offer an alternative to sacrifice?

- To what degree have the churches re-sacralized the eucharist? Re-created temples?

Personal Reflection

- Jesus replaces the Temple and all the needs that a temple fulfills. We have previously been taught that the temple is the place where we meet God. Rather, the sacrificial system is a human-constructed mechanism that helps us discharge our violence which we then experience as "divine." Jesus asks us to surrender this fundamental human dependence on temple and sacrifice. How does that make me feel? Is this unsettling? Liberating?

- How much of our human culture is still caught up in the sacrificial system?

- How does Jesus teach us to deal with our violence?

- Can I think of times when I have seen Jesus' way in action?

- How often, and in what different ways, is Jesus' life threatened by "sacrificial" violence? And how are the lives of those to whom he ministers sometimes similarly threatened?

Glossary

- *skeuos* — means "vessel" and in the Temple context this means part of the sacrificial apparatus.

- Robber — legally someone who steals with violence.

- Deconstruction — a mode of thought or action exposing the function of violence in a given structure of meaning, so overturning or abolishing its effect. Deconstruction of texts was the primary usage of the term.

Resources/Background Reading

- https://en.wikipedia.org/wiki/Temple_Scroll

Cultural References

- Movie, *The Sacrifice*, dir. Andrei Tarkovsky (1986)

- Movie, *Come and See*, dir. Elem Klimov (1985)

- Movie, *Magnolia*, dir. Paul Thomas Anderson (1999)

194

History to its End

Lesson Plan

- Lesson 1: Wisdom
- Lesson 2: Son of Man
- Lesson 3: New Paradigm

Learning Objectives

- To gain a sense of the late Biblical mutations: of Wisdom into Daniel's apocalyptic, of the Kingdom of God into the suffering Son of Man, of the cross into resurrection.
- To confirm awareness of the New Paradigm: that Christianity is the revelation of nonviolence, divine and human.

Synopsis of the Story as a Whole

- The ancient thought-form and genre of Wisdom does a quantum leap in 2nd century BCE into Daniel's apocalyptic: the in-breaking of divine nonviolence.
- Jesus deeply embraces this shift, exemplifying and realizing it in his cross and resurrection.

Key Words/Concepts

- Wisdom in crisis
- Books of Maccabees as background to Book of Daniel
- Nonviolent apocalyptic
- Resurrection as new transcendence — of the nonviolence of the cross

HISTORY TO ITS END
Lesson 1: Wisdom

Learning Objectives

· To understand Wisdom as a Biblical mind-set and genre of literature seeking the best outcomes for human life.

· To see the development of Wisdom thought around the figure of Woman Wisdom.

· To recognize the crisis in Wisdom thinking represented in the books of Job and Ecclesiastes.

· To understand how Jesus identifies with Wisdom and how Wisdom plays a generative role in the Gospel of John, both for Jesus and the disciples.

Core Biblical Texts

· Prov 8.22–31
· Sir 24.1–22
· Lk 7.34–35
· Jn 2.1–12

Key Words /Concepts

· Wisdom literature
· Woman Wisdom

Key Points

· Wisdom is a Biblical way of thought dealing with questions organic to this earthly life.

· Wisdom books like Job and Ecclesiastes talk about root problems, and Ecclesiastes sees them as insoluble.

· Personified Woman Wisdom is a central theme in Wisdom writings and becomes a key motif for Jesus and the Gospels.

This story begins with an introduction to the figure of Wisdom.

Wisdom has been something of a well-kept secret during this course — as it frequently is in Bible studies generally. But in a very clear sense Wisdom has been with us from the beginning. The ancient tradition of thought known as "wisdom" is all about the best way to lead life so that it turns out as well as possible. The opposite to wisdom is, of course, folly. When we say that there is a pathway of transformation in the Bible this implies a profound wisdom at work, seeking to make human life turn out well at the deepest formative levels. We can call this radical Wisdom. (We have already studied how the Book of Job does this: it is perhaps the greatest book of Biblical Wisdom.)

Also when we talk about semiotic shifts — shifts in human meaning — this is a wisdom concept. To change human meaning is to change the way human life is structured in our hearts and minds, and if we do this for the sake of life then it is the work of Biblical Wisdom. "Whoever finds me finds life!" (Proverbs 8.35.)

Wisdom Literature

To begin with we see that Wisdom is a genre of literature in the Bible. There are three canonical Wisdom books, Proverbs, Job, Ecclesiastes; and two more deuterocanonical books, Sirach and Wisdom of Solomon.

These books have a very different tone and content from the legalistic Deuteronomic texts or the passionate, thus-says-the-Lord prophetic texts. They are thoughtful and reflective, dealing in human existence as it is, seeking organic solutions to its questions. Nevertheless, they belong fully to faith in the Biblical God (the Lord) and provide a vital voice in the scriptures. Without the Wisdom writings we would not see how deep the human rabbit hole goes, and how the Bible refuses to abandon the problem in favor of some "off planet" solution.

Wisdom is actually present throughout the Bible; its stories and thought forms are scattered within the other major divisions. It is present in the Torah, in the saga of Joseph in Genesis. Joseph is a Wisdom figure, understanding the world through his dreams, and eventually organizing that world so that everyone is fed despite conditions of severe famine. His actions bring life in a situation of envy, attempted murder, false imprisonment, and famine. Among the prophets, Jonah represents an extended and highly skilled Wisdom parable, demonstrating the folly of murderous anger. And going back to Genesis, the story of the Garden of Eden has the hallmarks of a Wisdom analysis. All this material in the Bible wrestles with the challenging depths of human existence.

The book of Proverbs is hard to date. It likely has material from the 10th century (the time of Solomon) and perhaps before, but it probably reached its final form in the 6th century. In many ways it is very conventional, as you would expect traditional Wisdom to be. Age and experience accumulate a knowledge of patterns in life and they pass on this wisdom to the next generation.

Read Prov 10.4–5. "A slack hand causes poverty, but the hand of the diligent makes rich. A child who gathers in summer is prudent, but a child who sleeps in harvest brings shame."

Read Prov 12.16. "Fools show their anger at once, but the prudent ignore an insult."

The Figure of Wisdom Personified

On the other hand chapters 1 through 9 show a remarkable evolution. (It was likely added as prologue to the older material.)

At some point scribes of Israel began to see "Wisdom" in a personal and relational fashion. "She" becomes a person! How this happened, or even how the figure is to be interpreted (is she real or just a literary device?), remains undecided.

Read Prov 3.13–18.

"Happy are those who find wisdom, and those who get understanding, for her income is better than silver, and her revenue better than gold. She is more precious than jewels, and nothing you desire can compare with her. Long life is her right hand; in her left hand are riches and honor. Hers are ways of pleasantness, and all her paths are peace. She is a tree of life to those who lay hold of her; those who hold her fast are called happy."

Read Prov 1.20–22.

"Wisdom cries out in the street; in the squares she raises her voice. At the busiest corner she cries out; at the entrance of the city gates she speaks: 'How long, O simple ones, will you love being simple?'"

Read Prov 9.4–5.

"'You that are simple, turn in here!' To those without sense she says, 'Come and eat of my bread and drink of the wine I have mixed …'"

(Note, Jesus uses a Wisdom form of expression in the beatitudes: "Happy are …" is a Wisdom statement. And at Mt 11.25 he is using Proverb's word "simple," as in the above quotes, rendered in the Greek as "children" or "babes:" " … you have hid these things from the wise and prudent, and have revealed them to babes." [American King James version])

It becomes difficult to dismiss personified Wisdom as simply a literary device when we then see her depicted as a companion of God at the very beginning of creation.

Read Prov 8.22–31.

"The Lord created me at the beginning of his work, the first of his acts of long ago. Ages ago I was set up, at the first, before the beginning of the earth … when he marked out the foundations of the earth, then I was beside him, like a master worker [variant: a little child] and I was daily his delight, rejoicing before him always, rejoicing in his inhabited world and delighting in the human race."

All of this sounds more than simply poetic; it has the ring of a profound intuition about the way God is in relationship to what is "other." God doesn't create like an engineer, but as an artist, giving personal life to and through what he forms. God is supremely personal and cannot be other than in relationship to what he creates — he loves what he creates. Indeed, what God does outside of Godself reflects God within — he is essentially "in relationship." This insight is fully expressed in the concept of the

Trinity. (The Biblical God is not the neutral First Mover of Aristotelian metaphysics.) Thus God and Wisdom, "the first of his acts," are in relationship, a relationship that makes Wisdom real and a companion to God. As noted the word for "master worker" can also be read (with a very small notation change in the Hebrew) as "little child" which seems to fit better contextually. The former is usually used though, because it is used in the Wisdom of Solomon (7.22) and is less relational/more technical, and easier to fit with the philosophical tradition. But God delights in Wisdom and Wisdom delights in us. It seems a "wisdom thing" to do so — to delight in other persons. There is no need for a separate sacred place if the world is full of delight — no need in fact for a temple. Instead, through Wisdom we find transcendence in each other. We find the fulfillment of God's purpose in creation.

Wisdom as Tree of Life

In the early 2nd century BCE, Sirach, another Wisdom book, was written. This is considered Deuterocanonical by the Roman Catholic Church, Apocryphal by the Protestants. Jesus knew the teaching of this book and was informed by it. Parts seem to have been used and developed by him.

(See Sir 4.10, 6.23–8, and especially Sir 28.1–5; compare Mt 11.29–30.)

Read Sir 24.13–22.

Wisdom is depicted as a great tree. "I grew tall like a cedar in Lebanon, and like a cypress on the heights of Hermon." In v.23 she is associated with the Torah, and in v.31 she forms a great river spreading across the Earth. As we have seen, in Prov 3.18, "She is a tree of life to those who lay hold of her." The implication is that through Wisdom, humans can reverse/avoid the expulsion of Eden, and attain abounding life. (God expelled Adam and Eve in order to stop them taking from the Tree of Life and so living forever.) In contrast, it is folly which leads to death. Without wisdom people come to harm. In Wisdom thought the retributive "God of wrath" plays almost no role. Instead we can choose to bring destruction upon ourselves by rejecting Wisdom, or choose life by following her paths.

Wisdom Associated with Breath and Logos

An important thing about Sirach is the way it sustains and develops the personified figure of Wisdom, showing how deeply embedded it was in Jewish thought.

Read Sir 24.1–12 (Wisdom praises herself in the presence of the Most High).

"I came forth from the mouth of the Most High, and covered the earth like a mist ..." (v.3; cf. Gen 2.6). Here Wisdom is associated with the breath or the word of the Most High, preparing the way for the Gospel of John and its prologue, "In the beginning was the Word and the Word was with God." We also read in the prologue that "All things came into being through him." In the very late Wisdom book (1st century CE), the Wisdom of Solomon, the same thing is said of Wisdom. Sofia (Wisdom) is the fashioner of all things. Also, a little later in the same book, the Word is identified in this role, in parallel to Wisdom.

Read Wis 7.22. " … for wisdom, the fashioner of all things, taught me."

Read Wis 9.1–2, "O God of my ancestors and Lord of mercy, who have made all things by your word, and by your wisdom have formed humankind … "

Thus the prologue in the Gospel of John uses Wisdom thought. It is Wisdom theology.

Wisdom In Crisis

In Sir 50.1–21 the scribe describes a Temple service that took place at some point between 219–196 BCE when Simon son of Onias was High Priest. It gives us a snapshot of the liturgy at that point in time. It is a glorious picture of heavenly splendor come to earth. It is also the last time that Wisdom literature basks in such confidence.

We have seen how Job questions Deuteronomic justice. Ecclesiastes questions the value of Wisdom itself.

Read Eccl 1.14–17.

"I saw all the deeds that are done under the sun; and see, all is vanity and a chasing after wind. What is crooked cannot be made straight, and what is lacking cannot be counted. I said to myself, 'I have acquired great wisdom, surpassing all who were over Jerusalem before me; and my mind has had great experience of wisdom and knowledge.' And I applied my mind to know wisdom and to know madness and folly. I perceived that this also is but a chasing after wind."

Read Eccl 2.12–26, 8.10–17 (all is vanity and injustice, and makes no sense).

We cannot be sure exactly when Ecclesiastes was written (it is certainly post-exilic), but it represents without doubt a sense of Wisdom's failure. Life does not make sense and there is nothing that can be done about it. Despite repeating some stock Wisdom formulae it recognizes in a near-fatalist sense that the wicked prosper and the righteous perish. The stage is set for an in-breaking of the apocalyptic viewpoint, a dramatic vision of heavenly power intervening to set the world to rights when nothing else can. It will take a crisis at the very heart of Judaism to shock this new thought-world into existence. (We will be looking at this in more depth next lesson when we study the Book of Daniel.)

Jesus and Wisdom

In the Wisdom of Solomon the figure of Wisdom accompanies and inspires God's people from Adam to Moses.

Read Wis 10–11.14. Note especially 10.16, "She entered the soul of a servant of the Lord," (Moses) and 7.27: "In every generation she passes into holy souls."

It is possible that Jesus saw himself as the presence and fulfillment of Wisdom in Israel.

Read Lk 7.34–35, " … the Son of Man has come eating and drinking, and you say, 'Look a glutton and a drunkard, a friend of tax collectors and sinners!' Nevertheless, wisdom is vindicated by her children."

As we have seen Jesus uses Wisdom formulae and expressions. His frequent command or invitation of "Come …" is a Wisdom speech.

This relationship between Jesus and Wisdom is confirmed in another way in the Gospel of John.

Jesus and the Feminine Figure of Wisdom

In John's Gospel there are a number of women who have a pivotal role in Jesus' ministry. In fulfilling this task there are remarkable associations with Woman Wisdom.

Read Jn 2.1–12.

At the Wedding Feast of Cana the Mother of Jesus spurs Jesus into beginning his ministry, the "first of his signs." Jesus addresses her as "Woman," a highly unconventional form of address for one's mother, but appropriate if the passage is signaling a very particular woman. In other words the mother of Jesus becomes a place-holder for Woman Wisdom (see Prov 9.2). This is confirmed when she is again addressed in this way from the cross (Jn 19.26–27). The Beloved Disciple is then introduced to her as son. This would be appropriate if the Christian disciple is being invited into a close relationship with Woman Wisdom, in and through Jesus. (Remember: the Gospel of John is not talking here in strict Greek terms of hypostases — distinct individual beings in some kind of heavenly realm. These are signs, symbols and pointers telling us to be in relationship, like Jesus, with the feminine figure of Wisdom.)

In the theological tradition Jesus himself has been identified with the figure of Wisdom, and so has the Holy Spirit. In other words Wisdom is a movable theme and identification. This also allows the Gospel of John's approach to see the Christian disciple in relationship with the feminine figure of Wisdom. John's Gospel recognizes that this feminine figure is not exhausted in the tradition and needs to be preserved in its own right.

Read Jn 12.1–3 (Mary anoints Jesus at Bethany: "the house was filled with the fragrance … ").

Mary is attacked by Judas on the pious pretense that the ointment should have been sold for the poor. Jesus defends her and points the whole thing toward his death and burial. There are a number of anointings of Jesus in the Gospels, one by a sinful woman (Lk 7.36–50) and one by an unnamed woman at Bethany shortly before Jesus' arrest (Mk 14.3–9). In every case the act is an act of love. The only other scripture to give such prominence to anointing is the Song of Songs (see Song 1.1–4; and at Song 1.12 there is the only Old Testament mention of nard used as a fragrance).

It is evident that these women (possibly they are all the same one) use a concrete language of love toward Jesus. The woman at Bethany anoints Jesus as Messiah, and that is the reason for the disciples' intense annoyance. Jesus understands the act in terms of his imminent death and burial. In any case it is a woman, motivated by love, who takes the initiative in symbolizing Jesus' exceptional status as he moves toward his death. The link with Woman Wisdom is again suggested: it takes a woman to break through the established taboos and protocols and demonstrate the unique character of Jesus' Messiahship. Through Jesus, Wisdom is transformed into love, love becomes death, death becomes life.

Lesson Questions

· In what ways do the Wisdom Books of Job and Ecclesiastes deal with bad things happening to good people? What do they conclude? How is God presented in these books?

· Wisdom literature is Earth focused — how the Earth and the people on the Earth can be transformed for the good. Why is it important to have Wisdom books as part of the Biblical canon?

· Wisdom's focus is life in its fullness. In what ways does it make sense that Jesus would associate himself with the figure of Wisdom? What about his teaching brings to mind a Wisdom teacher? How is he the fulfilment of the project of Wisdom?

· In what ways do logos and Spirit and Wisdom connect?

· Does Wisdom allow us to understand the more feminine characteristics of God? If so what are these?

Personal Reflection

· Wisdom teaches how to live a full life by choosing wisely. Is this generally true do you think?

· Woman Wisdom is described as going out into the streets, inviting people to her banquet. How have I experienced God's call? How is God inviting me into relationship?

· Do I experience God as mostly male or female? Does this matter? Does it affect/detract from how I understand God's nature?

· Does Jesus associating himself with the figure of Wisdom change the way I understand God and God's purpose?

Glossary

· Deuterocanonical — the "second canon," consisting of books approved as part of the Old Testament in a number of Christian traditions, including the Roman Catholic, but not included in the Hebrew Bible, and named Apocrypha in most Protestant churches.

· *Logos* — Greek for "word" or "narrative," with transcendent meaning when it is God's Word in the Old Testament. It is used as a synonym for Wisdom and identified with Jesus in John's Gospel.

· Anointing — use of oil by Old Testament prophets to signify blessing and ordination, for kings and priests. The Messiah or Christ means "the anointed one."

· Hypostasis — a technical term meaning an underlying essential reality, literally "sub-stance."

Resources/Background Reading

· *Mary Magdalene: A Biography,* Bruce Chilton (2006)

· *Written That You May Believe: Encountering Jesus in the Fourth Gospel,* Sandra Schneiders (2003)

· *The Divine Dance,* Richard Rohr, with Mike Morell (2016)

Cultural References

· Movie, *Babette's Feast,* dir. Gabriel Axel (1987)

· Movie, *Chocolat,* dir. Lasse Halström (2000)

HISTORY TO ITS END
Lesson 2: Son of Man

Learning Objectives

· To understand the crisis of the early 2nd century, the seedbed of classic apocalyptic.

· To use the Deuterocanonical Books of Maccabees as historical background for the Book of Daniel and the community that produced it.

· To grasp the essential revelatory content of Daniel as nonviolence.

· To gain a textual understanding of the mysterious figure, "one like a son of man."

· To discover how the book of Daniel acts as a matrix for Jesus' self-understanding.

Core Biblical Texts

· Daniel Chapter 7

· Daniel 11.29–35 & 12.1–4

Key Points

· Apocalyptic literature and thinking is a unique Wisdom response to the violence of successive empires, the last and worst being Alexander the Great's.

· The Books of Maccabees are essential contextual reading for the Book of Daniel.

· "One like a son of man" signifies a divine breakthrough of nonviolent humanity.

Key Words /Concepts

· Antiochus Epiphanes

· "The wise" in the Book of Daniel

· Son of Man

· Apocalyptic

· Kingdom of God

Wisdom Becomes Apocalyptic

In the view of Ecclesiastes the project of Wisdom – that if you set out to live a right kind of life you will do well – appeared to have failed. The failure was dramatically confirmed by the events of the early second century, described below. In response Wisdom thought becomes apocalyptic in the Book of Daniel. The premise of apocalyptic literature is that in order for good to prevail, for the righteous to live, God has to intervene directly. This book, the last of the four major prophets, was written at the time of the Syrian king, Antiochus Epiphanes, in 167–164 BCE.

Read Dan 11.29–35.

Here there is an account of Antiochus' profanation of the Temple. In the very same breath it tells of a nonviolent group who fall by the sword. They are called "the wise" and their action consists in "giving understanding to many" (v.33). However, they are subjected to violence and they "fall by sword and flame." Their nonviolence is inferred both from the fact that there is absolutely no mention of resistance, and from the transcendent horizon toward which their lives are directed. The atmosphere of nonviolence throughout the book must derive from this deeply alternative response. The wise fall by the sword, unresisting, but this is in order that they might be "refined, purified and cleansed, until the time of the end, for there is still an interval until the appointed time" (v.35).

In other words the violence produces suffering not resistance, and this is possible because of a future dramatic change in time, one which brings the present world order to an end.

Read Dan 12.1–4.

Here we find out about the end toward which the wise are looking. It is the first clear description of resurrection in the Bible. It tells how many of the dead will awaken to everlasting life and "those who are wise shall shine like the brightness of the sky ..." (12.3).

Wisdom, from being a broad picture of living well, has shifted to a key of (at least passive) nonviolence vindicated by a transcendent act of life. The only way we are going to make the world turn out well for life is through resurrection. In this thinking resurrection is not a reward of "salvation" in a heavenly hereafter, but as the only way a God of Wisdom can bring about the fulfillment of his project of creation. The violence of the world may destroy you — but the resurrection makes everything right and becomes our hope.

The spiritual and historical daring of this move can hardly be exaggerated. But it has a deep and logical consistency with the overall purpose and tenor of the Hebrew Bible. That is why it was accepted as scripture. Moreover, the germinal insight about nonviolence carries within it the promise of unbounded life in an essential way — an existence where there is no violence to destroy life, within or without, will necessarily bring a life beyond death. And vice versa!

Crisis Behind the Book of Daniel

(Some of this historical material was already covered in Story 3, "The Land And Its Loss," but it's vital to return to it for the perspective of the Book of Daniel and its spiritual breakthrough.)

Between 167–164 BCE the Seleucid king of Syria took over Judea. The invasion was the political consequence of a cultural revolution already undertaken by a group of citizens in Jerusalem, Jewish men converted to the Greek way of life and viewpoint. The following assault on the Holy Place, supported by a faction in Jerusalem, shook the Jewish world so profoundly that some of the faithful found themselves thinking about time and history in a dramatically different way.

We need to take a step back to understand this fully.

The threat begins with Alexander the Great who conquered the known world in a lightning campaign at the end of the 4th century BCE. He brought with him an enormously attractive material and intellectual culture. Amphitheater, agora, hippodrome, gymnasium, baths: suddenly the world was full of new opportunities for excitement and display, physical and mental. After Alexander's death, power was divided among his military leaders. Two particular dynasties arose in the area of Israel — the Ptolemies based in Egypt (Cleopatra was a member of this family), and the Seleucids who were centered in Damascus and Syria. At first Judea was under the control of the Ptolemies and left relatively undisturbed. Then it fell to the control and influence of Syria and in 175 a new king took power, Antiochus Epiphanes IV. From that time on the Greek or Hellenistic world made rapid inroads into the minds and sensibilities of many prominent citizens in Jerusalem and Judea. For them the old ways of the Jewish religion seemed hopelessly outdated: the new Greek world beckoned brightly.

The story of these critical times is told in 1 & 2 Maccabees, books of irreplaceable importance for the understanding of Jewish experience in the lead up to Jesus.

Read 2 Macc 4.7–15.

This describes the events from 175 BCE when Antiochus Epiphanes became king, and a Jewish aristocrat named Jason (name changed from Yeshua) purchased the office of High Priest. Jason introduced Greek customs and practices to Jerusalem. (See also 1 Maccabees 1.10–15 for reversal of marks of circumcision.)

Read 1 Macc 1.16–64.

This describes the subsequent campaign of persecution and outrage against Judaism unleashed between 167 and 164. It includes the construction of a pagan altar on top of the Temple altar of burnt offering, something called the "desolating sacrilege" (a profanation that makes empty). The rest of 1 Maccabees tells the story of resistance begun by Mattathias, a member of a priestly family, of the tribe of Levi. Mattathias and his sons were nicknamed the "Maccabees" (meaning "hammer" in Hebrew). They led a successful rebellion and founded a new royal dynasty known as "Hasmoneans." The kings named "Herod" in the Gospels (Herod the Great, Herod Antipas) are representatives of the rump of this dynasty. (The Hasmoneans are not of Davidic lineage and so are naturally opposed to the thought of a Davidic Messiah.)

Read 1 Macc 2.15–48 (the beginning of the Maccabean rebellion).

All This Provides the Background for the Book of Daniel.

Read Chapter 11 of Daniel.

The story of Antiochus Epiphanes is told in a detailed newspaper-report fashion, totally unlike the vague generalizations of prophecy. (See verses 29–35 for the crisis of 167 BCE.) This makes Daniel "prophecy after the fact," meaning it is written in the genre of prophecy/prediction to show that everything has been foreseen and planned for by God. The effect is deeply comforting. It shows that the horror of the present crisis already has its solution in the designs of God. But this is not simply a pious fiction to make people feel better. There is a profound spiritual truth at the heart of the book, revealing God's deep designs and helping to bring them into being.

Meanwhile all the description of Antiochus is accurate, but it makes a mistake about the place of and circumstances of his death. Antiochus died in Persia in 164 BCE, but verse 45 is vague and seems to have him dying somewhere on the borders of Judea. This suggests to scholars that, unlike other details, the author did not know this item for

fact. So the work was likely written before certain information of Antiochus' death, and in the near area of Jerusalem. Which makes the Book of Daniel written in the very thick of the crisis, between its outbreak and 164 BCE.

The vision of Daniel chapter seven reflects the trauma of the crisis with an immediacy and rawness suggesting again real-time character. It also provides the deep spiritual insight which justifies the prophetic fiction of the book. It is its spiritual insight which makes the whole thing prophecy, radically changing the perspective by which history is to be viewed and understood. We will return to chapter seven shortly.

Back to Maccabees Again

Not only do Maccabees give us the political circumstances of the crisis, they provide invaluable information about the reaction of the Jews. In the aftermath of the assault on Judaism many Jews chose to flee to the desert rather than accept pagan rituals and laws. The account comes after the introduction of the heroic figure of Mattathias and in contrast.

See again 1 Macc 2.29–41.

It describes how this group was pursued into the wilderness and overrun on the eve of the Sabbath. They refused to fight on the Sabbath and so profane it (v.32). They said, "Let us all die in our innocence; heaven and earth testify for us that you are killing us unjustly." So their enemies "attacked them on the sabbath, and they died, with their wives and children and livestock, to the number of a thousand persons" (vv.37–38).

Here we have a picture of a group of profoundly faithful Jews who have entered into an experience of God where they are willing to die rather than defile the sabbath, the quintessential Jewish celebration of creation at peace. There can be little doubt then that this group is the same as the "wise" of Daniel 11 and 12. The feeling of intense devotion is the same, the timescale is exactly the same, their nonresistance is the same, and what happens to them in the crisis is identical: they fall by the sword.

The Maccabees are more secular minded, using the standard arguments against nonviolence. They justify fighting on the Sabbath to prevent them all from perishing. "When Mattathias and his friends learned of it, they mourned for them deeply. And all said to their neighbors: 'If we all do as our kindred have done and refuse to fight with the Gentiles for our lives and for our ordinances, they will quickly destroy us from the earth'" (1 Macc 2.39–40).

So now we have the complete picture. The Maccabees, the people who finally triumph through violent rebellion, are not the authentic descendants of David and they refuse the response of the most faithful of their generation. We know they quickly became corrupt, appointing themselves as High Priests. At the time of Jesus, the Temple was compromised by this history. It is very possible that the community that produced the Dead Sea Scrolls was part of the reaction to this corruption, sharing much of the same spirit of those who fled to the wilderness. (There were no fewer than eight separate copy fragments of Daniel among the scrolls, making Daniel second only to Isaiah with twenty one manuscript copies.) The wilderness was the place where people went to meet God, awaiting a breakthrough of a just life on earth. John the Baptist represents the same movement away from the Temple to the wilderness and apocalyptic. Finally, Jesus stands at the cusp of this movement and a radical Wisdom of nonviolence.

The Structure of Daniel

The Apocalyptic genre finds its classic example in Daniel (see also 1 Enoch, 4 Ezra, 2 Baruch, Revelation). Apocalyptic provides an account of human reality from a "heavenly" point of view, characterized by heavenly beings and their messages, dreams and visions of scenes of divine power, condensed symbolism and time frames leading to "the time of the end." (The "Little Apocalypse" in chapter 13 of Mark, with parallels in Matthew and Luke, presents Jesus' own use of the genre, quoting Daniel.)

There are two parts to the book that are are held together by the Wisdom figure Daniel.

Part 1: Chapters 1–6 of Daniel are a collection of six tales about a Wisdom figure, Daniel, at the Babylonian court during the exile, similar to the Wisdom figure of Joseph in Genesis, and told in 3rd person. Daniel can interpret dreams for the king and in doing so, he saves people's lives.

Part 2: Chapters 7–12 are a series of 4 apocalyptic visions, narrated in the 1st person.

(There is also a linguistic division. Chapters 1 and 8–12 are written in Hebrew, and 2–7 in Aramaic. The reasons behind the language variation are unknown.)

History as Violence in Daniel

Daniel, as Wisdom figure, is able to read the meaning of history. That meaning is continuous through both parts. In the second court tale Daniel interprets a dream of Nebuchadnezzar about a statue made of composite material (2.31–45). The statue represents four successive empires, and this fourfold succession is repeated in Daniel 7 with four mythological beasts emerging from the abyss.

1. Babylonian Empire
2. Median Empire
3. Persian Empire
4. Greek Empire

The final empire is that of Alexander the Great. The "beast" has ten horns, representing the generals who inherited his empire. Three horns are then displaced by "a little one" coming up among

them and this horn is Antiochus Epiphanes (Dan 7.4–5).

The interpretation of history revolves around military empires of continually increasing violence. These empires are irresistible to smaller kingdoms like Judea, and the violence of the final empire is concentrated in the Syrian king who brings that violence directly to bear on the Jews. There is no way we can miss the centrality of the issue of violence to the Book of Daniel!

God's Response

Read Daniel Chapter 7.

There is the vision of the beasts arising from the place of chaos, of limitless violence. Thrones are set up, signifying God's final intervention of justice. One like "a son of man" or "a human being" comes into his presence, and an everlasting kingship and dominion is conferred on him (vv.13–14). The distinguishing mark of this figure is likeness to human beings, as opposed to the fierce armor of the beasts. Interpretations sometimes say that he is an angelic entity, but then the humanity becomes mere appearance. The point to concentrate on is the contrast with the violence of the beasts and the transcendent humanity (nonviolence) of the figure which deals with this acute problem at hand. Later on (v.21) we are told that the figure is in fact the same as "the holy ones" against whom the horn made war. These figures are tied symbolically and existentially to the actual people of Israel who are being persecuted. At v.27 we hear explicitly the goal of the whole episode is that "the kingship and dominion and the greatness of the kingdoms under the whole heaven shall be given to the people of the holy ones of the Most High; their kingdom shall be an everlasting kingdom, and all dominions shall serve and obey them."

In other words earthly authority will be given to the persecuted people of the covenant. One "like a son of man" is a symbolic figure representing God's people who are victims of imperial violence, and hence he is a symbol of the assault on God's own designs themselves and thus also a heavenly figure. There is an identity overlap between human beings and heavenly beings, which is typical of apocalyptic. But God's designs are always for a people living fulness of life here on earth, and so God's final judgment is to turn all earthly kingship and rule over to his chosen people.

Because we have seen that the "son of man" is a figure without violence there is no other way to conceive of this final kingdom other than in terms of nonviolence.

There is indeed a cosmic battle underway. This is confirmed in chapter 10 where we read about an angelic or heavenly being who contends for Israel against "the prince of the kingdom of Persia"

(v.13) and "the prince of Greece" (v.20). But the issue to be dealt with is always the violence taking place on earth. God's method of defeating the empires is shifted to the heavenly dimension precisely because no human military method is envisaged. The authors of Daniel took the issue out of human agency not because they needed a military force greater than any on earth, but because they intuited that God's method was completely different from those employed by the empires. It is the breakthrough of the revelation of divine nonviolence.

Jesus Belongs to the Matrix of Daniel

If Daniel was so popular with the community of the Dead Sea Scrolls there is no reason to think that Jesus did not know this text and had not drunk deeply of its message the same as they.

The theme of the "kingdom of God" so central to Jesus' teaching cannot be separated from the urgent image of the *malkut* (kingdom) given by God to the human one and the holy ones in Daniel.

If Jesus went to Jerusalem knowing that he would be killed then his action would be one of extreme folly — uncharacteristic of everything else he said or did — unless he expected resurrection. The only scripture to give clear warrant to this expectation was Daniel.

Buckets of ink have been spilt over the question of whether Jesus saw himself as "the Son of Man." The question has almost always been approached textually — trying to figure out whether one saying or another about "the Son of Man" could be authentic according to various criteria.

The question is much more about what is historically credible in terms of Jesus' action and motivation. Once we agree he went to Jerusalem knowing he was going to die, then what possible scriptural scenario could be in his mind to justify his action? Not only does Daniel give hope for resurrection,

it presents "one like a son of man" who is involved with lethal suffering and is vindicated by God.

Twinning this figure with the Servant of Isaiah (see Story 4) provides the template for Jesus' actions and a credible description of his own inner horizon of meaning. Jesus, identifying with Wisdom, would have assumed the authority to unite these two figures into a single seamless pathway. The project of the Son of Man/Suffering Servant is to take authority over the violent order of the world and replace it with a time of wisdom, peace, nonviolence, and love.

Notes:

_____

_____

_____

_____

_____

_____

_____

_____

_____

_____

_____

_____

_____

_____

_____

_____

_____

_____

_____

_____

_____

_____

_____

_____

_____

_____

Lesson Questions

- Why is apocalyptic the natural progression of Wisdom literature?
- In what way does apocalyptic answer the crisis of Wisdom described in the book of Ecclesiastes and Job?
- Why would the "son of man" figure appeal to Jesus?
- Why does Jesus seem to identify himself more with the Son of Man than Messiah?
- Apocalyptic language and imagery are dramatic and surreal. Why is it important to understand these texts as symbolic of a new reality and not literal or prognostic? (For example, some churches have used passages in Daniel and the Book of Revelation to predict imminent battles or contemporary world crises with violent intervention from heaven.)

Personal Reflection

- "One like a son of man" can mean just an ordinary "human being" but it is also the chosen figure in Daniel who brings peace to the Earth through the direct intervention of God. It was Jesus' preferred form of self address. How are both of these meanings important in how I understand and relate to Jesus?
- How do I feel about apocalyptic imagery and language? Those who used it (the "wise" in Daniel, the oppressed Christians of the early church, and Jesus himself) were characteristically non-violent, yet the images are often intense and disturbing. Why do you think this is? What is its purpose?
- Can I think of a piece of literature, art, or music that might in some ways be trying to convey something different or new?
- Why does resurrection necessarily imply nonviolence?
- Can I make the leap of faith to believe in the power of nonviolent love that overcomes death, violence, and empire?

Glossary

- *malkut* — Hebrew for "kingdom," used in Daniel chapter 7.
- Apocalyptic — a term meaning "unconcealing, withdrawal of a veil," referring to a "heavenly" understanding of earthly events, here interpreted as in-breaking of divine nonviolence. Also a genre of writing representing heavenly visions.

Resources/Background Reading

- *Invitation to the Book of Revelation,* Elisabeth Schussler Fiorenza (1981)
- *The Apocalyptic Imagination: Introduction to Jewish Apocalyptic Literature,* John Collins (2016)

Cultural References

- Movie, *Apocalypse Now*, dir. Francis Ford Coppola (1979)
- *2666*, Roberto Bolaño (2013)

HISTORY TO ITS END
Lesson 3: New Paradigm

Learning Objectives

· To see how Jesus entered into the horizon of meaning given in Daniel, including themes of "kingdom" and "Son of Man," and their profound connection.

· To suggest the possibility that Jesus had an initial approach depending on the proclamation of the kingdom, but afterward this changed into an expectation of suffering.

· To see the resurrection as the "natural" sequel of the cross, once we understand that Jesus is fulfilling the divine revelation of nonviolence.

· To grasp the emergence of a new paradigm, seeing how the seven stories interconnect, and how in Jesus produce the final sign of the resurrection as revelation of divine nonviolence.

Core Biblical Texts

· Mk 10.32–34
· Mt 26.63–65
· Jn 14.2–7

Key Points

· The prophecy of Daniel provides the most natural source for Jesus' characteristic message of the kingdom and its accompanying theme of "Son of Man."

· Jesus began his ministry with proclamation of the kingdom and expectation of the coming of the Son of Man, but at some point he understood the Son of Man must suffer.

· The Resurrection is only to be understood as consequence of the nonviolence of the cross. And the nonviolence of the cross can only be grasped when it is lifted up and made transcendent by the resurrection.

· The New Paradigm of this course is understanding the Resurrection as revelation of divine nonviolence.

Key Words /Concepts

· Kingdom of God
· One like a Son of Man
· Resurrection
· Divine nonviolence

Jesus' Self-Association with the Son of Man

We have looked at the dramatic events of the early 2nd century BCE in Judea and their expression in the Book of Daniel. How did these get translated to the single drama of a Galilean prophet who was condemned to death on a cross?

We have argued that the Book of Daniel provided Jesus with the horizon of meaning for the last days of his life in Jerusalem. But what about before? Was it always like that? Did Jesus always see "the Son of Man" in terms of suffering?

Jesus announced the "kingdom of God" as something imminent in his time. In Daniel God confers kingdom and authority on "one like a son of man." If Jesus announces the kingdom of God, it is credible that he should also relate in a special fashion to this figure. In the text of the Gospels he uses the term "Son of Man" in various ways connected to himself. It is plausible that for Jesus "the Son of Man" would also be arriving very soon and he, Jesus, was linked to this figure in a very unique way.

At the same time we need to recognize how Jesus maintains a deliberate distance between himself and a direct one-to-one identification with "the Son of Man."

Read Mk 8.38.

"Those who are ashamed of me and my words in this adulterous and sinful generation, of them the Son of Man will also be ashamed when he comes in the glory of his Father with the holy angels." (See also the parallel at Mt 10.33 as an obvious "editing up" of the saying toward a more formal or dogmatic identification.)

Jesus makes no metaphysical claim about himself, and this fits with a more faith-filled and open-ended approach. If he makes a direct identification this quickly has a feeling of violence. Jesus plays his part to bring in the cataclysmic change that Daniel is talking about, but he remains personally humble and nonviolent. This encourages people to enter into the change themselves, personally and meaningfully, rather than just submitting to an extraordinary cosmic individual.

Jesus and the Kingdom of God

It is essential to underline how Jesus in his preaching of the kingdom also opted for very organic, transformational images of its coming — of seeds growing, and the need for waiting through an arc of time for the harvest.

Read Mt 13.31–33 and Mk 4.26–29.

This description — something growing and a harvest which is its moment of fulfilment — is very much a Wisdom approach.

When and how did Jesus expect the harvest? Did he at first believe that his message of transformation — inspired by his own nonviolent relationship with the Father, and his healings and feedings as its concrete demonstration — would be enough to inspire the people and create a mass movement of human change? (Something like John the Baptist looked to have done at the Jordan?)

Read Mk 9.1: "And he said to them, 'Truly I tell you, there are some standing here who will not taste death until they see that the kingdom of God has come with power.'"

This appears to point toward a rapid advance of the kingdom message and its harvest.

Read also the parallel at Mt 10.23.

"When they persecute you in one town, flee to the next; for truly I tell you, you will not have gone through all the towns of Israel before the Son of Man comes."

These twin traditions — of when the kingdom/Son of Man will come — seem also to connect the two things, kingdom and the Son of Man, suggesting a link between the two. We get the sense that Jesus expected a very quick arrival of these conclusive events of God's plan of redemption. The seeds are growing, the leaven is working, the harvest is close at hand.

But at some point Jesus finds his organic approach is not working.

Read Mt 11.20–24 (these cities had chosen death/sheol rather than repentance).

It seems then that at a pivotal moment Jesus changed his approach. His understanding of God and the kingdom had not changed, but his understanding of humanity and its deeply ingrained rivalry and violence were clarified. He understood that more was needed. He had to take on the absolutely exceptional role of Servant/Son of Man in order to release the core knot of human opposition to the kingdom. At this point he begins to predict his passion.

Read Mark 10.33–34.

The Son of Man must suffer. Compare John 12.27–34 (the Gospel of John attests to the same association of Son of Man with suffering — where it speaks of

the Son of Man being "lifted up" it is referring to the crucifixion.)

Twinning the Son of Man with the Servant of Isaiah (see Story 4) provides the template for Jesus' actions, especially after he turns his face to Jerusalem. The conjunction of these two key prophetic figures becomes a credible description of Jesus' own inner horizon of meaning.

Read Mt 26.63–65.

Thus when Jesus was faced with the interrogation of the High Priest he answers in a way that leaves the High Priest in no doubt. The Temple authority asks Jesus about Messiahship which is, of course, what the High Priest is worried about. It seems totally credible, from a spiritual perspective, that at this point — when Jesus has been stripped of all earthly power/ violence — that he powerfully invokes the Son of Man. The High Priest knows the scriptures well enough to understand this: that a "Son of Man" figure is a much more profound threat to his Temple role than a Messiah. The latter is political, the former is a world without violence, an end entirely to Temple holiness and the in-breaking of God's very presence. It is for this reason that he declares Jesus' response "blasphemy."

From the overall study we have done it fits entirely that Jesus really did make this answer. In which case Jesus has been led through the course of his ministry to the point where he fully embraces and demonstrates the nonviolence of the Son of Man figure. He is completely without power, but at that moment he claims the powerful coming of the Son of Man! By uniting the figure of the Son of Man with the figure of the Servant, Jesus fully realizes the nonviolent revelation of God, bringing a qualitatively new sign and meaning into human history.

Resurrection

Afterward the Resurrection is the "natural" outcome. The Book of Daniel itself claims resurrection for "the wise" who fall helpless victim to violence. In the revelatory imagination of the author, resurrection is a consistent and necessary destiny for the nonviolent faithful who fall under the lethal violence of the world. The resurrection must be itself, therefore, an event of nonviolence. It fulfills the way of the wise (they "shall shine like the brightness of the sky," 12.3). The resurrection of "shame and contempt" for the wicked (12.2) is not a punitive expression, but declarative. The way of violence is declared absolutely and finally to be what it is — a dead end. (This is also the sense at Jn 5.29.)

Jesus' resurrection has to be understood in the same pattern. It can only be grasped as consequence of the nonviolence of the cross. It belongs to the revelatory imagination of

Biblical nonviolence. The inner transcendence of forgiveness realized in the cross is fulfilled in the transcendent life of resurrection.

This is the doubled sense of John's Gospel "lifting up," the intimate doublet of cross and resurrection, both together as the same thing.

But it did it really happen? The New Testament record is sure that it did. What could Paul's early

tradition of appearances of the Lord (1 Cor 15.5-8) amount to if the body was still in the tomb? Simply put, it would be some kind of mass illusion: a conclusion which all those people, including Paul himself, could not have avoided over time if the whereabouts of the body was known, or even just suspected. If the dead body was known about that meant the world was still under the control of Rome and the Temple establishment. Violence had won. The New Testament's integral witness to forgiveness and nonviolence (up to and including martyrdom) could never have been begun, let alone sustained, without grounded belief in the reality of resurrection.

At the same time resurrection cannot simply be a supernatural miracle. It cannot be "seen" without a profound change in the eyes of the witness herself. Without that shift resurrection remains in the generative order of this world — one more event of violent anthropology, a figure from the dead who would presumably be seeking vengeance. In the Gospel of John the story of Mary Magdalene at the tomb is the perfect illustration of this change. She undergoes a conversion, "turning" twice before she recognizes the Lord and speaks her word of love. Then Jesus says he is ascending "to my Father and your Father" (John 20.17). The Father of nonviolence is now the Father of Mary and of all the brothers and sisters of Jesus to whom she is sent. The resurrection,

therefore, is the final semiotic shift in the whole series, the one that brings to completion the whole project of "seven stories."

Jesus' resurrection is the event of God's nonviolent life in the midst of time and history. It is the fulfillment of Daniel's vision, because Jesus carried through nonviolence to the very end and so brought to completion God's anthropological project of life.

The fact that it happens in the midst of time, not "the end," is simply a matter of perspective. Viewed from the side of Jesus' resurrection, time has already reached its end. The rest of us are "catching up," already rising to life or to shame! He is the firstborn of many brothers and sisters (Romans 8.29). For a Christian the Risen One is just as present in this room as you or me, or even more so; because our reality is false (based in the fascination of violence), and his is true (based in love). We are used to the Lukan version of the Risen One disappearing into heaven, but there is also the Johannine abiding ...

Read Jn 14.2–7.

This is normally translated as "there are many dwelling places in my Father's house." While this is broadly accurate it misses the verbal connection between the noun "place" and the verb "to abide" used extensively in John's Gospel (monai, dwelling places, is derived from the verb, menein, to abide). "Abide" signifies the intimate connection between Jesus and his disciples. If Jesus goes to prepare a place or dwelling for us it is not simply something for after death. Rather it is the new human space made possible by Jesus' resurrection. "I will come again and will take you to myself, so that where I am, there you may also be" (John 14.3). This is the resurrection of Jesus in its future and present effects among humanity.

New Paradigm: Transformation

We can see now the benefit of an historical, anthropological understanding. It has enabled us to read the Bible as God's deep design, working through the core problem of human existence — violence.

How do these readings fit together in a coherent whole? If the traditional "salvation" reading of the Bible makes it so simple, how can this one explain itself easily in comparison?

We have to remember all the time that the "salvation" reading is cut-and-dried because it is legalistic. "God decides, so it is." In the anthropological understanding you have to read, so to speak, from underneath.

When we fit together the sequence of the stories in this way we get a cumulative change of

meaning, a complete semiotic shift. It is an evolutionary reading which sees that God is trying to change humanity from within.

At the same time, the Gospel message is all of the change rolled into one. It is the simplest, most direct expression of a total transformation in human existence brought about by God. Believe the good news, and be converted; the kingdom of God has come! The outpouring of the Holy Spirit is the apocalyptic "end times" event realizing and illustrating this change. "God's love has been poured into our hearts through the Holy Spirit who has been given to us" (Rom 5.5). What are the fruits of the Spirit? Love, joy, peace, patience, kindness, generosity, faithfulness, gentleness and self-control (Gal 5.22-23). All of them are realization and practice of nonviolence. And joy is the consequence when we know our lives have been transformed!

To receive the Holy Spirit is to enter humanly into the nonviolent life of God. It is an anthropological reality, i.e. an experiential event manifesting itself in multiple ways. The gift of tongues (1 Cor 14.1–5) can readily be understood as a complete restructuring of our basic sign-making capacity which is speech/language. Something which completely de-organizes our language and makes it in a new way can directly be appreciated as reconstitution of human meaning. It is a total audible semiotic shift! Miracles of healing will naturally accompany this change. If the old order of meaning keeps people imprisoned within a system of violence — including blame, guilt, hate, anger etc. — then to free someone from this order will necessarily be accompanied by new body sense, including events of release and healing.

At the same time, of course, the Holy Spirit is a sharing of God's own life. The human body and God's Spirit now belong to the same frequency, the same essential pattern. In the past we saw "spirit" as belonging to a different plane of being, "up there" beyond the clouds. But in reality "spirit" is our deepest mode of communication with each other and with the world. If our communication is violent then spirit will be violent. But if God's nonviolent Holy Spirit is poured out to us through the death and resurrection of Jesus it is because we are now in deepest communication with the Father/Mother of Jesus. "Behold I make all things new!" (Rev 21.5, KJV).

Lesson Questions

· What aspects of Jesus' preaching about the kingdom are reminiscent of wisdom literature (use of nature) and in what ways are they apocalyptic?

· The Son of Man figure in Daniel brings in God's kingdom non-violently. How does Jesus take this even further by his association of the Son of Man with the Servant figure of Isaiah?

· Why is the resurrection the culmination and fulfillment of the Wisdom and Apocalyptic teachings of the Bible?

· This course has demonstrated that the key human problem is violence, and that through the Bible God has been showing us a different way of being human. How is Jesus the ultimate revelation of this new humanity?

· Jesus says in John 14.9 "Whoever has seen me has seen the Father," and in Mt 11.27 "No one knows the Father except the Son and anyone to whom the Son chooses to reveal him." How does the Jesus revealed through this course help us to better understand God?

· The Holy Spirit is the New Testament apocalypse. Can we see how it is necessarily a nonviolent apocalypse?

Personal Reflection

· Apocalyptic is a way of making good on Wisdom's promise of life in its fullness even when worldly wisdom/justice sometimes appears to fail. (For example, the child who dies without having fully lived.) God intervenes directly to put things to rights. Resurrection is the ultimate vindication of the poor, oppressed, suffering — all those denied life — by means of fullness of life and goodness. Does this change the way I understand resurrection?

· The Bible is an evolutionary document that through key insights shows us a different way of being human, without rivalry and without violence. Why is this evolutionary revelation necessary for true transformation?

· The New Testament asks the question "Have you received the Holy Spirit?" Should we ask ourselves this question one more time now we understand it as God's Spirit of nonviolence abiding in our bodies?

Glossary

· New Paradigm — a fresh and transformative understanding of Christian revelation grounded in divine nonviolence.

· The Son of Man — a titular figure found in the Gospels derived from Daniel's "one like a son of man."

· Holy Spirit — Communication of the nonviolent character and very being of Jesus' God.

Resources/Background Reading

· *Resurrection of the Son of God,* N.T. Wright (2003)

Cultural References

· Movie, *2001 Space Odyssey*, dir. Stanley Kubrik (1968). Puts human evolution — from ape to spaceship — on the screen, but without shift to nonviolence.

· Movie, *Beauty and the Beast,* dir. Bill Condon (2017). Love transforms the violence of human selfishness.

· Movie, *The Matrix Trilogy,* dir. the Wachowskis (1999-2003). The final destruction of the city of Zion is stopped by self-giving death of Neo, "the One."

Notes:

_____

_____

_____

_____

_____

_____

_____

_____

_____

_____

_____

_____

_____

_____

_____

_____

_____

_____

_____

_____

_____

_____

_____

_____

_____

Notes:

Notes:

_____

_____

_____

_____

_____

_____

_____

_____

_____

_____

_____

_____

_____

_____

_____

_____

_____

_____

_____

_____

_____

_____

_____

_____

_____

_____

Notes:

Glossary of Terms

Alienation — a term with a philosophical background meaning profound human separation from others and social structures of well-being. (*S2, L3*)

Anointing — use of oil by Old Testament prophets to signify blessing and ordination, for kings and priests. The Messiah or Christ means "the anointed one." (*S7, L1*)

Antitheses — the passage in the Sermon on the Mount where Jesus contrasts previous Biblical teachings with his new teaching. (*S1, L3*)

Apocalyptic — a term meaning "unconcealing, withdrawal of a veil," referring to a "heavenly" understanding of earthly events, here interpreted as in-breaking of divine nonviolence. Also a genre of writing representing heavenly visions. (*S3, L2 & S7, L2*)

Apocrypha — a number of books included in the LXX (Septuagint) considered to be not authoritative for faith; Luther included the deuterocanonical books under this heading. (*Method, L1*)

Ark of the Covenant — a box containing the stone tablets with the ten commandments and acting as a sacred force in the vanguard of the people. Later it was kept in Solomon's Temple. (*S6, L1*)

Avenger of Blood — one of the meanings of *go'el*, a kinsperson whose job is to execute the one who killed a family member. (*S5, L2*)

Beatitudes — the passage in the Sermon on the Mount consisting of wisdom sayings beginning with "blessed are you …." (*S1, L3*)

Canon — the rule or list which establishes which books are to be included in the Bible. (*Method, L1*)

Cities of Refuge — designated cities (named in the Book of Joshua) where someone who has killed accidentally may flee and be protected from the automatic vengeance of the *go'el*. (*S5, L2*)

Consequential — the ethic of positive or negative consequences flowing naturally (mimetically) from nonviolent or violent actions, thus bringing their own judgment. (*S1, L3*)

Covenant — term for an ancient treaty or bond, protected by sanctions, which in the Bible applied to the committed relationship between God and his people. (*S2, L2*)

Critical — refers to the exercise of judgment about the thought-world and social pressures affecting the composition of a text. (*Method, L1*)

Dead Sea Scrolls — a treasure trove of ancient Jewish manuscripts discovered in 1946 in clay jars in caves above the western shore of the Dead Sea, their contents covering all the books of the Old Testament except Esther, and including deuterocanonical works and other unique writings proper to the sectarian community at their source. (*S3, L2*)

Decalogue — the ten commandments. (*S1, L3*)

Deconstruction — a mode of thought or action exposing the function of violence in a given structure of meaning, so overturning or abolishing its effect. Deconstruction of texts was the primary usage of the term. (*S6, L3*)

Deuterocanonical — the "second canon," consisting of books approved as part of the Old Testament in a number of Christian traditions, but not included in the Hebrew Bible, and named Apocrypha in most Protestant churches. (*Method, L1 & S7, L1*)

Deutero-Isaiah (Second Isaiah) — second part of the Book of Isaiah comprising chapters 40-55, written by a different author from the previous chapters towards the end of the exile and in the early days of the return. (*S4, L1*)

Dominant Biblical Interpretative Worldview — Deuteronomic texts that establish a violently retributive God. *(S3, L1)*

Essene — a group originating in the second century BCE, who found a solution to military occupation and corrupt government by complete separation, both spatially and in terms of mindset and lifestyle. *(S3, L2)*

Exile — the captivity of the Jerusalem population in Babylon from 597–538 BCE after the the fall of the Southern Kingdom of Judah. It ended when the king of Persia, Cyrus the Great, decreed that they could return to their land. *(S4, L1)*

Fundamentalism — a faith attitude to the Bible which considers the text to be inerrant (without error) and literally true, in order to preserve the "fundamentals of the faith." It arose in response to the scientific method of literary and historical criticism. *(Method, L1)*

Generative Violence — René Girard's theory that violence gives rise to human culture and yet always continues to produce more violence. *(Method, L2)*

Gilgamesh Epic — an ancient Babylonian writing, dating from the 2nd millennium BCE, describing the adventures of a king, Gilgamesh; a number of its concerns and stories are paralleled in the first chapters of Genesis. *(Method, L1)*

go'el — denotes a person who is the nearest relative, next-of-kin, the one given the duty of restoring his or her kinsman's alienated rights to liberty or life. *(S5, L2)*

ha' satan — the accuser or adversary, a social category and role in Hebrew culture, not a metaphysical enemy of God. In the New Testament "Satan" is the name for rivalry and violence as a constant "cosmic" force in opposition to Jesus. *(S5, L1)*

Hapiru — a form of a common name given in the Ancient Near East to a dispossessed class of people characterized as vagrants, mercenaries, migrant laborers, living on the margins of society (sometimes also spelled Habiru). *(S1, L1)*

Hasmonean — the name for the dynasty of kings (non-Davidic) resulting from the Maccabean revolt and ruling through the 2nd and 1st centuries BCE. *(S3, L2)*

Hermeneutics — a scholarly discipline offering coherent principles of interpretation. *(Method, L1)*

hilasterion — literally "a covering place," a place where the effect of sin is covered over and annulled by blood; used to refer to the cover above the Ark in the Holy of Holies. *(Method, L2)*

Historical-Critical Method — investigation of the historical reliability of events described in the Bible, and of the circumstances of their being written down. *(Method, L1)*

Holy Spirit — Communication of the nonviolent character and very being of Jesus' God. *(S7, L3)*

Hypostasis — a technical term meaning an underlying essential reality, literally "sub-stance." *(S7, L1)*

Ketuvim — the writings of the Jewish canon coming after the Torah and Prophets (*Nevi'im*), including late additions Daniel and Chronicles. *(Method, L1)*

Key Biblical Frame Story — the event of the Exodus and its multiple tellings and interpretations. *(S3, L1)*

Levite — a member of the tribe of Levi which was set apart for sacred duties in the land, eventually exclusively in the Temple. *(S6, L1)*

Liberation Theology — a theology that grew out of the big changes in thought in Latin America and elsewhere from 1968 onwards. It tells us that God's revelation is properly to be interpreted and understood from the perspective of the poor and oppressed. *(S1, L2)*

Literary Criticism — the investigation of the literary and rhetorical character of Bible writings affecting their interpretation. (*Method, L1*)

Logos — Greek for "word" or "narrative," with transcendent meaning when it is God's Word in the Old Testament. It is used as a synonym for Wisdom and identified with Jesus in John's Gospel. (*S7, L1*)

Maccabee — the nickname (meaning "hammer") given to Mattathias and his sons who led the revolt against the persecuting king Antiochus Epiphanes IV. (*S3, L2*)

malkut — Hebrew for "kingdom," used in Daniel chapter 7. (*S7, L2*)

Mimesis — the highly developed human quality of imitation, especially imitation of another's perceived desires. (*Method, L3*)

Mirror Neurons — function of brain neurons discovered in 1980s and 1990s through experiments with monkeys, demonstrating ability internally to imitate the action of others through motor neurons firing when those actions are observed. (*Method, L3*)

Mishna — a book of Pharisaic interpretation and codification of the laws of the Torah (traditionally numbered at 613) published around 200 CE, but developing from the beginning of the Common Era. (*S3, L2*)

Nephilim — giant mythic heroes and figures of violence in the early Biblical worldview. (*S2, L1*)

Nevi'im — "Prophets" in the Hebrew Bible, including narrative from Joshua through Kings, and "Latter Prophets," Isaiah, Jeremiah, Ezekiel and the twelve minor prophets. (*Method, L1*)

New Paradigm — a fresh and transformative understanding of Christian revelation grounded in divine nonviolence. (*S7, L3*)

Original Sin — the idea of a primary sin, committed by Adam, that is passed on to his descendants, with deadly legal and metaphysical consequences. (*S2, L1*)

parisim — the violent men, in Jeremiah

and Jesus' denunciation, who make the Temple their headquarters. (*S6, L2*)

Penal Substitution — the need for divine justice to make Christ a substitute to endure punishment in the place of human sinners if they are to be forgiven. (*Method, L2*)

Pharisee — a group originating in the two centuries before Jesus, who sought to resolve the tensions of military occupation and corrupt government by increased and detailed attention to purity boundaries and rule keeping. (*S3, L2*)

Proscriptive — a command imposing a restraint or prohibition. (*S1, L3*)

Purification — primarily a temple ritual to prepare priests and people for offering sacrifice, but extended progressively to cover many other situations. John's baptism at the Jordan could be seen as purification, for the sake of a life without sin in the land, and to preserve the people from wrath. (It was also a marvelous semiotic code for a completely fresh beginning as an Israelite.) (*S3, L3*)

Qumran — an archeological site on the shore of the Dead Sea thought to be home to the community which produced the Dead Sea Scrolls and associated by many scholars with the Essenes. (*S3, L2*)

ra'ah — Hebrew for "destruction," "evil," "violence," "disaster." (*S5, L3*)

rab ereb — Hebrew for "mixed multitude." A Biblical term that describes the group that left Egypt under Moses. (*S1, L1*)

Redeemer — the English translation associated with the root *gaal*, a term applied to Christ but needing its full anthropological content in order to see its meaning. (*S5, L2*)

Relational — referring to the structure of human relationships rather than a system of rules. (*S1,L3*)

Retributive — the ethic that justice is achieved by reciprocal compensating violence against the perpetrator. (*S1, L3*)

Return from exile — the physical return of a group of Judean exiles from Babylon to Jerusalem; also the spiritual return — led by God — that was still in process in Gospel times. *(S4, L2)*

Revelation — in this Seven Stories study the word refers to revelation of generative human violence alongside its progressive transformation through divine love. *(Method, L3)*

Robber — legally someone who steals with violence. *(S6, L3)*

Sacrifice — the act of killing or destruction that evokes the original violence against a surrogate victim and renews its benefits. *(S6, L2)*

Sacrificial Crisis — the moment when the order of a group breaks down and violence builds to the point where the remembered solution of killing a victim is activated, and sacred order is re-established. *(Method, L3)*

Sadducee — the priestly class representing a conservative set of beliefs and the need to preserve the Temple as the last remaining independent symbol of Judaism. *(S3, L2)*

Satisfaction — the surrender of some element of life on the part of an offender to make good the loss of status on the part of the one offended. *(Method, L2)*

Scapegoat — a Biblical term used in common parlance for a designated group victim unjustly blamed for a general social crisis. *(Method, L3)*

Semiotic Shift — the concept of how human meaning changes through pivotal stories, signs and symbols, above all through the Biblical narrative. *(S1, L2)*

Septuagint (LXX) — Greek translation of the Old Testament produced by Jewish scholars around 200 BCE, used frequently in first century CE New Testament. *(Method, L1)*

Shell Stories —term used in the Seven Stories for the Land and the Temple, institutions providing the physical-social background and necessary continuity for transformative meaning over time. *(S3, L1)*

Sign — a manifestation of divine power. For a violent mindset this implicitly involves some form of violence. In Jesus' mind it is God's vindication of nonviolence by means other than violence. *(S5, L3)*

skeuos — means "vessel" and in the Temple context this means part of the sacrificial apparatus. *(S6, L3)*

Sons of God — the gathering of companions or heavenly court around God, sometimes understood as angels (e.g. Job 1:6). *(S5, L1)*

Tabernacle — an elaborate transportable tent acting as a sanctuary during the wilderness wanderings and housing the Ark (perhaps non-historical). *(S6, L1)*

Tanakh — Hebrew acronym for the Torah–Prophets–Writings. *(Method, L1)*

Targum — an Aramaic version of the Hebrew Scriptures, often a very loose translation of the original text. *(S4, L1)*

Temple — a sacred space created and defined by formal use of sacrifice. *(S6, L2)*

Temple Holiness — a sense of purity and proximity to God constructed by means of animal sacrifice. In the case of the Jerusalem Temple this was overlaid with the national and spiritual history of Israel. *(S6, L1)*

Temple Theology — an understanding of the Temple, chosen by God as his house, (strictly speaking a place where his name would dwell), a space where he may be encountered by his people. *(S6, L1)*

The Fall — traditional theological concept figuring a vertical fall from communion with God, with a background Platonism of the soul becoming immersed in the material world. *(S2, L1)*

The Son of Man — a titular figure found in the Gospels derived from Daniel's "one like a son of man." *(S7, L3)*

Torah — first five books of the Bible, comprising the "Teaching" or "Law" of the Jewish faith. *(Method, L1)*

Traditional Christian Biblical Frame Story — the Fall, a metaphysical change from the presence of God to alienation from God. *(S3, L1)*

Wisdom — in the Bible a genre of writing specializing in rules of how to live life well; plus a personified figure, a Woman who is God's first offspring and accompanies him in the work of creation. *(S2, L2)*

Wrath — the human attribute of anger and violence that becomes an attribute of God both because of its "sacred" power and because the prophets saw it as cyclical and retributive. Jesus subverts this interpretation in every sense. *(S4, L3)*

Zadok — High Priest at the time of David, important in the Dead Sea Scrolls as true priestly ancestor. *(S3, L2)*

Zealot — a general term for a rebel against Rome in the 1st century CE, but then referring to a specific group of militants during the Roman-Jewish war, 66-70 CE. *(S3, L2)*

Made in the USA
Middletown, DE
12 July 2018